Bomb Detection Dogs

by

Charles and Linda George

Content Consultant:
Sgt. Michael Peck
San Mateo County Sheriff's Bomb Squad and Range

RiverFront Books

An Imprint of Franklin Watts
A Division of Grolier Publishing
New York   London   Hong Kong   Sydney
Danbury, Connecticut

RiverFront Books
http://publishing.grolier.com
Copyright © 1998 by Capstone Press. All rights reserved.
No part of this book may be reproduced without written permission from
the publisher. The publisher takes no responsibility
for the use of any of the materials or methods
described in this book, nor for the products thereof.
Published simultaneously in Canada.

Printed in the United States of America.

Library of Congress Cataloging-in-Publication Data
George, Charles, 1949-
   Bomb detection dogs/by Charles and Linda George.
   p. cm.--(Dogs at work)
   Includes bibliographical references (p. 45) and index.
   Summary: Tells about the use of dogs for bomb detection and then
describes their selection, training, and accomplishments.
   ISBN 1-56065-751-0
   1. Police dogs--Juvenile literature. 2. Bombings--Prevention--Juvenile
literature. 3. Bombing investigation--Juvenile literature. [1. Police dogs. 2.
Bombing investigation. 3. Dogs.]
I. George, Linda. II. Title. III. Series.
HV8025.G27   1998
363.2'32--dc21

                                        97-41177
                                           CIP
                                           AC

Editorial credits:
Editor, Christy Steele; cover design, James Franklin; photo research,
   Michelle L. Norstad

Photo credits:
Andrews Air Force Base, 11, 16, 19, 24, 27, 37
Steve C. Healey, 14
The Image Works/Dorothy Littel Greco, 7, 13, 30, 40; Topham, 34
David Macias, cover
Michael Stapleton Associates, 20, 43
New York City Police Department, 8
L. O'Shaughnessy, 4, 22, 29, 38
Unicorn Stock Photography/Mike Morris, 32

Table of Contents

CHAPTER 1

About Bomb Detection Dogs

Bomb detection dogs risk their lives to help people. They use their strong sense of smell to find bombs, guns, and mines. A bomb is a set of explosives or a holder filled with explosives. A mine is a bomb that is hidden underground or underwater. Dogs can often find hidden explosives more quickly than people.

Bomb detection dogs search for bombs on airplanes and before major public events. They also search for guns and other explosives.

Handlers

Specially trained handlers work with bomb detection dogs. Handlers volunteer to work with bomb detection dogs. Volunteer means to offer to do a job. Like bomb detection dogs,

Bomb detection dogs use their strong sense of smell to find bombs.

handlers risk their lives when they search for bombs.

Handlers are members of law enforcement agencies. A law enforcement agency is an office or department that makes sure people obey laws.

Some handlers are members of bomb squads. A bomb squad is a group of officers that protects people from bombs. Bomb squad members know how to find, disarm, and dispose of bombs. Disarm means to make harmless. Dispose means to throw away.

Dogs must let their handlers know when they have found bombs. This is called indicating a find. Each dog indicates a find in a different way. Some dogs sit next to the bombs. Others bark or point at the bombs with their noses. Some wag their tails or paw the ground. The dogs never touch the bombs. These signals show the dogs' handlers where the bombs are. Bomb squad technicians then disarm and dispose of the bombs.

Bomb detection dog handlers are members of law enforcement agencies.

History

People first noticed that dogs could find bombs toward the end of the Vietnam War (1954-1975). This caused the University of Mississippi to begin studying dogs. They studied how dogs' senses of smell could be used to find bombs. Law enforcement agencies became interested in the university's work.

The New York City Police Department (NYPD) began testing bomb detection dogs in the early 1970s. The department trained dogs to recognize different bomb scents. Then the trainers hid disarmed bombs. The dogs quickly located the hidden bombs. As a result, the NYPD added bomb detection dogs to its bomb squad. Other police departments soon added bomb detection dogs to their bomb squads.

Other law enforcement agencies also started using bomb detection dogs. The U.S. Air Force began using dogs to find bombs at airports and

The NYPD began using bomb detection dogs in the 1970s.

in airplanes. Air force handlers trained dogs to work in airports around the world.

Bombs

Bombs can cause dangerous explosions. Even small bombs can make airplanes crash. Other bombs can hurt people on busy city streets. Bombs may even kill people.

It is against the law for people to make bombs. People who try to make or hide bombs are arrested if police catch them. But some people secretly make bombs. They use bombs to hurt and scare other people.

People try to smuggle bombs in many ways. Smuggle means to illegally take something into or out of a country. People smuggle bombs in suitcases and briefcases. They hide bombs in calculators, cameras, and envelopes.

Sometimes smugglers ask airplane passengers to carry packages onto airplanes. Bombs are hidden in the packages. Other

The U.S. Air Force began using dogs to find bombs at airports and in planes.

times, smugglers put bombs in baggage when no one is watching. Travelers pick up their baggage without knowing that the bombs are inside.

Airline Safety

Airport managers try to keep airplanes and passengers safe. Airports hire security guards to help them do this. Security guards ask passengers if strangers tried to give them packages. They ask travelers to keep their baggage in sight. By doing this, security guards prevent some bombs from being smuggled onto airplanes.

Bomb detection dogs work at some airports. Trained dogs can smell bombs and find them quickly. Dogs are cheaper to use than expensive equipment. Dogs also move around much more easily than sensing devices. Dogs can squeeze into hard-to-reach places. People only use bomb detection dogs when they suspect that a bomb is present. Handlers help the dogs search for bombs.

Trained dogs can smell bombs and find them quickly.

Some airports have bomb detection dogs on duty all the time. These dogs often search for bombs even if there are no bomb threats. A bomb threat is a warning that a bomb has been placed or sent somewhere.

X-ray machines also help airports look for bombs. X-ray machines take pictures of everything inside packages. All baggage entering an airplane is X-rayed. Security guards search the bags if they see anything that looks suspicious.

Even so, bombs sometimes make it onto airplanes. Many people want all airports to use bomb detection dogs. There are not enough bomb detection dogs to search every airplane in the world. But the number of bomb detection dogs is increasing. Dogs trained to sniff out explosives can save thousands of lives. These bomb detection dogs keep airplanes and other public places safe.

X-ray machines take pictures of everything inside packages.

CHAPTER 2

Best Breeds

Most bomb detection dogs are male. Male dogs are usually larger and stronger than female dogs. But some law enforcement agencies also use female dogs.

Law enforcement agencies receive their dogs in different ways. They usually buy their dogs from breeders or receive dogs as gifts from community members.

Requirements

Bomb detection dogs must be intelligent and healthy. They need stamina. Stamina is the energy and strength to do something for a long time. Dogs selected to become bomb detectors must be active. They must show a desire to search and retrieve. Retrieve means to bring an object back.

Bomb detection dogs must be intelligent and healthy.

Selected dogs also have to be friendly. They will be around many strangers during their searches. They must be calm and not easily excited. An overly excited dog might make a bomb explode accidentally.

Most dogs have good senses of smell. But some breeds have special skills. These skills make them well-suited for detecting bombs. German shepherds and Labrador retrievers are the breeds trainers choose most often.

German Shepherds

German shepherds are the most popular dogs for police and bomb detection work. These dogs are smart, faithful, and easy to train. German shepherds also react quickly to risky situations.

German shepherds have stronger senses of smell than most other dog breeds. This makes them excellent bomb detection dogs. For example, fox terriers' noses have about 147 million sniffing cells. German shepherds' noses

German shepherds have stronger senses of smell than most other dog breeds.

have 220 million of these cells. People have only five million sniffing cells. More sniffing cells means a better sense of smell.

Many people respect German shepherds. Some people fear them. Not many people will challenge a full-grown German shepherd.

Labrador Retrievers

Labrador retrievers are also common bomb detection dogs. Most Labrador retrievers are calmer and gentler than German shepherds. They are also faster runners. This makes them good at searching large areas of land.

Sometimes bomb detection dogs need to find mines hidden in water. Labrador retrievers are good swimmers. This helps the dogs find underwater mines.

Labrador retrievers are common bomb detection dogs.

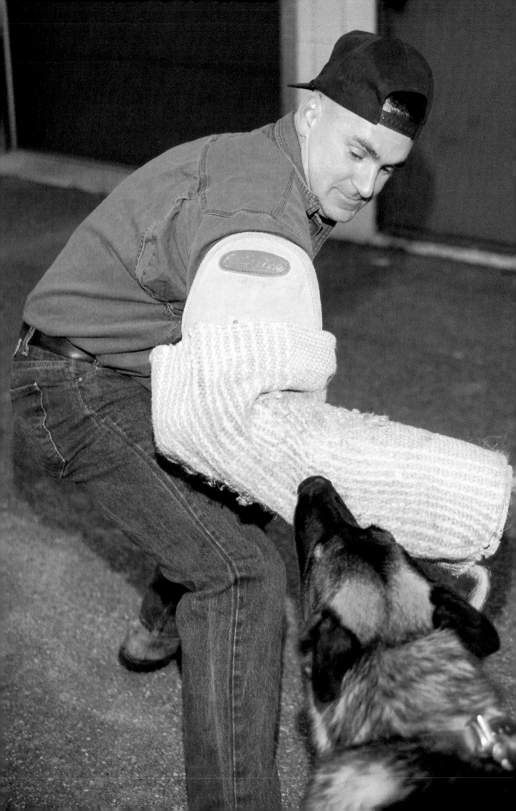

CHAPTER 3

Training

All dogs selected for bomb detection must pass obedience training. Obedience training is teaching an animal to do what it is told. This includes teaching basic commands such as sit, stay, come, and heel. Heel is a command that instructs a dog to walk alongside its master, usually on the left side.

Police bomb detection dogs also go through training to become police dogs. They learn how to help police officers. They learn how to search, chase, and hold suspects. A suspect is someone thought to have committed a crime. Police dogs learn how to attack suspects without being too fierce. This is called a controlled attack.

Police bomb detection dogs learn how to attack suspects without being too fierce.

Handlers must know their dogs' personalities.

Handler Training

Handlers must know the skills and characters of their dogs. They learn about dog behavior and how to care for dogs. Trainers teach handlers how to give commands to their dogs.

Some bomb detection dogs work for the military. Many military handlers train at Lackland Air Force Base in San Antonio,

Texas. Handlers take a six-month training course offered by the government. Other schools offer similar programs.

First, all handlers work with dogs that are partly trained. Later, handlers are paired with the dogs that will be their partners. These dogs are already fully trained.

Training exercises build trust between dogs and their handlers. Handlers pet and praise their dogs when the dogs perform well. Some handlers give the dogs treats. Other times they allow the dogs to play for a few minutes. The dogs learn skills quickly because they want attention from their handlers.

Scent Association

Law enforcement agencies have different dog training programs. Most training programs are 10 to 14 weeks long.

During training, the dogs learn scent association. Scent association is the ability to identify a specific smell. People generally smell a mixture of scents. Dogs can smell single scents, even when hundreds of scents are in the air. This makes dogs able to remember the scents of many explosives.

Trainers teach dogs scent association by using specially scented objects. These objects have the scent of the explosive that trainers want the dogs to find. Trainers tell the dogs to sit every time they show interest in the scented objects. They praise the dogs and give them toys. After a time, the scent brings back positive memories to the dogs. This makes the dogs want to search for the scent.

One training device is an eight-inch (20-centimeter) piece of plastic pipe with small holes in it. This is called a dummy. The holes must be too small for the dogs' teeth to enter. Scent from the explosive is put inside the pipe. Trainers place caps at each end of the pipe to seal the material inside. The scent escapes through the small holes.

Trainers spend two or three days teaching dogs the scent of each explosive. The dogs remember each scent. Dogs can detect at least 12 explosive materials by the end of training. They can also detect thousands of other scents.

A dog is ready to find a target after it has learned scent association.

They learn these other scents during advanced training and while they work on the job.

Finding the Target

A dog is ready to find a target after it has learned scent association. A target is something that smells like explosives. At first, the target is the dummy filled with explosives. Later, the target may be a real explosive device like a disarmed bomb or an unloaded gun.

First, a trainer places the target on a flat surface. The trainer tells the dog to find the target. The trainer praises the dog for each successful find. Next, the trainer hides the target in tall grass. The dog cannot see the target easily. The dog must find the target. After the dog has mastered this, the trainer hides the target in many different places. The trainer may hide the target in boxes, vehicles, and buildings.

After a time, the trainer puts other kinds of explosives inside the target. The dog learns to find more scents.

Obstacles

People sometimes hide bombs in difficult and hard-to-reach locations. Dogs must be able to reach these places to find the bombs. During training, the dogs climb ladders. They cross junk piles or other obstacles. An obstacle is an object that gets in the way. Trainers have dogs search through warehouses, cars, trucks, and

The trainer hides the target in many different places.

Dogs climb ladders during obstacle training.

houses. A warehouse is a large building used for storing goods. Sometimes handlers bury targets or hide them in trees. This makes dogs work harder to find the targets. The dogs also learn to search in both high and low places.

Searching must be done as quickly as possible. Trainers help their dogs find targets. Lives might depend on finding bombs quickly.

Bomb detection dogs are ready for work when their advanced training is finished. They work with handlers to search for real bombs, mines, or weapons hidden by criminals.

At work, handlers give dogs the same commands the dogs received during training. Dogs are rewarded if they find bombs.

Partners

Handlers take their dog partners home after completing bomb detection training. The dogs live with their handlers and become special members of handlers' families.

Bomb detection dogs are allowed time to play when they are not working. They are treated with care, respect, and kindness. The dogs are not spoiled, because spoiled dogs might not listen to their handlers. Lives might be lost if the dogs are not obedient.

CHAPTER 4

Special Jobs

Bomb detection dogs are ready to work at any time. They help bomb squads work on bomb threats.

Sometimes the dogs search large public areas before entertainment events. This helps make sure that the performers and their fans stay safe. Teams of dogs and their handlers may check areas before political meetings. Bomb detection dogs still search airports, too.

Finding Mines

Some bomb detection dogs travel to places where there have been wars. They search for land mines. Land mines are mines buried

Bomb detection dogs may search large public areas before entertainment events.

underground. Some land mines are only four and one-half inches (11 centimeters) wide. They are only two and one-half inches (six centimeters) high. They are small but deadly. A single land mine can kill several people.

Bomb detection dogs train for an additional seven to 20 weeks to find mines. Mine detection training is like bomb detection training. Dogs learn scents to detect mines.

Soldiers leave many land mines in the ground when wars end. Land mines hurt and kill thousands of people each year. About 100 million land mines lie buried in more than 60 different countries.

In 1979, the Soviet army invaded Afghanistan. The army buried many land mines. The mines were still there when the army left Afghanistan in February of 1989. Today, the United Nations is running Operation Salaam. Operation Salaam includes training and sending bomb detection dogs to find mines

Many bomb detection dogs train for an additional seven to 20 weeks to find mines.

in Afghanistan. These mines are mostly on roads and pathways. Mine detecting dogs find the mines so people can disarm them. This allows the people of Afghanistan to return safely to their homes.

Gun Detectors

In 1994, a bomb detection dog was searching for bombs in a Greek airport. The dog came to a car and indicated a find. Its handler searched the car and found a gun. The dog thought the gun was a bomb. This is because gunpowder smells like explosives in bombs.

This find gave law enforcement agencies a new idea. They decided to train bomb detection dogs to find gunpowder, bullets, and guns. Sometimes the guns have been used to commit crimes. Finding the guns helps police officers find the people responsible for the crimes.

Bomb detection dogs train for an additional four to eight weeks to learn how to find guns. Trainers use scent association to teach the dogs the scent of explosives in guns.

Some bomb detection dogs are trained to find guns.

CHAPTER 5

Dogs on the Job

Hundreds of bomb detection dogs work hard every day. As a result, bomb squads have found and disposed of many bombs. The dogs and their handlers have saved hundreds of lives. They have been making the world a safer place for many years.

Brandy

In 1972, a Trans World Airline jet took off from John F. Kennedy Airport (JFK) in New York City. An unknown person called the police and said there was a bomb on the airplane. The police told the pilots. The pilots flew the airplane back to JFK.

Hundreds of bomb detection dogs work hard every day.

Bomb detection dogs search airplanes to find bombs.

A bomb detection German shepherd named Brandy searched the airplane. Brandy had been trained to find bombs. She found the bomb. Bomb squad members disarmed it. The bomb was set to explode 12 minutes later.

Charlie
A Labrador retriever named Charlie was the first dog trained as a gun detector. He found guns, ammunition, and shell casings by

detecting gunpowder. A shell casing is the metal or paper case that holds gunpowder. Charlie learned to detect 19,000 different explosives.

Charlie helped law enforcement agencies search for guns and other explosives. He helped officers look for the Unabomber in Los Angeles. The Unabomber was a bomber who sent many bombs through the mail.

Bingo

A German shepherd named Bingo was a police bomb detection dog. An airline manager called Bingo's bomb squad to look into a bomb threat. Someone had reported a bomb on an airplane that had taken off. The airplane flew back to the airport and landed. The passengers quickly left the airplane.

Bingo's handler brought him on the airplane. Bingo searched the airplane and found the bomb in one of the plane's bathrooms. The bomb squad put the bomb in a special container. Officers took the container to another part of the airport and disarmed it.

There was a timer on the bomb. The bomb would have exploded in 15 minutes.

Better than Machines

Bomb detection dogs are faster, safer, and more effective than machines used to find bombs. People using machines do not know where bombs are. They might search areas for hours without finding bombs. Dogs waste no time searching areas with no bombs. They go directly to areas where the scent of explosives is present.

Some mines are buried so deep that metal detectors cannot find them. Dogs can find these mines. They can even detect explosives wrapped in plastic.

Risk and Retirement

There is no special safety equipment for bomb detection dogs. Most bombs are so powerful that safety equipment would not offer much protection. Bomb detection dogs may die if bombs explode while they are searching. Some

Bomb detection dogs work five to 10 years before they retire.

dogs and their handlers have given their lives to help people.

Bomb detection dogs work five to 10 years before they retire. They live the rest of their lives with their handlers. Sometimes their handlers cannot keep them. In these cases, the law enforcement agencies find good homes for the retired dogs.

bomb (BOM)—a set of explosives or a holder filled with explosives

disarm (diss-ARM)—to make harmless

dummy (DUHM-ee)—a piece of plastic pipe with small holes in it that is filled with the scent of explosives

heel (HEEL)—a command telling a dog to walk alongside its master, usually on the left side

land mine (LAND MINE)—a bomb buried underground

obedience training (oh-BEE-dee-uhns TRAY-ning)—teaching an animal to do what it is told; includes basic commands such as sit, stay, come, and heel

smuggle (SMUHG-uhl)—to bring something in or out of a country illegally

stamina (STAM-uh-nuh)—the energy and strength to do something for a long time

target (TAR-git)—something that smells like explosives

Curtis, Patricia. *Dogs on the Case*. New York: Lodestar Books, 1989.

George, Charles and Linda. *Police Dogs*. Mankato, Minn.: RiverFront Books, 1998.

George, Charles and Linda. *Search and Rescue Dogs*. Mankato, Minn.: RiverFront Books, 1998.

Green, Michael. *Bomb Detection Squads*. Mankato, Minn.: RiverFront Books, 1998.

Ring, Elizabeth. *Detector Dogs: Hot on the Scent*. Brookfield, Conn.: Millbrook Press, 1993.

USEFUL ADDRESSES

The Canadian Police Canine Association
8004 4A Street
Calgary, Alberta T2K 5W8
Canada

Dogs Against Drugs, Dogs Against Crime
517 Spring Mill Road
Anderson, IN 46013

K-9 Concepts
406 East Madison
Broussard, LA 70518

The United States Police K9 Association
P.O. Box 26086
Shoreview, MN 55126

The Washington State Police K9 Association
P.O. Box 1302
Renton, WA 98057

INTERNET SITES

Chomi's Detection Dog Applications Web Site
http://www.erols.com/chomi/

K9_cops
http://www.acmenet.net/~streetcops/k9cops.htm

Police Dog Homepages
http://www.best.com/~policek9/index.htm

Workingdogs.com
http://www.workingdogs.com

INDEX

48

Contents

Pam Isherwood

RAF Greenham Common is used by the US Air Force as part of a NATO agreement. At present, there is no obligation for the US government to obtain Britain's consent before firing missiles from Greenham Common. Hence the base is referred to in the text as 'USAF Greenham Common'.

Introduction

Greenham Common women's peace camp has existed now (June 1983) for 21 months, maintaining an unbroken presence outside the air base, despite two bad winters and continual harassment by the authorities. The ideas and vitality exemplified by the peace camp are in dramatic contrast to the bleakness and dreadful purpose of the base – two opposing value systems right next to one another but on opposite sides of the fence. The peace camp is a remarkable manifestation of women's determination and vision, an inspiration to many thousands of people in this country and abroad. As well as being a round-the-clock protest against cruise missiles, it is also a resource – a women's space in which to try to live out ideals of feminism and nonviolence, a focus for information and ideas, a meeting place, and a vital context for women to express their beliefs and feelings.

The peace camp does not exist in isolation, but is supported by a wide network of individuals, women's groups, peace groups, CND groups, religious groups and union branches, who send money, food, warm clothes, firewood, equipment, and offer their homes, telephones, cars, time and energy. Thousands of people all over the world have sent letters, cards and telegrams of support and encouragement. It is a testimony to people's support for the peace

camp that it has existed almost entirely on donations since the beginning.

Through contact with the peace camp and the actions associated with it, many women have discovered that they are not alone in their beliefs or their fears for the future. This growing network of women is a source of inspiration and strength to us. Like so many women, we have found this a context where we can express our opposition to the diabolical madness of the arms race.

Women outside the main gate, USAF Greenham Common

Eleni Leoussi

Opposing cruise missiles

The growth of the peace movement in Britain and Western Europe was stimulated by NATO's decision of December 1979 to site US cruise and Pershing II missiles in several European countries in the 1980s. This decision gave rise to sickening discussions on the possibility of a 'limited nuclear war' in Europe. In addition, the British government's commitment to Trident submarine-launched nuclear missiles to replace and 'upgrade' the existing Polaris system – and to be paid for by British taxpayers – is another major focus for opposition in this country.

Like most government decisions, the decision about cruise missiles was taken over our heads and without our knowledge. It was also taken over the heads of most MPs, our elected representatives, despite the fact that the government purports to be acting in our name, defending 'freedom and democracy'. It is the presence of 20 or so peace camps outside military bases, and the campaign of nonviolent direct action associated with them, which has been largely responsible for opening up a public debate about cruise missiles and disarmament in general. As the first peace camp in this country, Greenham Common women's peace camp has played a special part in this. Also, following the lead taken by the peace camps, the Campaign for Nuclear Disarmament (CND) has sup-

7

ported and organised nonviolent direct action at national level for the first time in its 25-year history – a recognition of the ineffectiveness of going through the 'proper channels'.

The issue of cruise and Trident missiles and nuclear disarmament did eventually surface 'officially' in the 1983 general election, thus breaking the political consensus on defence which had lasted for 20 years. Disarmament was a central issue for the Labour Party, reflecting growing public awareness and deep concern over the escalation of the arms race. However, this issue was apparently not sufficiently important to people to win the election for Labour. Indeed, the new Conservative government, firmly committed to cruise missiles and increased defence spending, will interpret its election success as a clear mandate for its defence policies and will feel even more confident than before about suppressing opposition to nuclear weapons. Despite the Conservative election victory, the majority of people in this country are against cruise missiles (54 per cent, according to a Gallup poll published in the *Daily Telegraph* in February 1983), including a group called Tories against Cruise and Trident.

Mrs Thatcher's commitment to US military policy is as uncritical as it is uncompromising and her re-election is undoubtedly a major setback for the peace movement. Even if a Labour government had been elected, crucial differences of opinion would still have existed between Labour politicians as to what they would do about disarmament. A Labour government would have been under great pressure not to depart from existing military commitments both from within its own ranks, and from British military and financial institutions, and international organisations such as the EEC and the International Monetary Fund, both dominated by the United States.

In discussing the campaign against cruise missiles it is as well to acknowledge some of the realities of the situation at the outset. Cruise missiles are pilotless aircraft, each carrying one nuclear warhead, launched either from sea, ground or air. Their maximum range is 1,500 miles and, once fired, they travel at about 500 miles per hour. They fly very low, thus eluding enemy radar, and find their target by means of a computerised map which matches the terrain to radar altitude readings.

There are 4,000 cruise missiles being produced and the plan is to deploy 464 land-based cruise missiles in Europe: 96 at Green-

ham Common; 64 at Molesworth; 112 at Comiso in Sicily; 96 in West Germany; 48 in Holland; and 48 in Belgium.

If they are as accurate as their makers claim, cruise missiles could hit military as well as civilian targets in the USSR. They could also be used to fight a nuclear war in Europe, and would make the escalation from the use of conventional to nuclear weapons easier. The missiles stationed at Comiso will have the capacity to hit Middle Eastern targets, thus heightening the possibility that US nuclear weapons could be used to intervene in a Middle Eastern conflict.

Each one of these 464 cruise missiles would have the capacity to destroy 15 towns the size of Hiroshima. The official scenario is that, in times of grave international tension, the missiles and their warheads would be taken from their silos and loaded on to trucks. A cavalcade of US troops, tanks, the 55-foot long launching vehicle and a security system protecting even against chemical weapons, would accompany the bombs through the countryside. They would thus avoid the possibility of being destroyed in their silos, and in their new positions would be free to destroy areas of the Soviet Union, Eastern Europe, or other pre-programmed targets. At Greenham, there will be a unit of 12 men (called Quick Reaction Alert) constantly on alert in one of the silos, ready to put this scenario into action at any time should the order be given.

The fact that cruise missiles will not be launched from Greenham but from somewhere within a 50 to 100 mile radius, makes that entire area a likely target. This highlights the irony of talk of cruise missiles as 'defensive' weapons. Far from being protected by them, the very fact that there will be 96 at Greenham (and 464 in Europe as a whole) means that this entire area is more vulnerable to attack. While Soviet surveillance systems are not yet able to detect cruise missiles once in flight (although within the next two years it is expected that they will be able to) they would receive satellite information when the missiles were taken from their silos and transported around the countryside.

The missile silos at Greenham Common – enormous mounds of reinforced concrete – are nearly complete. Cruise missiles and their launching lorries can be brought into the base by air. Blockades of the base, though of great symbolic importance in showing the strength of people's opposition, cannot physically stop cruise missiles. Blockades would have to be *massive*, recurrent and planned entirely without police knowledge to disrupt the functioning of the

9

base substantially. Virtually every day for at least the last 18 months, huge container lorries have been going in and out of the air base. Some people believe that much of the equipment needed for the missiles, and perhaps the missiles themselves – though without their nuclear warheads – may be at Greenham Common already.

The two superpowers, the USA and USSR, have been developing more and more sophisticated weapons and guidance and detection systems for decades. There is much discussion and argument as to the strength of these arsenals, each side underestimating its own capacity and overestimating the capacity of the other, seemingly to justify continued escalation of the arms race. The economies of both superpowers are in effect war economies, where vast wealth is invested in the research and development of ever more deadly weapons systems, and literally millions of people are involved in this process in some way. In the West, private companies make enormous profits at every step: mining uranium, processing it and enriching it to 'weapon grade' plutonium, designing and producing the various components, and so on. In the Soviet bloc this process is organised through state departments and industrial enterprises.

It is against this background that the superpowers talk about disarmament. Not surprisingly, political and economic systems so heavily dependent on arms industries produce more weapons, not fewer. Years of sporadic talks have got virtually nowhere. Both major power blocs continue utterly entrenched in their existing commitments. It has been said that if there is some agreement in the current round of arms limitation talks in Geneva this year, NATO will not deploy cruise missiles in Europe, but such agreement is hardly likely. What is needed is intervention at every stage in the process: millions of people making clear their opposition by, for example, putting political pressure on governments, refusing to make the various components for the missiles, refusing to transport or assemble them, and refusing to build the silos or supply materials.

At the beginning of June 1983, NATO defence ministers confirmed their earlier decision to deploy cruise and Pershing II missiles if the Geneva negotiations fail, but Denmark and Greece both had reservations and Spain abstained. The Dutch government is openly debating whether to reduce its nuclear role in NATO and has not yet agreed that cruise missiles should be deployed in Holland. US Assistant Secretary for Defense Richard Perle said

that the decision to site cruise and Pershing II missiles in Europe had 'proved politically difficult to implement.' (The *Guardian*, 3 June 1983.)

The governments of Western democracies depend on people's consent for their legitimacy. The great majority of people support the government, if not wholeheartedly then tacitly, by not objecting to what it does. Over the past two or three years many people have begun to question a 'defence' policy which needs ever more horrendous weapons at enormous expense. There are now enough nuclear weapons in the world to totally destroy a city the size of Cardiff every half hour for the next 57 years. Indeed, there are sufficient to destroy the whole world many times over. More and more people – women particularly – are recognising that the only hope we have of reversing this terrifying situation is to withdraw our support from a system which in no way deserves our cooperation or respect.

Greenham Common women's peace camp is an initiative by a small group of women who felt desperate about the prospect of cruise missiles being sited in this country, convinced that this would make Britain more of a target than ever, and angry that resources are being squandered on weapons of mass destruction. It is the strength of these ideas which inspired us to write this book. It speaks in a variety of voices as different women describe their dreams, explain their ideas and experiences, and express their fears, optimism and vision. More and more women are acknowledging their fear of nuclear weapons and gaining confidence to take action. This is a struggle not only for survival but for a life worth living – a life not continually overshadowed by the very real possibility of annihilation through nuclear war.

Fear is the starting point and, given the dreadful potential of nuclear weapons, it is absolutely reasonable to be afraid.

A private nightmare

As a person who has lived most of their life, I still do not wish to die by lingering on with some form of radiation sickness. I worry when I look at my dear grandchildren and my heart aches – will they ever have the chance to grow up? I worry about this beautiful earth of ours, it belongs to all of us, why should it be destroyed by the few?

This fear is on my mind every day, and I have dreams about the terrible slaughter and burning up a nuclear war would bring. My most recent dream was:

I was walking along a long road, weeping and looking for my husband. The earth was opening up, and the bodies of thousands of screaming naked people were falling into this abyss.

All members of my family and friends worry about this third world war happening, especially the young people with children. I think some of them are living in dread. I know lots of people try to push this into the back of their minds, but I think it is getting harder to keep it there now. I'm sure most people are getting the feeling that we are heading towards some dreadful calamity.

Mrs Smith

The horror of nuclear weapons and the possibility of nuclear war had frightened and worried me [Alice] for years. I chose the people I discussed this with. Many men laughed off my bad dreams, until I stopped bothering to talk about it to them. I had a feeling that many women felt as I did, however, and finally put an advertisement in *Spare Rib*, asking women to contact me if they had had dreams about nuclear war. All through that summer in 1980, I received letter after letter from women talking about their own bad dreams. Later, I put a similar advertisement in *Sanity*, which is read by men as well as women. The response was so immediate and so many women replied that I began to get a strong sense of an undercurrent of anxiety, which was having far-reaching effects on people's lives. This anxiety emerged in dreams and worried thoughts, plans for the future and an overriding feeling of desperation and pessimism.

I don't think about the future any more. I never think more than a year ahead. I can't conceive of the future and I think it's a result of the fear of war. I've been aware of the bomb since I was eight or nine. I was very frightened then but I suppose I got used to it. But now I can't conceive of the 1990s; I feel I mustn't sink into thinking like that but I can't help it. Then I think that I'm not going to sacrifice anything now, any sort of enjoyment I might have, for the sake of the future. That's why I work hard for a while and then stop, because there seems no point. I run the risk of people saying I'm crazy, but I can't stay with anything because I want to do as many things as I can. I find I don't want to get closely involved with anyone. It's hard to think of people you know dying. I've got my family to think about and I don't want any more worries. I don't want to think about anyone else dying.

I think that the fear of war has increased in the last couple of years, and I'm sure I'm not the only one to have private nightmares about it. My dreams about war are all quite similar. They take place after the bomb has dropped, and involve people running around madly, trying to get away. Or else everyone is dead and I'm alone, trying to look for someone I know. In the dreams, I know there's no escape and that to run around blindly is pointless. All I want is to find someone and die with someone I know. I always feel an incredible desolation, a sense of loss, that all these people are going to be dead in a short while, myself included.
Ruth

No one knows just how many people have repeated nightmares about the nuclear holocaust. Such dreams highlight the enormous strength of feeling which, if it could be acknowledged and mobilised, would be freed for positive action. One of the most common features of the letters was that each woman felt completely alone in her fear. She had no idea that other women felt the same. This was before the women's peace movement became such a growing force. At the time, there seemed no positive way in which this energy could be channelled. Most of the women's dreams and statements that appear in this chapter date from that time. Since then, I and many of the women who replied have been able to turn this energy outwards in a positive direction and become actively involved in the women's peace movement.

Many women who have visited the women's peace camp at Greenham Common, or become involved in actions associated with it, have done so after a period of growing fear and anxiety about nuclear war. These fears are not much talked about. They usually remain the private concern of individuals too nervous of being thought hysterical to share them with others. We have to try to come terms with these dreadful feelings of despair and paralysis or else we are submerged by them. What propels people into action is that the feeling of impotence becomes so unbearable that we have to try to do something about it.

The press characterises women's actions at Greenham and elsewhere as 'naive', 'sincere', 'emotional', thus seeking to denigrate them by using attributes that are thought to be 'female' or weak. What is left out of their stories is that this kind of response is not the easy option it is believed to be. It is easier to think about cruise missiles in the abstract language of political debate, where death is discussed in facts and figures, than to think about one person's death from radiation sickness. In order to be able to respond emotionally to the fact that our planet may be destroyed by nuclear weapons, each person must struggle through the layers of apathy and paralysis that surround this issue.

Many people believe that a nuclear war is more likely now than at any other time since the Cuba crisis of 1962. People see the cold war re-spiralling. Through newspapers and television they get a picture of Reagan and Andropov becoming increasingly intransigent, increasingly hostile to arms reduction, warning of war. According to recent opinion polls (The *Observer*, NOP, 8 November 1981, and The *Guardian*, Marplan, 24 January 1983):

49% of people interviewed think a nuclear war is likely in their lifetime

87% believe they and their families would not survive if nuclear weapons were used against Britain

57% think US defence policy is making nuclear war more likely

53% think American bases should be removed from Britain

58% of women do not want Trident nuclear submarines

67% of women do not want cruise missiles

We are repeatedly told of the importance of a nuclear deterrent against the Soviet threat, but many people now fear the USA almost as much as the USSR. More people in Britain are now in favour of unilateral disarmament than ever before.

In an opinion poll conducted by *New Society* in 1980 most people who said they were worried about nuclear weapons were either unwilling to do anything, or felt that nothing could be done. Many people are both anxious and fatalistic about the nuclear war they increasingly expect, and are increasingly certain that they will not survive. If the findings of the various polls are turned into personal statements they have a very different impact.

I worry about nuclear weapons.

I believe a nuclear war will happen in my lifetime.

If there is a nuclear war, I am sure I will die. I will either die from the initial blast, be vaporised or crushed, or I will die in the ensuing weeks from radiation sickness.

To confront the issue like this turns the abstract into the concrete, the impersonal into the personal. This is the reality behind the beliefs stated in the opinion polls, because the use of nuclear weapons will **directly** and **personally** affect every individual.

We all live with the threat of nuclear war. It is a fact of life, a possibility that permeates our lives whether we choose to think about it or not. At this minute there are enough nuclear weapons targeted on various countries to blow up the world many times over, were a war to be started by accident or design. We are surrounded by information that tries to block out this fact. Nuclear terminology – words like 'overkill', 'megaton', 'theatre war' – has become commonplace. Even the image of a nuclear explosion, the mushroom cloud, is a term in general use. We read not of nuclear

weapons and what they actually do, but of abstract 'warheads'. In the debate over cruise missiles, for example, the government has focused on 'dual key control' and how 'cruise is an answer to the Soviet SS20s'. This euphemistic argument leads to a curious sense of unreality, when we realise that what is being talked about is the deaths of millions of people.

It is, of course, in the interests of those politicians who support the nuclear arms race to ignore stark realities in their presentation of the 'facts' to the people, and to concentrate on euphemisms instead. It is also not surprising that most of us accept this with a certain amount of relief. What we have to come to terms with otherwise is a picture so terrifying that our whole being revolts against it and we develop mental strategies to defend ourselves.

But many people are finding it increasingly difficult to ward off their fear. Often it comes out in nightmares. In dreams we may deal with information and feelings which we cannot assimilate in waking life. The women who describe their dreams in the following pages often felt them to be a way of expressing to themselves fears that were too desolating to consider while awake.

It was a bright, grey winter's day. There was, to my certain knowledge, half an hour to go before the bomb dropped. I was walking, stumbling down a country lane, naked hawthorns on either side. I was with my two children. I felt at once calm, philosophic. There's only half an hour to go anyway. I mustn't frighten the children. I felt how easy it would be to die. Somehow personal annihilation was no threat. I could cope with death, whether it came suddenly and unknowingly, or slowly and tragically, watching my dearest girls ill, knowing my far-flung unreachable friends and family to be suffering too. If only. 'If only' was the crunch. 'If only' meant if only I could know that the sick fields and waters, trees and mountains could renew some day, if only the bare hawthorns could leaf again. So thinking I looked lovingly at the twigs and branches. Clearly, in sharp tender focus, young small green leaves sprang into sight. Their pale unfurling vulnerability, their promise of hope, their pledge of spring and rebirth, pierced me with emotion. I still knew there was half an hour to go, and that the world could not, would not revive. The eternal promise of the leaves had been betrayed,

and I awoke. I was startled to find that my predominant emotion was that of wonder and gratitude that I had been able to see those beautiful leaves before the world died.
Kate

I was in a jeep driving through a very wasted landscape. It looked like a desert but I knew it was a long time after a nuclear war. I was going away from one area to somewhere safer, but everywhere looked very blasted, like the Great Salt Lake of Utah, but it was just what had happened to the landscape as a result of the war.

The atmosphere was very thick. I couldn't see any stars, but the headlights of the jeep were working. I was driving along with someone else, who seemed to be a friend, but I couldn't tell the sex of the person. There was some trouble with the jeep, and it seemed fairly unlikely that we would get to our destination, which I felt to be London or some other big city, because there wouldn't be enough petrol.

My friend was driving, and I was holding between my knees a giant piece of ice. Inside the block there was a fish, and this was the last fish, which I had to get to London, which was the last place where there was still some clean water where the fish could survive. [A mythological character, Finn McClure, is told about a certain fish by an old woman. This is the fish of knowledge, the idea being that real power is knowledge and real knowledge is in the thoughts and words of creatures, stones and trees. Finn McClure catches the fish and by eating it gains the knowledge.]

This fish I was holding was the fish of knowledge, and if we could keep the fish alive there was some hope for continuance in the world. But if we couldn't it would be the end. There was a feeling that this was necessary, it was inevitable, we had to do it, it was all we could do, but the likelihood of actually doing it was fairly remote. The heat from the engine was starting to melt the ice, and I had to keep shifting it, and try to steer by non-existent stars.

When I woke up – still on the journey – I felt quite calm.
Noa

I have dreamt many times of the first few moments after a nuclear explosion.
On one occasion there was a horrible smell of burning flesh (although I have no idea what burning flesh smells like). Children were screaming, running with their hands lifted up for help, and their skin was peeling off. There was no blood. In fact there was no liquid, everything was hot and dry. I was somehow watching all this.
The dreams started after showing *The War Game* to children at the school where I teach. I'd seen the film eight years ago, but this time it was more shocking, more immediate. The kids were appalled and frightened, but on the surface I switched off. The

only way to cope was to cut off from it because it is so horrific. Two weeks later I dreamt about nuclear war four nights in succession. I still have the dreams sometimes but wake up with a different feeling. At the time it was fear. I'd wake up and realise that the war must already be here. It's in our heads and we are thinking and dreaming and making plans. Now I don't feel that kind of panic, I think I've accepted it, and that it's in everyone's heads. My mother, who lives in a totally different environment, talks about it, asking me if I think nuclear war will be so different from the last war.

They – men, the powers that be – have won the war already in a way, by planting it in our heads . . . The problem is so monumental that it tends to make action seem meaningless. Strength of numbers is nothing. Feeling so impotent and powerless adds to the guilt which I feel surrounds the whole issue.

There are times when walking down the street, touching things, the concrete, I think this is all going to go. It's disbelief, and once I get through the disbelief, panic. When I go it's never going to be replaced, it's the end.

There isn't the language to deal with this. It's like trying to imagine infinity. It's so vast that I am totally pessimistic. I go on marches in a very half-hearted way, knowing that at the end I'm just going to feel very depressed and panicky.

It's incredible that I or anybody else is talking about accepting it, almost tolerating it, but having exhausted the possibilities I can see no way out.

I'm very conscious of not reading or finding out more. It's bad enough dreaming about it. Men I know haven't ever described that feeling of panic, which women talk about – all the women I know have felt real fear over this threat. Of course they have a different perspective.

In the cold light of day I feel numb. It's not going to get me because I've accepted it, but in the dreams it's still full of panic and disbelief. Although I see myself in the dream, I don't feel myself in it and I'm incredulous. The strangest thing about the dreams, and the connection between them and how I feel about them when I'm awake is acceptance. We all take the image that is given to us. While I resent that I'm drawn into it, feel so angry about it, I live in this society and must take some of the blame for the feeling of inevitability that surrounds this issue.

Many years ago now, I had a nervous breakdown which

started with an anxiety attack in which I felt I couldn't breathe. I remember vividly the feeling – the same as in the dreams and when I think about war – total horror and panic, and yet tolerance at the same time. In the dream the siren goes off and I can watch the panic rising. I know that I can either surrender to the panic, or sit down and somehow refuse to be sucked into that state. When I wake up I won't allow that panic to get to me. But when I had the breakdown I felt somewhere deep inside that I had made a choice, wanted to be a victim of fear and panic, that it was somehow easier than the other choice.
Carol

Individuals have to come to terms – however they can – with living in a world under threat of total annihilation. Many simply drive it out of their consciousness, and those who try to confront this reality can run the risk that others will call them mad.

Women run that risk in any case:

16 times as many women as men are treated for depression;
many more women than men have 'breakdowns';
one out of every eight women spends time in mental hospitals;
millions are prescribed tranquillisers every year.

We are facing the ultimate insanity – destroying the world we live in. This insanity is the 'real' world. Yet if women talk plainly about how this insanity affects their lives now, before the event, they are called mad themselves.

So many people are depressed. They can't see a way of getting out of the terrible situation we're all in, where all our lives are threatened, and some people have severe mental problems from this. I was working in a psychiatric hostel for a couple of years before I gave up my job to come here [Greenham], and people were actually having breakdowns because of the violence of society. One woman I was working with was having nightmares every night about the nuclear disaster, the end of the world, and it meant that she just couldn't carry on with her ordinary life because it was meaningless to her, because she felt so hopeless, that there was nothing she could do about it. She'd collapsed under that pressure and had been labelled mad and locked away because of it. Supposedly for her protection, she'd been pumped full of drugs and put away from society.

She *knew* the reality. She just let it in and that was why it was so devastating for her, because she was isolated in that position. The attitude of the authorities was very much: don't talk to her about that because it'll just drive her more insane, whereas we should all have been admitting that this affects us all. She wasn't *mad* to be having breakdowns about it. We should all be changing society so no one needs to have a breakdown.
Sarah

Nobody really knows the effects of these bombs. It seems like the biggest gamble that we could possibly ever take, and here we are, it's happening now. The politicians want to hide away from the reality of the situation we're in. They're in it as deep as everybody else. They're just part of the whole spiral that's taking us down. It's as if there's a certain part of their personality that can't look at the reality of what's happening and can't look realistically at the part they're playing in that reality.

We fear many, many things, nuclear weapons being one, and it's necessary to block off things that really are so dreadful . . . we split off certain sections of our lives. We're taught right from beginning school. We begin to section off our thinking into certain avenues until, at the end of school life, children are specialising, they're going into different rooms to think about different things. They have different teachers to talk about different subjects. When you compartment your feelings it's a certain way of thinking that brings about a neurosis. That's all right on a temporary basis, but it doesn't help the *whole* person, the *whole* mind, the *whole* life, and neurosis will out, eventually. I think it's very important for people to start trying to face the situation and at least allow themselves to feel the truth and the reality of it.
Jayne

Dreams have brought the whole subject home to me in a way that thinking about the possibility has never done, because they make me feel so helpless. I am frightened in the dreams about my own survival and the survival of the people who are close to me, but what sets them apart from other anxiety dreams is the way they involve everyone and everything.
In one dream I am with my friend, and we are standing with crowds of

people outside, and we are all watching the sky. It is as if we know something is going to happen; there is a portentous feeling, we all know the bomb is going to drop, but can do nothing about it. It makes me feel empty and desolate, like stone — and this is the feeling I wake up with which makes the dream so hideous. It's a very different feeling from being emotional and upset: that tears up my stomach. This is far away from that kind of gut feeling, there is not even that response left, and that is what makes me feel so desperate. Knowing that everyone else is going to die makes the horror of the dreams seem all-embracing, somehow bigger. I watch other people in horror, although I feel it most in myself. I think of my insides, I don't think of anyone else's insides.

I wake up from such dreams in a state of shock and they stay with me for a long time afterwards. I wake up thinking, this is the end of the world. I don't think this is the end of me, or the end of England, but the end of the world, even though I can't possibly absorb this thought. I don't even know what it means. I wake up and the reality of the dream is far worse than the dream itself. I know that I have dreamt the palest reflection of what would happen.

They make me feel as if I should be listening to them in some way and I just don't know in what way. There is the possibility that they are a vehicle to release the worry I feel but am not always aware of. I'm cynical about the thought that I am dreaming about something that is going to happen.

But waking up after such dreams isn't a relief because of their content. I'm just as horrified when I wake up and know that these images are in my head.
Wendy

One of the ways we normally differentiate ourselves from our dreams is by a process of reality testing: we test the reality of the world we have woken up into against the reality of the dream world we have left. We wake up and realise that the monsters who pursued us such a short time ago are not actually in the room. We perceive that our life is not actually threatened in the way it seemed in the dream. The more frightening the dream and the more overwhelming the anxiety, the harder this process is, as anyone who has ever woken in terror from a nightmare will acknowledge. Dreams about nuclear war are different in this respect from other dreams. There is no waking up from this nightmare. We wake and know that the threat of nuclear war is a real one.

Yet politicians suggest that people need not worry, that they should have faith in a government which has rationally considered the options and decided that disarmament is naive and deluded. In a debate in parliament, John Nott, then minister of defence, claimed that he:

> knew of the apprehensions about nuclear war among ordinary people, worried about their children's future. But these natural apprehensions were misplaced provided Britain stuck to her course and did not gamble wildly on some different one.
> *The Times*, 4 March 1981

We are told not to worry, that our deaths are not our concern, and that we should leave the matter to politicians and nuclear strategists who are all the time planning and preparing for war. The government requires local councils to make plans for their areas: to work out how they would keep essential services running, organise civil defence training, provide emergency centres and decide which open spaces to use as mass burial and cremation sites. Many councils are convinced that such proposals are no more than a cruel confidence trick and that there is no defence against nuclear weapons. This is brought out in the following extracts from the *Emergency War Plan*, published by Lambeth Council, London.

> Since it is impossible to predict both the pattern and scale of attack and the weather conditions at the time (especially the wind strength and direction), it is assumed for planning purposes that no part of the UK would escape the effects of nuclear attack . . .
>
> *Post-Attack* . . .
> There may be extensive disruption to the normal services of water supply, waste disposal, refuse collection, sewerage, and fuel and energy supplies.
> There may be large numbers of casualties lying where they had died, and large numbers of survivors may be living in conditions in which peacetime standards of hygiene would be difficult or impossible to achieve.
> Until more usual and permanent arrangements could be made for the resumption of . . . services . . . , the rapid improvisation of public emergency sanitary measures would be of paramount importance. These measures may include:
> - The collection of the dead.
> - The disposal of the dead, probably by mass interment or cremation without formal identification.
> - The collection and disposal of human waste.
> - The collection and disposal of refuse.

- The provision of communal sanitary facilities.
- The provision of communal cooking (in co-operation with the Borough Emergency Feeding Officer) and water storage facilities . . .

Radiation Malaise

Persons exposed to 'radiation' from fallout may contract radiation malaise, the severity being dependent upon the intensity of the dose. The signs and symptoms of the malaise are initially nausea, vomiting, diarrhoea, headaches, apathy and dehydration; in severe cases after a latent period of about a week the following signs will appear:
- diarrhoea with blood in stools,
- fever,
- haemorrhage from all skin surfaces,
- ulceration of tongue, throat and bowels,
- loss of hair . . .

Emergency Feeding . . . 6: Emergency feeding will not be commenced until the radiation hazard has reached acceptable levels; until that time householders and others must exist on stocks of food and water stored in the refuge room prior to attack. On being instructed to commence emergency feeding operations it will be necessary to ensure that food, water and outside areas to be used are decontaminated. The following guidance is given: . . . Special protective clothing will not be issued. Exposed parts of the body should be carefully washed with soap and water . . .

Compare the view that radioactive fallout is something we can just wash off, with Dr Helen Caldicott talking about the effects of plutonium which would be released into the atmosphere after a nuclear explosion and which is very easily absorbed into our bodies – our blood, bones and internal organs.

Plutonium is one of the most carcinogenic substances known . . . One pound, if uniformly distributed, could hypothetically induce lung cancer in every person on earth . . . [it] has a half-life of 24,400 years and, once created, remains poisonous for at least half a million years.

Plutonium is a chemically reactive metal which, if exposed to air, ignites spontaneously to produce respirable particles of plutonium dioxide . . . These particles can be transported by atmospheric currents and inhaled by people and animals. When lodged in the tiny airways of the lung, plutonium particles bombard surrounding tissues with alpha radiation. Smaller particles may break away to be absorbed through the lung and enter the bloodstream. Because plutonium has properties similar to those of iron, it is combined with the iron-transporting proteins in the blood and conveyed to iron storage cells in the liver and bone marrow. Here, too, it irradiates

nearby cells, inducing liver and bone cancer, and leukaemia.

Plutonium's ironlike properties also permit the element to cross the highly selective placental barrier and reach the developing foetus, possibly causing . . . gross deformities in the newborn infant. Plutonium is concentrated by the testicles and ovaries, where inevitably it will cause genetic mutations which will be passed on to future generations.

Dr Helen Caldicott, *Nuclear Madness*

Thus children born to people whose parents survived Hiroshima are more likely to be born deformed; the radioactive particles which are absorbed so easily into the body are still active years later.

Our skin absorbs these radioactive particles.

They sink into the earth.

They are absorbed by all animal and plant life.

The danger lives on for thousands of years, lessening only gradually.

The people of Hiroshima are separated from us by 40 years and half the world. They are still dying from the effects of that 'small' bomb.

Each cruise missile is 15 times as lethal as the bomb that was dropped on Hiroshima.

The prospect of a nuclear war is so terrifying that we refuse to think about it. It is easier to be numb than to consider what we can do to prevent the use of these weapons and stop the mentality that fuels the arms race. It is as if we are frozen.

I freeze when I cannot follow a line of thought: when it will threaten my equilibrium.

In my dream a monster is chasing me. I run stumbling down a path. I can hear my heart beating and look down at my feet which will not go fast enough. I glance over my shoulder and see the monster moving with effortless strides closer and closer towards me. Now all I can hear is the thumping of my heart and I stumble and fall. Time stands still. I am motionless, frozen. The monster takes the last pace, reaches down

and I awake, sweating and shaking.

This is a common dreaming experience, when fear renders us immobile, rooted to the spot, speechless, dumb. We often describe this in terms of cold:

Suddenly I was frozen, I could not move.
My blood ran cold with fear.
I felt myself freeze up when she began to speak.

When something happens in a dream that is so frightening that we freeze, we have one option left: we wake up, our release. The 'worst possible' is about to happen and we protect ourselves from it happening. In a dream we have created this phantom and ultimately we have the power to destroy it too. On waking, it becomes a mirage, half-glimpsed and then, thankfully, we turn away from it.

To be frozen also describes a waking state, an absence of emotion. To be frozen, to be numb: I can no longer feel. If I felt this emotion it would overwhelm me, therefore I block it out. Avoid it. Numb myself.

Polar explorers have often experienced an irresistible desire to go to sleep in the snow. If they give way, then the instinct for self-preservation is lost and death becomes inevitable.

It is easier to be numb and 'cold' than to be responsive and 'warm' when the stimulus is so threatening. To lie down in the snow and refuse to move any further: this is the anaesthesia when the struggle for life is given up. It no longer matters, the only thing that matters is to lie down, to sleep, to be invulnerable, to freeze.

Being frozen indicates a certain blindness – a voluntary turning away. I choose not to look at this, to be implicated, to be threatened, and so I will keep myself as still as possible, until I cannot move and am turned to ice. Then I will be motionless and passive. I will not be responsible.

It is far easier not to have certain thoughts.

It's estimated that in a nuclear war, in 30 days 90 per cent of Americans would be dead. Now I cannot accept that. Apparently there are some people who say, 'well, it's going to happen.' They've lost their most primitive, most powerful instinct, and that is for survival. So they are sick. But unfortunately it's become a collective psychosis in a way, because we all practice psychic numbing, and push it back here . . . We go to work . . . and we have the babies and we cook the cakes, and pretend it's going on forever. But you know that what I've said is true. We are all children of the atomic age, and somehow we've become passive. We are all responsible. This is the most serious medical issue ever to face the human race.

Well, what choice is there? Do I just go along and be a hedonist

and enjoy myself and practise medicine? When my kids are going to be blown up? Knowing what I know, what else can I do? What am I here for? Am I here just to enjoy myself? . . . We are the curators of every organism on this earth. We hold it in the palm of our hands, and this is the ultimate in preventive medicine: to eliminate every single nuclear weapon on earth, and close the reactors at once. For if we do not, we are participating in our own suicide.

Dr Helen Caldicott, *Critical Mass*

The most disturbing aspect of dreams about nuclear war is the way they relate to the very real threat of destruction that hangs not simply over our own lives, but over the future.

The effects of nuclear weapons lie in our heads as well as in radioactive fallout. The damage that is being done *now* to people's vision of the future and their faith in future generations is incalculable.

Personal responsibility

I've got two young children, and I've taken responsibility for their passage into adulthood. Everyone tells me they are my responsibility. The government tells me this. It is my responsibility to create a world fit for them to grow up in. I can't say I'm responsible for my children not catching whooping cough and *not* responsible for doing anything about the threat of annihilation which hangs over them every minute of the day. There were two things that really brought this home to me. I took my daughter to London Zoo one day as a birthday treat. Where we live in Wales it's very quiet. Every plane that went overhead frightened her, and she put her hands over her head saying, 'Mummy they're going to bomb us.' Suddenly I became really conscious that they *could* be: that's about as much warning as we would get. It seemed terrible that I was allowing her to grow up with this fear. I was forced to think about it, but then put it to the back of my mind again. Some time later, when I was about seven and a half months pregnant, I watched *Horizon*, about the 'Protect and Survive' plans. We in Wales would not be hit directly, and it became very plain to me that I would have to sit and watch my children die. Children are much more susceptible

to radiation than adults, and I would have to watch them die in agony and then die myself. Suddenly it became obvious to me that I had to do something for my children.
Susan Lamb, 1983

We might be frightened simply of thinking about nuclear weapons at all and what they mean. The horror is so awful we push it to the back of our minds. Thinking about them means we will have to ask ourselves difficult questions, perhaps recognising that our sense of security may be misplaced, that the future we plan and save for, the home we live in, the friends and families we love are all at risk and no security at all. For each woman associated with Greenham and the thousands who identify with it, the necessity for taking personal responsibility has grown out of feelings of anger and desperation.

As Helen Caldicott says, 'We are the curators of every organism on this earth.' This means that we are *all* responsible for the preservation of life. If we do not take up this responsibility we are likely to destroy the world. This is a difficult idea to accept, for we are not used to defining responsibility so broadly. Many women are saying we must take a fundamentally different attitude, one which encourages rather than denies individual responsibility, which acknowledges the connection between caring for each other and caring for the planet. No one will change this disastrous course for us, we must do it ourselves – by proving that there are other ways of organising, which do not depend on violence; by pointing out that relying on threats and violence threatens life itself; by acknowledging that each person is responsible in their own way for the world in which we live.

I used to wake in the middle of the night in a complete panic, having dreamt the nuclear nightmare, the post-holocaust dream. I was tired of this fear being thrust upon me. I felt I had to do something and not just build a bunker in my back garden! I'd heard of near catastrophes through computer error, through mismanagement, through negligence, and was appalled at the planning and contemplation for mass murder that was going on all around me.

When I heard about the women's peace camp initially, I must have pushed the idea into the back of my mind, because I felt that the sacrifices that needed to be taken in order to make

such a direct action were too great for someone like me with two small children and a seemingly secure, cosy world.

But one day I had a letter from a woman in the peace camp telling of the threat of eviction that the women here faced. What was needed was a strong physical presence of women and it was something I could do. So I packed my sleeping bag up and drove the 200 miles or whatever it is up to Greenham Common not knowing what on earth to expect. I'd never been to a peace camp before. I didn't really know what was going on here. But the warmth and the love that I was greeted with, the total absence of suspicion, was a fantastic feeling and I really felt that I'd made the right decision.

The camp itself is a permanent reminder to the government that there are many people who don't want to be part of the nuclear arms race. We're not just a bunch of women sitting around a base. We're speaking for thousands of people who don't want cruise missiles sited here. It seemed a strange kind of democracy to me that a decision could be taken without even parliament being consulted, let alone the public. I sensed this sick mentality all around me that was motivated not by the sacredness of life but by *fear* that was feeding the arms race. It seemed crazy to me that the government were pouring our precious energies, our resources, billions of pounds, into something that was for mass murder, instead of this money going towards our social services, our health and education.

But it's not just a question of costs and alternative military strategy. It's a moral question. There's really only one thing you need to ask yourself, and that is: would you pull the trigger? would you press the button? and if the answer is 'No', then you have to work with us and help this struggle for peace.

The peace camp's more than just a brave gesture of defiance. It's an experiment in nonviolent resistance, the taking of responsibility by ordinary people, not just for what's being done in our name, but for how we behave towards each other. It was certainly my instincts that brought me here – a deeply based conviction that nothing in the world is more important than peace and that what's going on over there, behind those gates, is evil and only adds to our peril.

We plan to take direct action this weekend. We want to blockade the base for 24 hours by chaining ourselves to the

Decorating the perimeter fence, Greenham Common,
12 December 1982

gates, and we face possible arrest and imprisonment. I've been
accused of being cruel and hard-hearted for leaving my children
behind, but it's exactly *for* my children that I'm doing this. In the
past, men have left home to go to war. Now women are leaving
home for peace.

Sarah van Veen, March 1982

It is hard to accept that *each individual* is to blame for nuclear
weapons – ourselves, our families, our friends. Thousands
of people do not want them and genuinely feel the present situation
is not of their making. This year the government will spend
£16,000,000,000 or so on 'defence'. This works out at about £18 a

Decorating the perimeter fence, Greenham Common,
12 December 1982

week for every family. The army, navy, air force, weapons manufacture and research are all paid for with our money, from income tax, VAT, tax on cigarettes and drink. Of course, not everyone has equal power to effect a change – most of us do not have the same power as a cabinet minister, for example – but we all have the power of refusal in our own lives. If the government makes decisions we do not like we can go along with them – however reluctantly – or we can stand out against them and make our opposition clear. If we do not stand out against nuclear weapons, then we are – however reluctantly – supporting them.

The implications of this line of reasoning are enormous and

31

different for everyone. They are also frightening. We may be frightened

> of taking risks, not knowing what will happen to us,
> of standing out by making a personal statement,
> of being embarrassed in public,
> of being arrested, punished, or having a police record,
> of losing security, perhaps our jobs, or the respect of people we had thought were friends.

Probably every group of women who sit down to discuss nuclear weapons and what can be done about them find themselves talking about these issues. It is only by talking through such fears and seeing that others share them that they cease to be so monumental and become less of a block to taking action.

A fundamental principle of women's actions is that these personal issues are seen to be an integral part of the process, not an embarrassing diversion to be left at home and dealt with separately on our own. Crossing this barrier of silence and isolation is the first step in breaking the chain of powerlessness.

We are all responsible for opening up this issue, for making sure that cruise missiles are a subject for debate, instead of being quietly deployed all over Europe, which is what our governments intended. A majority of people in this country are now opposed to cruise missiles. Two years ago most people had not even heard of them.

On 12 December 1982, 30,000 women from all over Britain, as well as groups from Sweden, Holland, West Germany and Ireland, encircled the base at Greenham Common. In the weeks that followed, hundreds of local papers carried articles about women involved in the peace movement and letters expressing their views. Women were interviewed on local radio stations and invited to speak at meetings. People talked about the action at Greenham all over the country. There is now a chain of women's peace groups. In virtually every town, women are talking about what they can do to express their opposition to nuclear weapons in their own neighbourhood – for example, highlighting the existence of military establishments, the danger from nuclear power stations and nuclear waste, and the inadequacies of civil defence planning.

At present there are over a dozen long-term peace camps in Britain besides the women's peace camp at Greenham Common. Faslane and Holy Loch peace camps are outside nuclear submarine bases in Scotland. There are peace camps outside US Air Force

bases at Upper Heyford, Oxfordshire; Lakenheath, Suffolk; Daws Hill, near High Wycombe; Molesworth, Cambridgeshire; Burtonwood near Warrington, and Wethersfield in Essex. Other camps are protesting at the activities of RAF bases – Lossiemouth in Scotland; Bishopcourt in Northern Ireland; and Naphill, near High Wycombe, as well as against the chemical and biological warfare research centre at Porton Down and the Royal Ordnance factory at Burghfield. These peace camps and others which will be set up in the future all need continual support – money, food, equipment, ideas and encouragement.

People are campaigning against nuclear weapons through their trades unions. Local government employees in many areas are refusing to take part in training for civil defence programmes, which they believe to be wholly inadequate. There are peace education projects in some schools, introducing children to co-operative rather than competitive games and ways of working. Some civil engineers are discussing whether or not they should be designing and building nuclear missile silos. Some doctors – and, indeed, the British Medical Association – are recognising the enormous devastation nuclear war would bring, and emphasising that the present medical services would be unable to cope with more than a tiny fraction of the casualties.

The government spent more on 'defence' last year than on either health or education, and more than double what it spent on housing. It made very serious cuts in public spending between 1979 and 1983, especially in social services and health care. The cuts in public spending in socially useful services and increases in defence spending are two sides of the same coin. There are now fewer places in hospitals or day-care centres for the elderly and the sick, which means that they have to be looked after at home, invariably by women. Other women are involved in campaigning for nurseries and playgroups, for better pay for public service workers, trying to keep hospitals open, getting repairs done to council houses, and so on. Indirectly this is also a campaign against nuclear weapons, against the sickening waste and mismanagement of money, skills and resources invested in the arms race.

As these examples show, everyone has a point of contact with this issue through the areas we live in, the work we do, or the taxes we pay. Compared with the scale of the problem, these initiatives may seem fairly insignificant. However, we all have a responsibility to speak out against the threat of nuclear weapons.

I'm here at Greenham Common where they're building silos for 96 cruise missiles. I want to be here every day to remind these people of what they're doing. They're just ordinary guys who need jobs. If I weren't here every day, they'd be able to do their jobs with that much greater ease. I'm hoping to encourage them to leave their jobs. With my sign I say 'Can you stop for a talk?' and I do mean a *talk*. I don't argue with these people. Once you start to argue nobody listens to each other any more. I talk to them about the men in Germany who built prison camps and gas chambers before the war, never dreaming that they would be used for such atrocities. They needed work and thought they were doing something their nation needed. These people need jobs, but cruise missiles are far, far worse than any gas chamber. Each cruise missile is the equivalent of 15 Hiroshimas, and there are four cruise missiles on each lorry. If America makes trouble anywhere in the world this will have to be knocked out. The devastation that would entail . . . I no longer consider what I may achieve. To me it's important that I express myself about these missiles, and if I can encourage people to leave their jobs then that's great. There are so many ways people can express themselves. If we all gain that little bit of confidence to find our voices and do things then there's a hope of things changing. There's millions of people who don't like what's going on in the world. We've got to find ways of expressing ourselves.
Fran De'Ath, March 1982

After the second attempt to evict the peace camp at Greenham in September 1982, workmen began to lay sewer pipes, part of the expansion needed to house all the extra personnel who would accompany the cruise missiles. Several men arrived on the first afternoon and, with the aid of a large mechanical digger, began to turn over the earth and started to dig trenches. Women gathered at the edges of the site in small groups and stood silently watching. Some talked to the workmen, asking them whether they had considered the consequences of their work, how they felt about preparing the ground for cruise missiles. At first some of the men laughed to each other at the women, but quite quickly all the laughter stopped. The workmen were unable to look the women in the eyes, they looked embarrassed as they continued their work. Some of the women sang to the workmen, songs about the consequences of nuclear weapons, about the bombing of Hiroshima. All

Pam Isherwood

Police support construction workers by
breaking the women's blockade of the base,
Greenham Common, 13 December 1982

the time they looked into the eyes of the workmen, often they cried. The next day the group of workmen was smaller. Several construction companies now find it difficult to hire men to work at Greenham Common. Unwilling to lose the contract, one of these companies has written to all its ex-employees, asking if they would like a job at Greenham.

Many trade unions have passed resolutions expressing their opposition to working in the arms industries, and yet there is often no alternative employment or the firms involved use non-union labour, which makes these votes meaningless. In addition, parts for cruise missiles are made in West Germany, the USA, Canada and the UK. The dozens of companies engaged in supplying parts for weapons systems and preparing sites to house them are firms with such household names as Bendix, Singer, Goodyear and Tarmac.

There are obviously economic reasons for these facts, but one important result is that no one group of workers can be said to be responsible for the manufacture of nuclear weapons. The workers who laid sewage pipes could easily ignore the implications of their work, because all they personally were doing was laying pipes. Incidents like this underline the need to confront individuals.

This is reiterated over and over again in conversations with the police, magistrates, workers, whenever people reply: 'It's not a question of whether I agree with you, I'm just doing my job.' People often see themselves – and are encouraged to see themselves – as simply part of a corporate mass, and feel that the part they play is insignificant. It is individuals who make the silos, and the component parts for cruise missiles, and individuals who drag women away to police cells.

Unlike bad housing conditions, hospital closures or unemployment, nuclear weapons may seem very abstract. We never see them. They are strictly guarded in prohibited places. As far as we know, cruise missiles are not here yet. They are being paid for and will be controlled by the US, which makes them even more remote. But this government's commitment to nuclear weapons is having an impact now. Nuclear weapons are killing people now. People all across the world are dying of starvation, malnutrition, dirty water, pollution. The resources that are invested in arms could so easily be used to create better ways of living. Confronting individuals with the consequences of their work is only part of the process. We must all take responsibility for forcing men and women to work in the arms industries or support them in any other way.

Taking responsibility does mean changing our lives, changing what we think is important, how we spend our time and money, and it is something that everyone can do in their own way, making their individual contribution.

Taking direct action

When we heard that the women from the march to Greenham Common had stayed there and set up a peace camp outside the main gate, we decided to let people know what was happening by mimicking their action: we decided to live on the streets at Porth Square, Rhondda Valley, Wales. The press should be getting information about nuclear weapons across to people, but it's obvious that other people have to do their job for them. We must cut across all the misinformation which, either by accident or design, we are given. On the first day at Porth Square we didn't know what to expect. But we were in the street, and quite soon people's curiosity got the better of them and they started reading our leaflets and talking to us, even if at first they thought of us as a loony bunch of women. We went carrying four flasks. By the end of the first day we had 25 flasks lined up that had been given us. A man across the street brought us a bottle of whisky; his wife had not let him go to sleep until he brought something to keep us warm. Old people and children were the first to respond to us being there. Several old people came up and blessed us, saying they'd lost brothers in the first world war, sons in the second, and thank God someone was doing something to stop there being another war which would kill us all. We went out of

desperation and we came away knowing we could do it, because of the response of people – the way they opened their minds and talked. Every night people would come and talk to us. Perhaps they wouldn't go to meetings, but they could easily approach an individual and talk about their fears and what they could do. We can't leave everything up to committees, we must take action for ourselves. Women are often intimidated by organisations like CND. They could identify with us and would come and talk. Local people were very supportive. The action started a chain of letters to papers, and opened up discussion. The fact that people knew us all reinforced this.

Susan Lamb, April 1983

In August 1981 a group of women, children and a few men, marched from Cardiff to Greenham Common in protest at NATO's decision to site cruise missiles at Greenham. Much of South Wales is within a 200-mile target area based on Greenham Common, and it was women living in Wales who initiated the march. Some stayed and set up the peace camp. Other women in Wales decided to take supportive action, telling people about the peace camp and the issue of cruise missiles.

More and more women are using nonviolent direct action to express their opposition to nuclear weapons, informing other people and also the authorities of their opinions. The actions described in this chapter illustrate several points, including how an action might be organised; the reactions of the public and the police; and what women involved in the action felt about doing it. Most of them are connected with the Greenham Common women's peace camp. A few took place at Greenham, while others were inspired by the peace camp or were organised by women associated with it. This is not because we think these actions are more important, but simply because we know about them. Some of the numerous and imaginative actions that have taken place all over Britain are mentioned at the end of the chapter to give a sense of the scope of nonviolent direct action.

The first large action initiated by Greenham women in London was the die-in outside the Stock Exchange on 7 June 1982, coinciding with President Reagan's visit. Helen John from Greenham spoke to a massive CND rally in Hyde Park the day before, and invited

women present to participate in an action in London the next day:

'You're within the 200-mile area where these weapons are going to be put and that makes you not a defended area, but a target for certain. We're taking an action tomorrow. We're going to institute a die-in. That's a very simple thing to do – you just lie down and die, because that's exactly what's going to happen if these missiles come here.'

Many of the women who responded to this invitation had not been associated with Greenham before. However, it was clear to them that larger and larger demonstrations were not actually changing anything.

Groups of six or seven women met in Hyde Park to discuss the action, what we felt about participating, the legal consequences, and what each woman would do – who would actually 'die', hand out leaflets or act as observers and peacekeepers. By the end of the afternoon about 80 women had gone through this process. Many women had arrived knowing no one, and by the end had a strong sense of being included within a small and supportive group. Early the next morning, those who had decided to do the action met again in Jubilee Gardens, and the overall feeling was of strength and confidence mixed with varying degrees of apprehension. The police had gathered in large numbers in Jubilee Gardens and followed our small groups to the underground station.

The aim was to lie down and 'die' across five roads around the Stock Exchange, thus effectively blocking all traffic going through the City. The Stock Exchange – one of the world's financial centres – was chosen to highlight the connection between the vast sums of money spent on nuclear weapons and the consequences in human lives. The road each group of women would lie across had been decided beforehand, and when we arrived at the Stock Exchange, women quickly lay down. In each group there were women handing out leaflets and trying to talk to passing office workers, explaining why the action was taking place: that the women were lying down to symbolise the one million who would be killed instantly in a nuclear attack on London. It was an attempt to confront people going to work, doing their job, with the realities behind the nuclear threat.

Reactions of passers-by to this action were predominantly hostile. Most people resented their morning routine being disrupted in this unforeseen way. One man snatched a woman's bundle of leaflets, tore them up and proceeded to stamp on them.

Paula Allen

Die-in at the Stock Exchange, 7 June 1982

The leaflet read:

'In front of you are the dead bodies of women.

Inside this building men are controlling
the money which will make this a reality, by
investing our money in the arms industries
who in turn manipulate governments all
over the world and create markets for the
weapons of mass destruction to be purchased
again with our money.

President Reagan's presence here today is
to ensure American nuclear missiles will be
placed on our soil. This will lead to you
lying dead.

As women we wish to protect all life on
this planet. We will not allow the war games,
which allegedly protect some whilst killing
others, and lead to nuclear war which will
kill us all.'

Motorists shouted and swore at the women. It was hard for the leafleters to keep calm and keep talking. Some people, however, took the leaflets and showed support for what was happening.

The police, arriving on the scene rather late because their vans had been held up by the traffic jams, found the whole situation rather confusing. They stood about for some time, giving women conflicting stories: some were told they were arrested, others just dragged away. In the end nine women were arrested, seemingly at random. The police obviously believed that they should make some arrests, and it did not seem to matter whom they chose.

We had planned a time limit of 15 minutes on the action. As it

happened, we had underestimated the scale of disruption that 70 well-organised women could create by peacefully lying down in London streets. Once the action was over, it was possible to quietly disperse back into the rush-hour crowds. We made our way back to Jubilee Gardens in small groups, because it was important to meet together afterwards to make contact with each other again and to learn how to be more effective in the future.

If one person on their way to work had suddenly made the connection between the money spent on arms and the deaths of millions, then the action had been a success.

As important as an action itself is the organising that goes on to make it successful. Because people only see the result, and the aspects the media judge to be significant, these other processes go unseen except by those involved. For this reason, many actions can sometimes seem hard to identify with. They also appear spontaneous when this is often far from the truth.

While many women who took part in the Stock Exchange action spontaneously decided to join after the CND rally, other women had been thinking about it for some time. A few women had the idea of taking direct action in London. They talked about it with others until a plan began to emerge. Someone went to check the roads around the Stock Exchange and leaflets were written and printed to hand out on the day. It was decided that the action would be publicly announced, but not its location, for fear that the police would be at the Stock Exchange in force and prevent it happening. Only one member of each group knew the precise location. Photographers were contacted who could be trusted not to inform the police, and independent film-makers arranged to film the action. The time limit of 15 minutes was set for the duration of the action so that a realistic expectation could be defined. Women were allocated to phone newspapers on the day with details of the action and how it had gone. All of this was in addition to the work that went on in the groups the day before.

For many women, taking the first step is the hardest. Perhaps isolated at home or at work, where personal fears are not discussed, it is difficult to know how to begin and vital to have some means of meeting others who share our opinions. Tamar Swade, who started Babies against the Bomb, put a card in a newsagent's window asking other mothers with small children to contact her. Other women's peace groups have started from an informal meeting at someone's house, often after watching Helen Caldicott's video,

Critical Mass. Other women may already be members of women's groups, church organisations, the Women's Institute or the Housewives Register.

A year ago I started a branch of the National Housewives Register and groups of us met in different women's houses on the Isle of Wight. Our meetings were democratic and discussed issues, they weren't about our domestic lives. We talked about nuclear weapons, and there was a lot of pressure within the group to invite a man from the county council who visited schools and talked to meetings about civil defence. There were about 25 of us at this meeting. He horrified me. He was so smooth, gentle, kind and reassuring, very clever. I was not involved in the peace movement but I knew he was lying. I sat for three days afterwards, frantic and terrified.

I'd joined CND six months before although I hadn't become involved really. I rang up the local branch and went to see *Critical Mass*, which stunned me. It was the week before 12 December 1982. We cancelled everything for Christmas. We were going to have a party on 11 December, but hired the local cinema instead and showed *Critical Mass* to about 120 people. Women who were involved in the Greenham Common women's peace camp came to talk to the meeting.

I went to Greenham the next day, stayed overnight and joined in the blockade on 13 December. I had never done anything like this before and I was amazed at how strong I felt.

The CND meetings I had gone to used to drive me beserk. So I rang up a friend on the other side of the island and we arranged a meeting. About 15 women turned up. Now, four and a half months later, there are six groups on the Isle of Wight. They are all small, but each week they grow.

After Christmas we didn't know what to do, but it was clear that we should talk to as many people as possible. We decided to arrange a press conference in London and show *Critical Mass*. We didn't know about press releases, and so we got 100 cards printed like party invitations saying the Women for Life on Earth are holding a press conference, and sent them to every paper and magazine. About 50 journalists turned up to the meeting in a room above a pub in Fleet Street, including the editor of the *Financial Times*. We did it to get to journalists as ordinary people, not so they would necessarily print articles. I wanted to

get the message across to ordinary women though, who read women's magazines.

I couldn't speak for terror. All I said was 'hello' and turned the video on. Afterwards a very smart woman photographer wanted to take a photograph of me outside. She had a lot of make-up on and, when we got outside, she burst into tears, crying, 'What can I do about all of this?' All her make-up was running down her face. We talked for a while and I gave her a list of things she could do.

In February, when the court cases were going on in Newbury for the women arrested on New Year's Day at Greenham, we decided not to go to the court, because we knew there were going to be a lot of women there already in support. Instead, we hired a hall for our children and held a vigil outside the court house in the Isle of Wight. Women had never demonstrated like that before on the island. We dressed in black clothes and walked around the streets handing out leaflets, talking to people and explaining why we were demonstrating. We must have talked to 3,000 people that day. None of the leaflets were thrown on the pavements. Women read them, took them home, and many joined us in the street. When the evening came we decided to stay all night. We lit a brazier and hung our banner on the courthouse flagpole. People came to talk to us till 3 a.m., giving us fuel for the fire and hot food.

There was a CND meeting recently to discuss direct action. It was all very theoretical, people discussing it in the abstract. Then a hand went up at the back and a Scottish girl asked in a really quiet voice if you can take a baby into prison. She knows she's going to go to prison over this.

We're having a children's party on Sunday at Greenham which has been organised by the Isle of Wight women. Women will go on to the base with their children. I believe it's only when children are involved that things will start to change. People will see that it's for real. The lives of our children are threatened.
Sue Bolton, April 1983

All the components to make an action a success are invisible but necessary. Each in itself is straightforward, and most skills are easy to learn if there is an urgent reason to do so. Many women have not been in a position to pick up these skills and a great deal of ingenuity and imagination goes into learning them. It was probably

because the women from the Isle of Wight had never written a press release before, and sent cards that looked like party invitations, that 50 Fleet Street journalists turned up in a lunch hour to watch a 40-minute video film on the medical effects of nuclear war. If standard press releases had been sent, they could easily have been thrown into a pile with the rest and ignored.

Many people, both detractors and supporters, commented on the good organisation for the actions at Greenham Common on 12 and 13 December 1982. Women connected with the peace camp had organised firewood, water supplies, food, toilets, car parks, road signs, creche, lawyers and so on. They had produced a booklet with a map of the base, details about facilities available, notes about nonviolence, legal information, songs, and a programme for the two days. Everyone who took part in the blockade on 13 December registered with a co-ordinating group and was briefed about the action. Some women had been meeting beforehand and a few groups had already taken direct action together. The majority had never done anything like it before. Women who did not know each other joined into groups. Each person had a role to play and was immediately involved. The legal implications of the blockade were discussed early on in small groups. Anyone who did not want to be arrested knew that she could take a supporting role or, if blockading, that she could move out of the way when cautioned by the police.

Where there is a clear task, like trying to blockade the base for a day or 'dying' outside the Stock Exchange for 15 minutes, and everyone takes responsibility for her part in the action, it is much more likely to succeed and to be a positive experience for those taking part. It is important to provide legal back-up and practical support as well as support for court cases and press coverage, so that everyone feels confident. Spontaneous actions without this practical back-up can lead to people becoming over-stretched and feeling that they are not being effective.

The care that goes into planning women's actions is vital, giving each woman a chance to learn the necessary skills, talking through possible consequences, taking the time to make sure that each woman is feeling confident and wants to take the action. There is always an understanding that each woman is responsible for herself, and that no one should feel pressured to act in a way that she feels uncomfortable with. This absence of 'bravado' means everyone is certain that they are doing what is right for them and not what someone else thinks they 'ought' to do.

This is very important, because in other contexts we all too often wait to be told what we ought to do, and taking responsibility is about creating opportunities for ourselves. In the case of the Stock Exchange action, Reagan's visit to Britain was the opportunity. As the other actions described in this book show, such situations are all around us. We just have to pick them up and make use of them.

Thirty women lay in Downing Street in February 1983 while the US Vice-President, George Bush, was having dinner with Margaret Thatcher. They represented the 30,000 women who had embraced the base at Greenham on 12 December. They decorated themselves with symbols of their wish to live in a world free of nuclear weapons, thus bringing the Greenham fence to London. Those involved anticipated that they could be arrested and in the event 11 women were charged with obstruction.

We were all tense; catching the looks of the faces around me I was bemused that we were a 'threat' to our present government. There's something very ridiculous about that. We'd arranged a specific time to lie down. I remember thinking how classic that the clock hand seemed to stop moving.

As we got to Downing Street there was hardly any talking, but our senses were very attuned to each other. I asked the policeman on duty a few absurd questions to play for time while we felt out what we wanted to do. We all lay down. A second after I lay down, I looked up at the police staring down at me. Although we'd decided to be completely silent, I found the word 'Hallo' slipping out of me. I was cross with myself, for it had come out of weakness and fear. Then I became very calm. I felt very clear. It was as if a film had lifted – an actual space had opened up. Through becoming completely limp, not moving and seemingly abdicating all responsibility (to the police), it felt that it was I who was in control.

We reached out and touched each other, with bits of hands, shoulders, legs. It asserted that calmness, and centredness.

We were dragged off into the police van. In the van there was an undercurrent of violence. I was aware, as I lay in the bottom of the van, of a policeman rocking his foot up and down so that the hat that was in his hands hit against me. It took quite a lot of concentration to reclaim that prior state of mind.

In the police station, it was chaotic. There were masses of police to 'control' 11 of us. I was covered with photographs of people and places that I loved, a colour chart, statements of Hiroshima victims, and dreams that women had had of nuclear war. I started to read these out loud enough for them to hear, but not like a speech. Various police officers asked me to stop and 'just fill in these forms', 'you can read them later': language you might use to someone who was mad, but at the same time I don't think they see us as mad.

I was taken into a room with a woman police officer. My money and my watch had already been taken away from me and sealed in a plastic bag. Her job was to unpin all the photographs and statements and dreams. She asked me if I would take them off. I said I couldn't do that. She asked me if I would let her take them off. I said I would come to an agreement with her: I would read each statement she took off aloud. I started reading a dream very slowly. The room went very quiet. I couldn't tell you what she looked like, but I remember the impression of round-ness about her – her hands became very soft and gentle. She unpinned everything very carefully and slowly. She *placed* the papers on the table. She was listening. When I came to the end of the dream, she had been stooping down and we didn't really look at each other, but her face was flushed. I said lots of women have had these dreams. She said 'What was it that made you act this way?' I told her I'd been frightened for a long time, since I was 14, that I used to have fantasies of how to survive, and how I'd gone to Greenham and got involved.

After this, we walked slowly out of the room, and I joined the processing line . . .
Deborah Law, April 1983

The 11 women were kept in police custody overnight, harrassed, moved to another police station at 2 a.m., and left with blankets smeared with dried faeces – very unusual sanctions against people charged with the minor offence of obstruction. When they finally appeared in court (after one adjournment of the case), they were all given conditional discharges.

The police are sometimes said to be reluctant to arrest women taking nonviolent action because it is peaceful. Whilst individual police officers can be made to think about their actions by women who refuse to use violence, police operations are planned strate-

gies. The police reaction to the blockade at Greenham on 13 December is a case in point:

> Police were instructed not to arrest the Greenham Common demonstrators yesterday, and instead moved hundreds bodily from the gates around the base.
>
> Many of the 2,000 protestors who stayed the night had slept across the 16 entrances on the 9-mile perimeter in their attempts to shut the base.
>
> All day the police and a nucleus of 700 activists had a tactical struggle to get the upper hand. At the end last night, only two women and a man had been arrested and all sides were claiming a success.
>
> Assistant Chief Constable Wyn Jones, who was in charge of the operation said: 'We have been very conscious that these are ordinary law-abiding women who believe passionately in their cause.'
>
> He said hundreds of women had committed arrestable offences during the day but they were not 'vindictive or malicious'.
>
> They were not the sort of women who would normally come to police attention and he did not expect them to do so again.
>
> 'They were demonstrating because of their deeply held political convictions,' he added. 'I do not think the circumstances justify the full sanctions of the criminal law.'
>
> (The *Guardian*, 14 December 1982)

It would be nice to be able to take these much publicised words of Wyn Jones at face value. However, in practice, it would have been very hard for the police to arrest such large numbers of women. Television cameras and press reporters made aggressive police tactics unwise. There was obviously great support for the women's action all over the country.

All this did not stop many isolated incidents of police harrassment and outright violence:

My impression was that the police were being reasonably restrained and some seemed to be sympathetic. One put me down very gently on the grass with an 'excuse me'! Another, obviously exasperated, pleaded with me not to go back on to the road . . . Some police, however, were far from gentle; perhaps understandably through sheer exasperation. Some, I felt from studying their facial expressions, were being deliberately violent. I was dragged once by the hood of my cagoule, which was across my throat, which meant I couldn't breathe; I tried to scream but couldn't, and from the violence with which I was thrown down at the side, I was still retching and choking. I am sure that was deliberate. Another time I was dragged by the hair, which was up

in a plait. Several women told me they had been kicked on the head and in the stomach, though I only saw one incident myself. A woman lay at my feet having her head kicked by a policeman, whose number was covered by a plastic mackintosh. She was screaming and crying and the women around her were screaming at the man to stop . . . An elderly Swedish woman to whom I spoke was in a lot of pain, very pale and weeping, because she thought her arm had been broken. Later examination proved that it had not, but it had been viciously twisted, she said deliberately. The woman next to me had her face kicked and her glasses broken. I was trying to catch a policeman's eye to prevent them from trampling her further, and also trying to protect her with my body . . . My impression remains that they were obviously under orders to be restrained and most of them were managing to be reasonably good-natured. Some were deliberately violent from the outset, and some were unnecessarily violent through sheer exasperation. They were obviously not used to dealing with totally nonviolent women and some over-reacted.
Helen Steven, 13 December 1982

How the police deal with our actions varies a lot, depending on circumstances and on individual police officers. We often find ourselves talking about how the police behave and many women are understandably nervous of them. It is the police we come up against, but they are not our 'target'. Nonviolent women's actions in this country have so far not encountered concerted violent reactions from police. Reactions to nonviolent direct actions elsewhere in Europe have not been so restrained.

In March 1983, a group of women from Greenham visited Comiso in Sicily. Magliocco airport near Comiso is due to receive 112 American cruise missiles. These will serve a dual purpose: because they could reach 800 miles further south than cruise missiles elsewhere in Europe, taking in Libya and Egypt, they could be used either in a European conflict or a conflict which developed in the Middle East.

In 1981, two-thirds of Comiso's population signed a petition calling for the cancellation of the decision to site cruise missiles there, arguing that as well as being against the will of the people, the Paris Peace Treaty of 1947 forbade the use of Sicily for military ends. A march to protest against the decision on 4 April 1982 attracted about 75,000 people, the largest demonstration in Sicily

since the second world war. While local people are clearly not apathetic, there is a feeling that a decision taken by the Italian government will not be revoked, and local people are divided about Comiso being a focus for international attention.

A peace camp was set up outside Comiso in July 1982, as a permanent voice of protest, with supporters from Italy and the rest of Europe visiting and taking nonviolent direct actions to draw attention to the situation. In March 1983, women from Italy, England, Ireland, America, Holland, Germany, France and Switzerland, began a week of nonviolent actions beginning with the formation of a large circle outside the base on 8 March, International Women's Day. On 9 March, 40 women blockaded the main gate of the base and were subject to harrassment and increasing violence from the police. Women had their hair pulled out at the roots, they were thrown on to the side of the road on top of each other, and one woman's wrist was broken. On 11 March, 16 women blockaded the road. In the course of their action the violence became much worse and a woman from England had her wrist broken. Twelve women were arrested and taken to the prison at Comiso. They were later transferred to a nearby prison at Ragusa, and held in extremely bad conditions until their deportation on 17 March. After their arrest, everything belonging to the peace camp was taken by the police, and the remaining traces were burned.

The action taken by the women had been completely nonviolent at all times.

I found the whole experience of being at Comiso quite shattering. We held a meeting the evening after the trial of the women who had been arrested should have taken place. It didn't, because the women were deported instead. It was a mixed meeting, but it was agreed that the men would let the women speak, which they did, and what was said was very moving and powerful. I was glad that the men heard that. Someone asked me in what way my experiences in Sicily were different from my experiences in England. Obviously, people had the violence in mind. I said I thought that it was part of a continuum: it wasn't different in kind, just different in degree. The Italian police had swept out the peace camp, destroyed it and then burned it. There were about four days of vindictiveness and quite extraordinary violence. All because 16 women lay down in a road. Someone remarked that in England they were using the process

Women dancing on a missile silo, Greenham Common,
1 January 1983

of the law to get rid of the peace camp, whereas in Italy the police just marched in and destroyed the whole place, and then put everything that was left in a pile and burned it.

I felt that the end result was the same – the destruction of the peace camp. One went through the process of law and one didn't, but both were attacks on the peace movement . . .
Martha Street, April 1983

There are occasions when arrests have led to imprisonment in this country – when women charged with a breach of the 'peace' have refused to agree to be bound over to 'keep the peace', and when those arrested for obstruction refused to pay the fine. Direct action around a military establishment could lead to offences under the Official Secrets Act, which carry much harsher sentences.

Some women wanted to go on to the base on New Year's Day, on to the silos, to show their determined opposition to cruise missiles and to draw attention to the fact that the silos were already well under construction. In the event they were charged with a breach of the peace. It is easy to overlook the fact that the women involved were all aware that they risked very much more serious charges. The decision to take part in such an action, or to go to prison rather than agree to be bound over, is obviously not undertaken lightly – this was no New Year's party stunt.

As soon as we arrived at the camp a woman came down the path towards us and asked us if we'd heard the plan – to go on to the base at dawn and on to the silos, using ladders and carpets for the barbed wire! We were all amazed; it was such an incredible plan! I immediately felt really strongly that I wanted to do it. I had to try hard to hold back, to think about it rationally. We were worried about being charged under the Official Secrets Act.

But I knew my feelings about it would win over and that I'd end up going over the fence. It was because it was all centred around those missile silos. I think they're a focal point of all the negative things that are going on in the world – paranoia, greed, misuse of power, violence, a lack of imagination for alternatives. In my mind I saw them as revolting man-made boils on the earth's surface, full of evil. I wanted to let out all the feelings I have about the threat of nuclear war – the fear and the dread. And I wanted to concentrate on the future, to feel optimistic and get strength and hope that we can stop it. I kept thinking about celebrating life. What actually happened was that I did that. When we got on to the silos, even though we were so excited, I

stood quietly for a few minutes, with my eyes closed, and let it all drain out of me. After that I just kept thinking about being alive!

There were about 60 of us at the last planning meeting, all quite calm, but there was a nervousness in the air. The next morning it was very still and dark outside as we crept into the back of the van. The journey to the base seemed endless. I was leaning forward looking out of the window, so I could see when we arrived. The only thing I could make out in the back of the van were the white women-signs painted on the tabards we were wearing so that we wouldn't be mistaken for terrorists, to make it obvious who we were.

The atmosphere was electric when we got to the base. We got out of the van as quietly and quickly as we could and immediately made our way to the perimeter fence. By the time we got there the first lot of women were going over, and half of them were already waiting on the other side.

Ahead of us we saw the aluminium ladders. I remember seeing three on each side, leaning against the fence. It seemed ridiculously easy – there were streams of women going over the fence, over the carpet, making it so ineffectual. There was a queue to get over. Just then we saw vehicle headlamps in the distance coming towards us. My heart sank. We knew we'd been seen, and wondered whether we'd manage to get over in time. It turned out to be a small vehicle with only two police inside.

I was on the ladder, about to go over, I was on the carpet . . . They whipped the ladders away and I was left stranded on the top wondering how I was going to get down. I scrambled over the wire at the top, jumped down, and then I put the ladder back up. The two police were running from side to side with their arms out, backwards and forwards, saying 'Stop, go back' – as if we'd all stop and go back. I remember deliberately running wide in a curve to avoid them, and running like hell. I remember getting there and scrambling up the slope. It was covered in mud and very slippery. At the top there was a big ledge of concrete we had to climb on to. A woman leaned down to offer me a hand up. I said, 'Hang on a minute, I can't manage just yet.' I had to get my breath back, I was really puffing. I climbed up that last bit of concrete and felt really pleased – I'd got there!

Every now and again we'd link arms in a big circle and dance around the top of the silo. We were all ecstatic, overtaken by the brilliant feeling that we'd actually done it! We took off our

tabards and hung them on wooden posts to leave some trace and to remind the workmen that we'd been there, to make them think about it, and we planted a lovely colourful 'Peace 83' banner on the sloping side. The top of the silo was covered in bits of concrete rubble and wooden planks which we arranged into women's peace signs. When we began to explore the top of the silo we could see that we were only on one half of it. In between the two halves there was a deep rectangular pit with lots of steel reinforcing bars running across it like a grid. I suppose they were going to concrete it over. We went over to the far end and we could see the enormous airstrip. It looked really desolate. You could see for miles. There was nothing – just a watery sun coming up.

We were on top of the silos for about one hour and 20 minutes. A police car or two arrived first, then quite a bit later the buses arrived. I don't think they could believe how many of us there were. There we were on the top, celebrating New Year! The police walked around the bottom of the silo for quite a while, looking puzzled. Then some MoD police arrived and some military personnel.

When we saw the MoD police climbing up the side of the silo we all sat down around the edge of the big wooden peace sign, linked arms and just waited. They broke the circle and started lifting women down one by one. The police on the top picked up the women and passed them to the ones further down who dragged the women down the slope. One of the ones on the top was really nasty, much bigger than the rest, and he looked really threatening. I hoped he wouldn't be the one to get me. When they took a woman from the circle we all linked arms again and moved inwards, so the circle got smaller and smaller. The atmosphere changed but all the time we were friendly to the police.

One came to get me, and I went limp. He dragged me to the ledge and passed me over to two others, placing me on the ground on my front. I had my head facing down the slope . . . it was quite steep . . . They picked me up by the wrists and some-how my arms were pulled backwards as they dragged me. I thought they'd dislocate my shoulders. It was really painful. They said 'Get up and walk, you silly bitch. Are you going to get up and walk?' I was carried like that for about 20 yards or so. It was so painful I just said 'Please, put me down. I'll walk.' So they

put me down and I walked. For the rest of the weekend I was extremely stiff and under my arms felt very bruised.

I had a conversation with one of the police near the bus. The other one had gone off again to get someone else. I said, 'Why don't you think about what you're doing? Don't you ever think about what you're protecting here?' I was just met with stony-faced silence. I gave up and just sighed and said, 'How will we ever get through to you?' He said, 'You don't realise, you already have, but this time you've overstepped the mark.'

We were all whisked off to Newbury nick, singing all the way. When we arrived we were taken down to the cells in the basement and put into a small room, which was the biggest cell they'd got. The noise of our singing was deafening. The police seemed to be affected in the same way as the base personnel – completely awestruck that we'd done it and that we were so jubilant about it.

We'd asked on the bus what we were being charged with and they said breach of the peace which was a big relief! They spent the whole day processing us. We were taken to a little room at the end where there were two police. One read out the charge sheet and took down particulars – names and addresses. Afterwards we were put into different cells, smaller, like pens. There were little bits of paper stuck to the walls outside with our surnames listed – the kind of thing that if we hadn't been feeling so good we'd probably have felt really angry about. We kept asking where we'd be taken to. They either didn't know or they wouldn't tell us.

Our cell door was opened. I was called out and put into another cell down the corridor. It was a different kind of cell, with no bench, just a loo with no chain. The chain was on the outside, I suppose so they can check what goes down the loo. It felt horrible in that cell by myself.

We heard the cell doors being unlocked. We were let out and led outside. There was a riot van waiting, with cages like tiny cupboards with a grid, all painted white. We were told that we were going to Oxford. Two of the women had to sit in a tiny space in the middle between the cages, and they had their wrists handcuffed together behind their backs. I felt very frightened, and horrified that we were going to travel all that distance in such a confined space, locked in, with our hands handcuffed like that.

All of a sudden I realised how barbaric it was and that I didn't have to do it. They got one handcuff on my left arm and they kept trying to grab my right arm to get the other handcuff on it, while I waved my right arm about so that they couldn't grab it. I was determined not to be handcuffed. I said that we weren't going to get away, that I'd deliberately put myself in this position and that we weren't going to escape with police in the van and the doors locked. The more I went on the more determined I became and the more frightened. I said 'What if there's an accident? How on earth are we going to protect ourselves?' They kept telling me not to argue. I thought that sooner or later I'd have to give in to their authority, but then I thought, just because they're police in uniforms I don't have to do it. They were shouting by this stage and I was shouting back, 'You don't have to do this. It's not necessary. It's just spite and humiliation.' Finally they gave in. They let the other women out and took their handcuffs off and handcuffed us to each other in a line. I was on the end so I had a free hand. I remember feeling so relieved.

Juliet Nelson, May 1983

Most nonviolent direct actions do not lead to arrests or imprisonment, nor do they need to do so to make their point. On 8 March 1983, International Women's Day, about 7,000 women from all over Western Europe and from America and Asia demonstrated against cruise and Pershing missiles in Brussels. In London, a group of women handed out 'peace pies' outside the Bank of England at lunchtime. They had posters saying 'Bread not Bombs' to make the connection between the squandering of vast resources on weapons, and famine and malnutrition, especially in the Third World. Women brought cakes, each with a message about peace, either pinned to the cakes like little flags or tucked under them. This action had a pleasant, gentle atmosphere. It is unusual to be given something nice by a stranger in the street, and it generated constructive conversations about peace and disarmament with the people who passed by. One woman, dressed as a waitress, offered a cruise missile tò passing businessmen. But it turned out that none of them had ordered it!

Passing on information is a vital part of nonviolent direct action. Many people are involved in preparing leaflets, displaying posters, organising film shows and discussions. Brighton women's

peace group started a women's peace magazine, *Lysistrata*. A simple way of passing on information is to leave leaflets in library books, telephone boxes, on the counter in the post office or bank, in doctors' waiting rooms, or public toilets. Another way is through graffiti, especially drawing attention to military buildings, from bunkers to Territorial Army headquarters; or leaving messages in other public places, especially where people wait.

Women have collected signatures in support of the women at the peace camp, and expressing their opposition to cruise missiles. They have then sent these petitions to MPs or to the prime minister. Others have written letters to local papers, taken part in phone-in programmes on local radio, and done interviews for local radio stations. Many have been involved in demonstrations in their own town, or in vigils and pickets outside military establishments or outside courts, police stations or prisons, where other women are being held.

There have been several marches which have led to other actions. The Copenhagen-to-Paris peace march in the summer of 1981 directly inspired the Women for Life on Earth peace march from Cardiff to Greenham Common, and at the beginning of June 1982, from Cardiff to Brawdy in Pembrokeshire, the largest US submarine tracking station in Europe. Like the die-in at the Stock Exchange, this march coincided with Reagan's visit to Britain.

In the summer of 1982 there was a march in London organised by Babies against the Bomb. The whole procession was led by women in black mourning dresses, with push chairs, empty except for a 'tombstone' placard with the name of a child killed in Hiroshima or Nagasaki. During the Falklands War, women in Sheffield occupied the army recruiting office for a day, as a protest against the use of violence to resolve conflicts. On 12 October 1982, the day of the Falklands 'victory' parade in London, a group of women turned their backs as the parade passed them, symbolising their rejection of war.

In February 1983, women decorated the railings along the North London railway line with children's toys and clothes. This made a direct connection between the base at Greenham, decorated on 12 December, and the North London line, which regularly carries nuclear waste for reprocessing at Windscale in Cumbria. The waste trains travel at about 3 a.m., so that many people do not know that such lethal material is being transported through the middle of this densely populated area.

Women are campaigning against war toys, writing to manufacturers and politicians, and demonstrating outside shops. Two women from Yorkshire sent Mother's Day cards to Margaret Thatcher, as a reminder of her responsibility for their children's future.

Brighton women set up a peace camp on common land in the middle of the town. It started in the middle of February, when the women who had been arrested on the silo at Greenham started their prison sentences. Instead of lasting 14 days, as originally planned, the peace camp was very well supported for two months and provided an opportunity for many women to get to know each other and to plan other activities. Similarly, people in Sheffield squatted a disused building in the city centre and used it as a peace centre for several months. The city council had been promising to provide a permanent peace centre for a couple of years and they agreed to leave this building on the condition that this promise would be honoured.

On 17 January 1983 about 200 women went to the Houses of Parliament to tell MPs directly about their opposition to cruise missiles. Some made sure that their opinions reached the ears of other MPs by sitting down inside the House of Commons, where they were detained for several hours before being allowed to go. On 20 April 1983, a group from Brighton went into the Public Gallery

during a debate about holding a referendum over cruise missiles. Most MPs voted against the proposal, but the women took the opportunity to remind them of Mrs Thatcher's famous remark at the time of the Falklands War – 'The wishes of the islanders are paramount' – before being forcibly removed from the gallery.

This is necessarily a cursory list because numerous actions have happened over the past months. The strength and scope of this growing network was clear on 24 May, International Women's Day for Disarmament. This day was first celebrated in 1982 with 90 events all over the country and several events in other countries, notably the establishment of a women's peace camp at Soesterberg in Holland.

Remarkably little media coverage was given to the widespread action on 24 May 1983, despite press releases, interviews with journalists and television crews filming actions all day. Carrie Pester was one of the women involved in coordinating news of the actions.

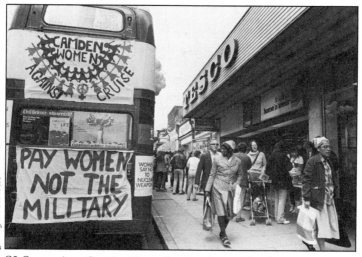

Jenny Matthews

GLC peace bus, Camden Town, London, International Women's Day for Disarmament, 24 May 1983

The day was a phenomenal success, involving several hundred thousand women in Britain alone. In every city, town, and most villages, women were saying no to nuclear weapons and informing others on the issue. Die-ins were held in many towns; women

61

encircled, invaded, and blockaded bases, communications centres and army recruitment centres; and they drew attention to local nuclear bunkers and areas designated as mass burial sites in the event of war. In Peckham, South London, crosses were hammered into the ground planned for a mass graveyard. In Plymouth, 500 women blockaded the entrance to the naval base and later staged a die-in in the city centre. Over 100 women in Hexham, Yorkshire, picnicked on their local nuclear bunker and then formed a chain to the nearby abbey. The events of the day are far too numerous to list. All the actions were organised on a local level by women's peace groups up and down the country, and, put together, they demonstrated an unprecedented commitment on the part of women everywhere to take action for peace.

Internationally, at least 20 separate actions took place in Connecticut, USA. We had reports of other USA actions in Washington, Philadelphia, Pennsylvania, Florida, Montana, Boston and Northampton. In New Zealand, another 20 actions took place, including 1,000 women in Wellington and 20,000 in Auckland. Other countries that contacted us about actions were Australia, Switzerland, France, West Germany, Sweden, Denmark, Norway, Italy, Eire and Zimbabwe. We even received a telex of support from Costa Rica. The knowledge that we are an international force gives us strength. Hundreds of thousands of people must have been utterly astonished at the lack of coverage of an event that had touched millions of lives.

Of course, national news headlines were not the main aim of the day. It was another opportunity for women everywhere to replace their fear with action, and for those who had taken action before to encourage those who hadn't. All the women who took part on 24 May will talk to their friends and neighbours and fellow trade unionists who will join them next time.

The women's peace movement is unstoppable. The lack of media recognition merely confirms the established interest's fear of that force. As a friend remarked, 'Which other country springs to mind where we are told dissent is not reported?'
Carrie Pester, May 1983

Nonviolence

'Since I've been taking action at Greenham I've encountered all kinds of violence, from the abuse and sometimes blows of individual police to the institutional violence of the legal and prison systems. On their scale, using their rules, I am powerless. If I try to use their means they will always manage to harm me more than I can dent them. I wouldn't be taking action like entering the high security area of the base and dancing on the half-built cruise missile silos as we did on New Year's Day if I didn't feel frightened and angry about what they are doing. But my anger and fear have to be channelled into creative opposition. Sometimes it's incredibly hard to lie down and sing as I am being manhandled by the police or sentenced to 14 days in prison. But every time that happens, 10 or 100 more women realise that they have been passive too long and start taking responsibility themselves for protecting life against the nuclear threat.'
Rebecca Johnson, May 1983

All the actions described in the last chapter recognise the validity of personal experience, feelings and ideas. They involve starting where we are now and building on what we can do, so that we

Ed Barber

define our own course of action for our own reasons. They are all public statements, bearing witness to beliefs and drawing public attention to the issue in a very direct way, whether they involve a few women handing out leaflets in the street and talking to passers-by, or 30,000 women forming a massive circle around the base at Greenham on 12 December 1982 and decorating the fence with personal belongings connected to real life.

Beyond this, the actions exemplify several important principles fundamental to nonviolence. They involve making contact with people, trying to generate discussion, not arguments that simply antagonise and alienate. If people are drawn into a conversation they are much more likely to be convinced by what we are saying and to support the action in some way. If they are hostile to begin with they can only change their minds if they are given the opportunity, if what people are saying seems reasonable. The women at Porth Square in Wales felt that one reason why their action was successful was that many people knew them already and felt able to talk to them as individuals, whereas they did not make contact with established organisations like CND. Handing out 'peace pies' outside the Bank of England was another way of opening up conversation with passers-by. More indirectly, going on to the silos drew people's attention to the fact that the silos are under construction, that they actually exist. Many actions try to

make connections between things that may seem separate: for example, highlighting the vast resources invested in arms while famine kills so many people, simply because money is spent on warfare rather than the necessities of life.

Keening actions try to make contact with people on a different level, touching them emotionally, without the use of words.

We went to the Houses of Parliament to keen on 18 January 1982 because this was the day that the politicians came back from the Christmas recess. We wanted to say right at the very beginning of the parliamentary year, 'It's enough. We've had enough.' Keening is something done traditionally by women and is now confined to mourning. It's a means of expression without words, without having to get tied up in various arguments, facts and figures, whys and wherefores. You can just show how you feel. At the camp at Greenham we've always had a nonviolent approach to protest. We felt that this was a nonviolent way of expressing our feelings to our representatives in parliament, who should take account of the people they represent. Had we just gone there and stood outside with a banner we could easily have been ignored, but by using sound we could actually penetrate the building. We didn't want to just shout slogans. Politicians are hardened to this sort of thing. They've had it said to them so many times by so many people that it doesn't touch them anymore. We made trees of life. We covered twigs with ribbons in suffragette colours – purple, green and white – and hung doves of peace from them and little sequins. We made them beautiful things. Our banner said:

> **Our hearts are breaking. Politicians, you must rethink nuclear policy in 1982.**

Nuclear weapons now exist and they seem to reflect the state that society is in – our expectations, our values, our priorities are just so *wrong*. It's difficult to think how to change things, but to show your feelings is a very good way of beginning.
Jayne Burton, March 1982

Confrontation is a central part of nonviolence, but confrontation without recourse to violence or aggression.

Confrontation: to meet face to face, stand facing; be opposite to; face in hostility or defiance; oppose; bring (person) face to face with (accusers . . .)

Claire Hershman

2,000 women take nonviolent direct action
by blockading the base, Greenham Common,
13 December 1982

This dictionary definition stresses the active part of confrontation. It is about stating opposition clearly, standing face to face. If we make use of the threat of violence in direct action, then we do not truly oppose, we are not opposite, because we are using aggression to oppose aggression. We confront by making connection, and by drawing attention to our real situation in a society working towards self destruction.

Military planners merely regard us as collateral damage. The fact that millions of people will die hideous deaths does not prevent the planning for nuclear war, nor the government's acceptance that a nuclear 'exchange' would be the 'answer' to international conflicts. If we use violence against this sickness, we mask the true nature of the situation. We do not possess the weapons of coercion and see no solution in possessing them. We must work in a different way and use confrontation to express our opposition in many imaginative ways.

Demonstrations are the most common way to show opposition but the strength or weakness of a demonstration is judged in numbers: many thousands and the demonstration is considered a success, only a few hundred and it has failed. Demonstrations tend to keep opposition within a static framework of 'acceptable' protest. We need to produce a change in consciousness, a questioning of violence as a valid option, opening up channels of debate. Nonviolence is not concerned with numbers primarily, but with creating a situation in which different options and responses can be explored.

The die-in outside the Stock Exchange in June 1982 made a clear connection between what weapons do, and people making money out of the arms race, challenging people who work in the City of London to think about their involvement in a system which makes money out of war and killing. Blockades at Greenham confront the police, who protect the base, with the reality of what they are protecting, and the construction workers with the reality of what they are building. This is very provocative in a way that an angry mob can never be, because it is easy to shut off from or deride shouted slogans. The use of aggression reduces people's options to two absurdities: complete acceptance or complete rejection. There is no room for questioning because no attempt has been made to reach us, and we are immediately excluded. There is no debate for us to become involved in.

The police and the courts expect violence to be the inevitable

result of confrontation. Women have been arrested for 'behaviour likely to cause a breach of the peace' on several occasions after taking nonviolent direct action. Breach of the peace means potential violence; it implies that had the police not intervened and arrested the women, violence would have occurred. Equating confrontation with potential violence artises from a deeply embedded assumption that violence is innate or inevitable. People assume that violence is a central part of human nature, or that because there has always been violence there always will be. People venerate cultures based on hierarchical principles that resort to violence to solve conflicts. Many people believe violence to be an inherent part of close involvement with other people. To step back and begin to question this assumption means that some deeply held beliefs are turned on their heads. Nonviolent confrontation assumes that nonviolence is at least as accessible (if not more accessible) a part of human nature as violence is.

It is important to differentiate anger and violence, whereas many people equate the two. Anger does not inevitably lead to, or express itself in, violence, and yet people often assume it does. When taking nonviolent action, your very vulnerability is your strength. For example, having put yourself in a position of apparent weakness by lying in the road, you trust that the motorists in the City or the truck drivers at Greenham will not run over you, and that the police will not beat you or kick you.

We must constantly put the responsibility for the use of violence back in the hands of the authorities, and this is only possible if we completely disown violence ourselves.

I've been quite badly bruised by the police, but they are accessible . . . just looking at them and saying 'This is my body. I'm protecting my life with my body because I don't feel protected by you and these weapons. Why are you trying to harm me? Why are you so threatened by me? Aren't you more threatened by cruise missiles?' I've not found a policeman able to use violence after that.

Rebecca Johnson, May 1983

By going limp on arrest we force the police to move us. They have to take the initiative and responsibility for doing this against our will and without our co-operation. Clearly, in confrontations with the police there is scope for very different responses. The police often discuss the use of violence as something forced upon

them to deal with an otherwise uncontrollable situation. When dealing with nonviolent women's actions, the choice is firmly in their hands. If they choose to use outright violence to deal with a nonviolent situation, the nature of their intervention becomes very clear. It is important to recognise that the police always have violence as an option, just as everyone has a choice to accept or reject the build up of nuclear weapons.

In all the actions described in the previous chapter, the aims are to make a strong and clear statement. This runs from each woman's conviction, through the means employed to make that statement, taking the action, to dealing with its immediate consequences. Using nonviolence as a process and a way of thinking, as well as a strategy for action, means it is more likely that the integrity of all these aspects will be maintained. This rests on the assumption that collectively as well as individually we can take control of a situation and define our own boundaries. We can never know exactly how others will respond to us, but we can maintain clarity over how we shall behave towards them. We make a decision to screen out various things which, normally, we would pay attention to. Feelings of fear, nervousness or anger have been considered and, temporarily, put on one side, so that there is a unity of thought and feeling that is very strong and clear.

As women, we are particularly used to responding to situations rather than defining them from the outset. In taking nonviolent action we set up the situation on our own terms and keep the initiative by not allowing ourselves to be deflected by attempts to undermine that resolve. Nonviolence, far from being weak, actually feels very strong to participate in.

This is brought out in the following account of the first blockade of the base at Greenham Common. It involved about 200 women and lasted for 24 hours, starting at 6.30 p.m. on Sunday, 21 March 1982, the spring equinox. On the Monday morning the people who usually work on the base wanted to get in to go to work. Instead of moving the women at the gates, the police opened up a gap in the perimeter fence, in effect creating a new gate which they controlled. When women heard about this gap groups volunteered to come round from the other gates to blockade here. The first two groups were arrested but the police must have decided that was pointless as more and more women were arriving at the gap. So they stopped arresting and pulled the women away from time to time to let the vehicles through.

For the last half-hour from 6 to 6.30 all the women who were there sat down in front of the gap. Before that we'd been doing it in shifts. We were pretty tired and bruised but our spirits were still high. When it came to 6.30 an inspector came over to the police and said, 'OK, lads, that's it' and they shuffled off in orderly rows. We leapt up. I can only say we had a sort of celebration. We hugged and kissed each other and felt wonderful. It was extraordinary. We felt as if we'd won a victory in a way – a moral victory. Somehow we found ourselves in this enormous circle. I don't know how many of us there were. There were enough to make a really big circle that took up the whole of the road, right from the base fence across to the other side of the road. We took up the whole of the space, dancing and singing for a while. It was lovely. Then one woman suggested that we should stand in silence to calm ourselves down. So we all stood in this enormous circle, smiling in silence for a few minutes. It seemed quite a long time. It was very restful and calming and we felt very close to each other.

The police had all gathered over by the van that was going to take them away. They'd been joking and laughing but they fell silent. They just stood there looking at us. I don't know whether they understood what our celebration and quietness was about, but it made them speechless. All the time we were silent they didn't move, they didn't speak. It showed them, I think, that what they'd done hadn't touched us in any way. We were still as strong then as we were at the beginning. All the hauling about they'd done, all the carrying us off, hadn't come anywhere near to affecting our determination to go on doing what we'd been doing. Then we broke the circle. There was more hugging and kissing and laughing, and then we broke into groups and walked back to the camp.

Lesley Boulton, March 1982

These feelings of strength are an important contrast to many people's view of nonviolence as passive, reactive and weak. It is important to differentiate between the surface appearance – women lying down in the road, or being dragged by the police – and the underlying reason for it. Some people take issue with what they see to be passive, 'feminine' behaviour, self-denigrating and subservient, which is not at all what the women involved in the actions feel. Though you appear to be surrendering your body, you

Climbing into the base, Greenham Common,
1 January 1983

are in complete control. You make a conscious decision to take part; you take the initiative and create the situation; and you can choose to leave. This is very different from other kinds of demonstrations where confrontation is very often out of control. People

71

jostle and scream at the police, are nervous and off-balance.

This feeling of calm and centredness leads to situations where we can do far more than we ever thought possible. Preparation before the action, and consensus decision-making are also vital in achieving this. Nonviolence should run through everything we do from the details of an action, the process of deciding these details, and how we behave towards each other. For example, women who planned to go on to the base at Greenham on New Year's Day decided not to cut the fence or damage it in any way, but to use ladders to climb over it, and to cover the barbed wire with layers of carpet, thus 'softening' and neutralising it. This decision was not made by a leader or committee but by those taking part on a consensus basis.

In this society we are most used to majority decision-making, which is not the same thing at all. In majority decision-making, a situation is defined to start with as a choice between a limited number of options. These options are framed as two or three competing points of view and everyone chooses between them. This leads to a situation where the person who puts the most forceful argument often dominates, and the options become polarised and fixed. It assumes that it is possible and sensible to decide between the options, and that everyone comes to a satisfactory final decision. Those who 'lose' the vote have no place in the final outcome. If they are regularly in the minority, their situation is intolerable. They are under pressure to accept, or at least go along with, the majority view, against their own better judgement.

In consensus decision-making, this does not have to happen. Everyone has the opportunity – some would say responsibility – to say what they think. As each person speaks, everyone's understanding of the situation deepens. The discussion is continually redefined and reworked to assimilate each person's ideas and feelings. The options are not pre-arranged in a fixed pattern and the fluctuating process of reaching a decision includes everyone. This process is crucial and just as important as the decision. No one side 'wins', but a co-operative decision emerges, based on everyone's ideas and understanding. Deciding through consensus means that, however idiosyncratic our ideas might appear, we have a responsibility to speak them and create an atmosphere where each of us feels free to say what we really think. In this way we can all find out how we feel and what we want from a particular situation. This process opens options rather than closing them off, and leads to a

greater sense of unity, which can be channelled into action. Because everyone is sure of the decision, it is possible to trust every member of the group and rely on them to provide help and support.

Where much bigger numbers are involved, briefing notes are useful as a starting point for many small group discussions. The following is a shortened version of the nonviolent direct action training notes drawn up for the blockade of the base at Greenham on 13 December 1982.

> The blockade will be done by groups of women at each gate. It will be totally nonviolent. The more preparation that can be done beforehand the better the action will be. Please come prepared to be flexible and adaptable to different women's needs.
>
> Women organising themselves into autonomous groups of about 10 makes a large decentralised action far easier to co-ordinate and service. More important, forming small groups allows women to get to know one another well; provides a basis of trust and mutual support for the action; makes decisions easier to reach; and avoids the need for 'leaders'. It also makes it easier to absorb individuals into the action at the last minute, forming the basis for a future network and future action. So please, if possible, join or form a local group.
>
> You will be expected to provide for your own physical needs – for example, tents, warm/waterproof clothing, food, water container and transport. You will also need your own 'support' people. No matter how big or small the group, it is essential that at least three women do not do the action itself but take on the following support tasks:
>
> ● legal observer (see page 111);
> ● someone who will see that during action the group is fed, warm, happy – *not* exhausted, miserable and hungry – and will look after people's belongings after arrest and so on;
> ● someone to look after transport/communications.
>
> Nonviolent direct actions do not have to be illegal but the blockade may be considered to be so. We may have to deal with hostility, violence and arrest. The following notes are to help your group to prepare for this. We are none of us experts and we all learn by sharing experience.
>
> 1. Exchange names, relevant experiences, fears and anxieties.
>
> 2. Make sure you understand the practical implications of action. Go through legal briefing (see pages 110–11).
>
> 3. *Before action*, think through all the other implications of what you are doing. Why are you doing this blockade? What do you hope to gain for yourself/for the movement? How will it affect other work you are doing? How do you feel about it? Sharing these feelings will help you ensure that the positives outweigh the negatives, and help sort out what roles you want to take.

4. *Action.* How will you do the action? Weave wool, link arms, sing, move, lie down? Will you talk to the police or be silent? How will you keep warm? Will you work in shifts? What do you like eating? What is it practical to eat?

How will you deal with disagreements/arguments/upsets within the group? How will you make decisions quickly?

How will you deal with confrontation? Nonviolence on your part does not, unfortunately, mean that people will treat you nonviolently. How do you feel about being kicked or shouted at? What if someone wants to talk to you? What if men want to sit down with you?

How will you support/peacekeep for each other? How will you deal with anger directed at you/coming from you?

How will you deal with arrests: going limp/total co-operation? How will you occupy yourself in a police cell?

Talking through all these questions – and there are many more – and sharing ideas and experiences will help.

Note: Pairing within a group is one form of peacekeeping. Each person can look after their partner, knowing in advance what situation they find really upsetting, and being able to support them.

A mental and emotional preparedness is not necessarily the same thing as nonviolent direct action training, which can sometimes be very mechanistic, stressing techniques, rather than talking about underlying assumptions. For some people nonviolence is just a tactic, and training sessions can, perhaps inadvertently, reinforce this idea, especially when time is short. A lot of nonviolent direct action training seems to assume that human nature is violent and aggressive, and that we must somehow overcome or subdue this. Role-playing exercises may actually set up a false situation – for example, where some people take the part of blockaders and others the police, those who play the police may be very frightened of police violence and so what they act out is a watered-down version of their own fears. This deliberately blanks out part of the real confrontation – the very humanity that nonviolence is meant to generate. What many women are stressing is that acting in a nonviolent way involves a state of mind that challenges assumptions about power. Each person has to think this through for themselves. It is the underlying attitude of mind that is important. If we have that, we will do the 'right' things at the 'right' time intuitively.

Nonviolent actions require imagination and flexibility to be able to respond as a situation develops and to keep up the pressure, not necessarily sticking to a pre-arranged plan if events render it

Ed Barber

Obstructing workers laying sewer pipes,
Greenham Common, 5 October 1982

ineffective. It is clearly impossible to lay down rules about this. We may decide to finish an action if there seems nothing more to gain, rather than sitting it out until we are dragged away and perhaps arrested. On occasions it may be useful for some people to get arrested to show that they are not intimidated. This will probably get further publicity and support for the action. On other occasions it may not be useful and it is certainly never necessary to be arrested to prove one's commitment. If the police are very angry we may decide not to give them any justification to use violence against us, and agree to move or leave. If they are very casual and patronising, we may want to confront them further. Sometimes it may seem appropriate to reinforce our physical presence by making a noise – humming, singing, chanting or keening. At other times silence may be more in keeping, generating a calm and dignified atmosphere. We need to be able to recognise the dynamics of a situation and decide how to behave accordingly, to achieve our purpose.

The authorities always try to impose their definition on any situation, reclaiming the initiative, and trying to define for us what we may or may not do. There is a danger that nonviolent actions such as blockades or die-ins may develop into a new orthodoxy, which becomes incorporated into what is 'acceptable' and 'allowed', as has happened with rallies and marches. Tactics, such as refusing to move when cautioned by the police or going limp on arrest, may become new 'rules' people expect to comply with, rather than choices to be made depending on the circumstances. It is necessary to focus always on what will be most effective in any particular situation. This is the challenge to our imagination and intelligence. If people really put their minds to it they can disrupt and confront without being violent.

Our obvious strength is that there are potentially so many of us, but unpredictability is equally important. The authorities simply do not expect to be continually challenged in creative, nonviolent ways. We can always take them by surprise, for they cannot anticipate what we will decide to do next. In this sense people do not know their own strength. We do not know what we can do because very few people have given it enough thought or begun to translate their ideas into action.

Nonviolence is not just the absence of violence or simply a tactic, but a total approach to living, both an ideal to aim for and a strategy for change. We cannot achieve peace through violence. It is a fundamental contradiction in terms. Means and ends merge

into one another and cannot be separated, so that anything won by violence has the seeds of that violence contained within it. In any case, the state can always meet violence with far superior violence through an extensive system of law, courts, police and, ultimately, the army. If we are saying that nonviolence is a possibility, that weapons are unnecessary, that nations as well as individuals can settle differences of opinion without resorting to violence, then we undermine our own argument if we use violence, for we show that even we – who profess a commitment to nonviolence – are not capable of it ourselves.

Nonviolence involves the idea of power stemming from our only real resources – our feelings, ideas, and ultimately our bodies – drawing on imagination and determination. No one individual should have any more power than anyone else; we are all dependent on each other's knowledge and skill. By contrast, people are used to thinking that power comes from independence, from controlling knowledge, from depriving others, from other people's dependence and acquiescence. Besides physical violence there is exclusion from affection, emotional blackmail, bartering of love, which are all part of a context that recognises the right of the powerful to coerce. Nonviolence suggests that power partly derives from our relationships with each other, and recognises our fundamental mutual dependence.

Without questioning the 'success' of violence in solving problems, many people assume that nonviolence cannot be effective. Much nonviolent action is symbolic, and it is true that there has been no really widespread, systematic campaign of nonviolent direct action in this country. But it is worthwhile asking what 'effectiveness' means. Actions are clearly effective when those involved in them experience their capabilities and their strength. That exciting feeling of empowerment is something that cannot be taken away. It becomes part of how we think about ourselves, as purposeful, effective people who can express ourselves clearly on an issue of vital importance. Speaking out is a liberating experience, both for ourselves and for others who identify with what we are saying. It affirms their beliefs and encourages them to speak out too. The campaign against cruise missiles is also effective in the sense that it is continually growing. More and more people are finding ways to express their opposition to nuclear warfare. Only through nonviolent means can we create a moral and political climate where such things become unthinkable.

Clearly this is an enormous task, which involves a complete rethinking of many fundamental assumptions. Violence is so ingrained in every aspect of society that ideas about nonviolence are often scornfully dismissed as naive and utopian. Yet violence, whether in protest against nuclear weapons or conflicts between nations, ultimately solves nothing. It merely redefines and extends conflict so that it becomes more entrenched. At root it only generates more violence.

A Memo for Peace
This poem is dedicated to the women at the Greenham peace camp; and to all those who live their lives in the struggle for peace and freedom.

let us assume
that the basic assumptions
are wrong

the assumptions
    that our leaders
    and politicians
    are right
    and we
    are wrong

    that those in power
    know what's best
    for us
    that they have
    our interests
    at heart (what if
    we assume
    that they have
    no hearts?)

    that They are Good
    and Grown Up and Wise
    and we are Bad
    and Stupid Children
    needing to be
    put down
    put right
    and shown
    How To Behave

Let us assume that
that is
not so
and let us
turn those assumptions

on their heads
til they rattle and groan
and beg for mercy
and for our
forgiveness

and let us remind ourselves
that we are many

who struggle
who cry out
who suffer in silence
even those who burned
to remind us
who march on marches
picket embassies
campaign and demonstrate
sign the petitions
write to newspapers
lobby MPs

who often go unheard

who join hands
who sing the songs
who write the words
who play the music
who surround the barricades
with clowns with children
who weave coloured ribbons
between the barbed wire
who offer flowers
to the guards
who light the candles
singing softly into night

who go to jail
we
who believe
in peace
and uphold the dignity
of human life
the sanctity
of our planet

who condemn
the killings
the rapes
the missiles
the poisons
the violations
the tortures
the cover-ups
the distortions
the pornography
the lies

the basic assumptions

we need to remind ourselves
that we cannot all
be wrong

and we who live with conscience
despite the discomforts
who raise our voices
despite the silencings

who gather strength
despite the pain

we who challenge
the basic assumptions

survive

beneath
the warmongers'
icecold indifference
the politicians'
stonefaced rhetoric
the uniform armed alertness

we rattle
and keen

cry out
one voice

for peace

Viv Wynant, 20 November 1982

79

Why women

I want to say very strongly that having women's actions in my view has got nothing to do with excluding men. It's got to do with – for once, just once – giving women a chance, *including* women. It's so women – who have been kept out of politics and all walks of life for so long, who've been pushed back into the home and been told that they can only function in one small closed-in area to do with children and nurturing – can come out of those areas and take part in politics and actually begin to affect and change the world, and that's Why Women . . . It's positive. It's so that women can get together. Women have been isolated as individuals for so long. They've had to struggle to join together and work on issues. This way women can join together. Hundreds of women can join together and find their strength, and it's essential at this point in our history that women's strength is utilised and seen and works and is regarded as important.
Katrina Howse, March 1982

The strength of the women's community at Greenham has been particularly important during the second winter, when women lived under very difficult conditions, sleeping under plastic, living

out in the rain and mud, continually harassed by the authorities. It is a remarkable manifestation of women's determination, courage and support for each other. The majority of adults in this country are women (52 per cent in 1982) but most women do not take an active part in politics, or are only peripherally involved. As time has passed it has become abundantly clear that Greenham is so successful *because* it is a women's peace camp.

It should not be at all surprising that women are involved in a campaign of nonviolent direct action, for nonviolence and feminism have some important principles in common. They both involve nonhierarchical, decentralised ways of organising, based on individual initiative, together with a recognition of our interdependence and the power of co-operation. This means that we want to work in supportive ways, sharing tasks, encouraging and caring for each other, respecting each other's ideas and experience, deciding things together. There is no role for permanent, separate leaders or experts. Since we all want the opportunity to develop and express ourselves, we should allow that opportunity to others. This may seem idealistic and in practice there are difficulties in this way of working, only too familiar to anyone who has tried it. It needs time to talk things over properly, to get to know one another, to decide things. There needs to be scope for individual initiative, without a few confident, assertive people taking over. We need to trust each other and respect our differences. While nonviolence involves caring and listening, it does not mean indulging people who are demanding, avoiding a difficult discussion or pretending things are all right when they are not. Rejecting centralised, hierarchical structures for informal ways of working can set up other kinds of exclusiveness based on strong personalities, women who are very articulate or dominating, cliques of close friends, or new rituals that become ends in themselves. Some women may feel frustrated in unstructured meetings with loose, seemingly rambling discussions. Many enjoy singing together and forming circles, and feel strengthened by it, but this does not appeal to everyone. Having said this, however, it is obvious that this way of working has great strengths and does include women in a way that other formal organisations do not.

Many women are justifiably sceptical of politicians or feel daunted and excluded by political parties, trade unions or CND groups, with their procedures, rules, committees, chairmen, written resolutions, impersonal discussions and agendas planned in

Lesley McIntyre

Brenda Prince

Women's Peace Camp, Greenham Common,
October 1982

advance. Most women have little experience of this way of working and often find it alienating and frustrating, as, indeed, do many men. Women respond emotionally to each other and to this crucial life-and-death issue, and do not tend to get bogged down in procedure or technical details about nuclear weapons. Obviously facts are useful, but they can sometimes become an end in themselves, a source of power and mystification, obscuring the need to try to do something about the situation.

I came to Greenham Common through the women's peace group in Sheffield. When we heard about cruise missiles, we decided to have a meeting about it. We were a fairly mixed group of women but very anxious about this issue. Our responses were almost entirely gut reactions against the whole idea of cruise missiles and all that they represented. I and one or two others had been involved in the peace movement before. Quite a lot of us hadn't been. We were feeling very angry and confused. We had a meeting and we talked. Some of the women wept in anger and frustration. This issue is very difficult for many women. They have a sudden shock of realisation. They don't have any background information. All they know is how they feel about it. They don't have any statistics; they don't have any facts.

Maybe, they think, 'I'll go along to my local CND meeting' – that's if they know one exists. They find that it's a very bureaucratic set-up, invariably run by blokes. There's a table at the top of the room and rows of seats. We all sit down and we are *informed* and we find ourselves talking to the backs of each other's heads. In that atmosphere, if you're a woman with no background to the peace movement, no political background at all, you go in and you sit at the back. You think, what I'm feeling is fear, panic, terrible distress. I want to express what I'm feeling, but there's no space for me to do it here. What are these blokes going to say? I can't stand up and cry. I can't stand up and scream. I can't even ask what I can do. They're all going on about SS-20s, missiles, rockets, the next demonstration, all kinds of political things that I don't understand. How am I going to find someone who feels the way I do? They don't seem to *feel* about it. All they seem to do is work with their heads. Some of us in our peace group have some experience of how women's groups work. Some of us didn't have that, but we were able to use what we knew – a completely different way of doing things. We *never* sat in rows. We introduced ourselves and tried to keep

the groups fairly small. If there were 25 or 30 women we would split up into smaller groups to talk. Everybody gets the chance to express themselves and their feelings. In the early days there were a lot of very distressed women, but there was space for them to express their emotions. And these things need to be done before you can sort out in your mind a plan of action for yourself.

Lesley Boulton, June 1982

By now we are involved in a widespread campaign that extends all over Britain, a decentralised network, growing all the time. Some women live at Greenham for days or months at a time. Others stay for a few days or visit occasionally, but support the camp in hundreds of ways, including raising money, publicising actions, writing to newspapers, taking photographs. Many belong to women's peace groups where they live. Besides initiating their own activities, local groups organise in their areas in preparation for large-scale actions, telling others about them, holding planning meetings and workshops, arranging childcare and transport. Equally important, small friendly groups give emotional support and encouragement.

The women's peace camp was originally set up on the basis of individual responsibility and initiative and this principle continues to be fundamental. At the same time, working together and keeping in contact with each other is vital. For local groups it is probably clear-cut who constitutes the collective, but it is less so for the peace camp itself, where women come and go. Potentially the collective could include anyone who has ever lived there. In practice, there are meetings at the camp and any woman who is interested is welcome to attend. There are also action planning meetings, often in Newbury and London, and in other towns. Particular groups tend to come together to plan an action and then send out information inviting others to take part. Ideas are discussed in smaller groups and passed on. There are no directives from above, and there is a framework provided for others to join in if they want. There is no 'official policy' beyond a shared commitment to women's actions and nonviolence.

The original march from Cardiff to Greenham Common was organised by women, calling themselves Women for Life on Earth. A few men went on the march and there were men living at the peace camp in the early months, but most of the women felt that

the way they wanted to run the camp would be jeopardised if men continued to live there. As a result, since February 1982, the camp has been exclusively a women's space. This decision was much debated, both at the time and since. It has been a source of great strength to thousands of women, but also a source of misunderstanding, alienation and hurt for some women and many men. One argument is that women's action is divisive, that the issue is too important to be left to women, or that we have no right to claim a separate space. Others maintain that men are perfectly capable of behaving nonviolently, or that the world will only change when men also take responsibility for nurturing and caring and are able to develop this side of themselves. While these last two points may have some validity, some women argue that we have helped men for far too long. It is their responsibility to develop caring and sensitive ways of thinking and acting, while we as women take the lead in this fight against extinction. Many women want a space where they can express themselves, develop confidence in working together and discover new ways of organising which are personal and informal. This is evidenced by the thousands of women who are involved with the peace camp or women's actions because they are *women's* actions.

The fact is that vast numbers of women identify with Greenham, and are prepared to engage in direct political activity often for the first time, because it is a women's initiative and builds on rather than suppresses women's strength. Embracing the base on 12 December 1982 spoke directly to women – decorating the perimeter fence with symbols of life was an idea that most women found inspiring. The strength of this action was that it was possible to incorporate the diversity of 30,000 individual responses into a strong and unified statement. All of us involved with Greenham have different backgrounds, but we are all affected by being women in a man's world. Different women want to take part in women's actions for different reasons. For some it is a matter of principle, for others largely a matter of strategy.

Sir – 'War is the male prerogative apparently, the most unacceptable face of patriarchy', says L. J. O'Carroll (Letters, December 30). Sarcasm. However, I notice this is true. I notice women don't, as a social group, kill each other in wars. I notice men do. I also notice that Mr O'Carroll is frightened of women holding hands with each other instead of with him, and by the

idea of a ' "baby-care" world-view' predominating.

I don't think any of this is biologically inevitable. I don't think that all men accept the war game or that all women reject it. I do think that for thousands of years society has been dominated by men as a sex, and that this has given us a split humanity.

Almost all of recorded history so far has been a series of men-only demonstrations, in which men have taken our property rights in the earth, in women, in children, in other men.

We have to say no to the men in power and to their claim on us, and we have to say it together, in solidarity as women, because it is by splitting us off from one another that men have put us at their disposal.

This sounds exaggerated; it is only as exaggerated as these images: a mother crying alone in a room because she is suddenly intensely aware that she may not be able to protect her child from a hideous nuclear death; nappies and teddy-bears hanging on the perimeter of a nuclear base.

There was a lot of singing by the women at Greenham Common that Sunday [12 December 1982]: I know I wasn't the only woman to find my voice there. It felt like a reclamation of life. Men can do it too – but not by trying, as so many times before, either to say it for us (better), or to shut us up. Yours sincerely,
Liz Knight
The *Guardian*, 5 March 1983

The world's major power blocs led by the Soviet Union and the USA oppose each other as if they were genuine opposites, as if to distract our attention from the fact that their similarities are much more striking than their differences. Each pours vast wealth – money, natural resources and brain power – into researching, producing, stockpiling and guarding ever more diabolical means of killing people. Nightmarish weapons which are continually counted, compared, gloated over, boasted and lied about. This sick *men*tality runs through every aspect of society – British, American, Soviet. It is based on greed, arrogance, cynicism, competitiveness and irresponsibility. It reduces people to the level of things and gives machines – clocks, dictaphones, assembly lines, computers – control over us. It disciplines and stereotypes us in the name of education; manipulates

our ideas and opinions through adverts, the papers and television. When we break down we go to the doctor's to be fixed, like cars to a garage. 'Reason' and 'science' are glorified and slavishly followed at the expense of feeling, intuition and spiritual insight. Animals are reared to be slaughtered in barbaric conditions. Air and water are polluted with poisonous 'wastes'. In the name of sterile, meaningless abstractions like patriotism and duty, mothers' sons are sent off to murder other mothers' sons. The police, the armies and the courts are all 'only obeying orders'. People in Africa, India and South America starve while these same continents export shipload after shipload of tea, coffee, meat, exotic fruit and vegetables to the rich countries of the world. This is 'civilisation as we know it', the 'peace' they are so proud about. We are left in isolation to deal with this system, this outrage, with its privilege, exploitation and rape. If we can't cope with it we're made to feel that we're weak, inadequate, over-sensitive. The world is run by a handful of mad old men, indulging their ghoulish, expansionist fantasies. Disenfranchised women, despite the vote, we are campaigning against cruise missiles, but in doing so we are also taking on the world.
Gwyn Kirk, April 1983

For many women the issue is about reclaiming power for ourselves, and not remaining victims of a male-defined world characterised by violence. While women feel saddened and pessimistic about the possible consequences of this violence all around us, it also makes us angry when we see what is going on in the world. It is often anger that forces us out of our feelings of powerlessness, and this anger has led many women to reject any involvement with men over this issue. The focus of Greenham has mobilised thousands of women and we are spreading this energy, finding ways to reach thousands more. It is vital that we recognise the diversity of women involved as a source of strength. We see the future and the role women have to play in the fight against nuclear weapons very differently.

Some look to women's tradition as 'carers': as mothers, teachers, looking after the elderly and the sick. They argue that this traditional role makes it impossible to contemplate mass destruction, perhaps even of the planet itself.

I think that most women are really in touch with what life is about. You can't even contemplate having a child without con-

sidering the value of that life and the struggle people have bringing up children, putting in all those hours and hours of caring. A lot of women do that not even with children, but with the home, making a wonderful place for people to get by day-to-day living. You just can't contemplate that being destroyed by some people's fear and the difference in ideologies of different countries. It just doesn't make sense. Life is so much more precious than that. Also, women can identify with women of Russia and Eastern bloc countries. We're just the same. A woman in Russia is the same as myself – the same emotions, leading the same sort of life. In no way will I be part of anything that will murder her. The myth that's been put around so long that we need armies, we need these missiles, men must protect women and children from other men in other countries. That's just completely out of hand. Women must come out and say

'We don't want this type of protection. It's this type of protection which is actually endangering our lives.'

We have to find our own strength, ways of using our energy whereby we can actually change the situation because it's a very, very small minority of people making these decisions, not taking into account people's lives – playing with our lives. The majority of people in this country don't want this. What we're doing here is a consciousness-raising thing, particularly for women, because most women don't take an active part in politics. They allow their lives to be run by rules and regulations, by parliament – mainly by the male structure. What we're saying is that women are powerful. We can all come out and say 'You can't do this to us.'

Sarah Green, March 1982

Some think of this role in a more mystical sense, a belief in women's spiritual insight and connectedness to the forces of life. This strand has roots in the earliest matriarchal religion which Judaism and, later, Christianity denigrated as 'paganism'. Some see the campaign against cruise misiles as part of their wider opposition to all forms of male violence. Some believe that women have innate good qualities and are better qualified than men to take up this issue. Others feel that women are less aggressive and more caring on account of their conditioning rather than any innate biological characteristics. Finally, on a tactical level, women's actions force the authorities – the government, courts and police –

Ed Barber

Breaching the peace, Greenham Common,
27 August 1982

to deal directly with women, which they are not used to doing.

Many women believe that nonviolent direct action is more likely to stay nonviolent if only women are involved. Of course, there are some men who understand nonviolence, just as there are some women who do not, but they may be more likely to provoke violence merely by being men. Many men are afraid of violence from other men, and the police, military personnel or construction workers are more likely to use violence against men than against women.

It is a tragedy that people should waste time and energy arguing about whether or not there should be mixed actions – women and men together – at Greenham, when there is so much to be done. There are 102 other American bases in this country, and a dozen other peace camps that need support. Hundreds of firms and 1.5 million people are involved in the arms industry in Britain in one way or another. Then there are the associated dangers of

nuclear power stations, the reprocessing, transporting and dumping of nuclear waste, to mention only a few things that need challenging and changing.

The different attitudes and experiences that enrich and strengthen the women's peace movement as a whole also lead to criticism from both sides: for being too feminist and for not being feminist enough. Obviously women who have spent years talking about feminism and being politically active will have a very different perspective from women who have never been directly involved in politics before. Each will come across attitudes that are hard to identify with. Many women have become involved because of their children or grandchildren. Most expect motherhood to be important for women in the future, though many hope to see the responsibility for childcare shared more. Others reject motherhood as an option and certainly as women's destiny. Still others do not want personal relationships with men. These different perspectives give rise to differences of opinion and emphasis, and to continuing, sometimes bitter, discussion. The important thing is that we build on what we share as women, our fear, commonsense, determination, and hope, developing our creativity and strength, while recognising and respecting our differences.

A public debate?

A group of women, children and men left Cardiff on 27 August 1981, to march 125 miles to USAF/RAF Greenham Common near Newbury, in protest at NATO's decision to site American cruise missiles there in December 1983. When they arrived 10 days later, they asked for a televised debate on this issue. This request was refused and so the peace camp was set up as a direct protest against cruise missiles and to get wider publicity. On 1 January 1983, people all over the world saw women dancing on a missile silo at Greenham on the television news.

In the intervening months there was some interest from local papers, local radio and television, sympathetic freelance writers and photographers, journalists and film crews from abroad, and occasional reports in the national media. Throughout the peace camp's first year, freelance writers and photographers found it virtually impossible to get mainstream newspapers or magazines to use their work. A Dutch television programme about Greenham so inspired a group of women in Holland that they decided to set up a women's peace camp at Soesterberg in May 1982, but this programme was not shown in Britain.

The national media only really began to take an interest in mid-November 1982, when 23 women were found guilty of

breaching the peace for occupying the security box inside the main gate of the base in August and for obstructing work on new sewer pipes in October. By a coincidence of timing, two weeks after this there were large-scale actions at Greenham: embracing and closing the base on 12 and 13 December. Suddenly the 16-month-old protest was news and reporters scrambled over each other to catch up on some of the background. At long last a public debate had begun.

As the peace movement has grown in size and strength, government propaganda against it has had to become more blatant. In January 1983, the government talked of mounting a £1 million advertising campaign to push its 'defence' policy. Politicians from opposing parties – Labour, Liberal and SDP – as well as national CND, vociferously condemned this idea. In any case it was hardly necessary, as the goverment has access to the vast resources of the mainstream media, and already puts out its policies, especially to schools, through its Central Office for Information.

Television and radio programmes are particularly powerful. They are also very transient compared to newspapers which you can keep and look at again. You get *impressions* rather than precise information because it is difficult to remember a lot of facts and figures when they are only said once. The order in which the news items are presented is also very important in contributing to the overall impression we retain.

A very clear example of this occurred on ITN's *News at Ten* on Thursday 31 March 1983. CND organised two blockades on this day at Greenham Common and at Burghfield (also in Berkshire, where Trident warheads are being made). On Good Friday, 1 April, there was a 14-mile 'human chain' linking Burghfield, Aldermaston (the nuclear weapons research establishment which also produces nuclear warheads) and Greenham Common. The following reports were culled from newspapers, but they are presented in the order chosen by *News at Ten*:

*The expulsion of three Russians for spying – two diplomats and a journalist. Five Russians have been expelled from this country in the past four months. The Russians, two of whom were interviewed, said that the charges were ridiculous.

*The breaking of the blockade at Greenham Common airbase in Berkshire by the police.

*A report of Mrs Thatcher's reply to a question in parliament: 'It would make far more sense for these women to go and link hands

Women lay siege to Stock Exchange

The Standard Monday 7 June 1982

WOMEN demonstrators, including actress Susannah York, blockaded entrances to the Stock Exchange today in a peace protest.

Police made 10 arrests as the women, daubed with red paint, lay down in the streets around the building.

The 40 demonstrators, including several women from the long-running sit-in outside Greenham Common air base, timed their protest to mark President Reagan's visit to Britain.

Ms York said: " As a member of the peace movement, I have to try to help stop Cruise missiles, Trident, and all nuclear weapons systems.

" We want to try to take our lives back into our own hands and safeguard our children's future."

The demonstration ended peacefully after police threatened to arrest the whole group.

A spokesman for the women said: " There has been no trouble with the police and no violence. We have decided not to make any more moves today

The Stock Exchange was chosen because its members controlled the money invested in arms industries to create nuclear weapons.

However . . .

There were nine arrests

Nobody was daubed with red paint

There were about 70 demonstrators

The Women's Peace Camp

The police didn't threaten to arrest the whole group

A spokes*man* for the women?

No-one would have said 'we have decided not to make any more moves today'

---

round the Berlin wall, if by doing so they can persuade the Soviets to take it down, to remove the guns, the dogs, and the mines there to kill people attempting to escape to freedom. If they do not succeed in this way they will prove that the freedom of the women of Greenham Comomn and of all our people needs to be defended.'

*A report of the Secretary of State for Defence Michael Heseltine's visit to Berlin. He said, 'I have a simple message for those watching the protests: raise your eyes above the demonstrators and banners and look over their heads to the Berlin wall – for this represents the real world. This is where the marching has to stop. There will be no protests behind this wall.'

As the cold war atmosphere between East and West intensi-

fies, diplomats from different countries are being expelled on a tit-for-tat basis. What a convenient time to announce the decision to expel three more from Britain and for Heseltine to spend two days in Berlin. It seems no accident of editing that Thursday's blockades and the human chain planned for Good Friday were sandwiched between these others 'events', thus creating a context supporting the government's view that Britain needs a 'deterrent' against the 'Soviet threat'.

Most people do not have any direct contact with the press until they become involved in some kind of campaign. It is only then that you realise that getting media coverage is not a straightforward matter. Hundreds of journalists have visited the peace camp since it started. In September 1982, the caravans were removed in a second attempt to evict the women and since then they have lived very much in the open, where everything they do is potential 'copy'. The press are specifically invited to cover particular actions. Since the autumn of 1982 a lot of this work has been co-ordinated from London as well as Greenham. Some women work hard to get media interest, preparing press releases and telephoning newspapers and magazines. Not everyone wants to talk to the press. Some people do not feel sufficiently confident. Some are exhausted with answering the same questions time and again or are sceptical about what will be published. Others want to communicate directly with those responsible for the situation – individual construction workers, politicians, police or military personnel – without going through an intermediate channel which they consider an unnecessary diversion.

Press coverage, or lack of it, plays a crucial part in any political campaign in helping to mould public opinion, though the apparent advantage of being able to reach millions of readers and viewers has to be weighed against the inherent danger of misrepresentation. It is very difficult to see the bias in reporting. It is only when you are involved in something that gets media coverage that you can compare your own experience and knowledge of it with how it is reported, and see what the discrepancies are.

The reports have been mixed and, taken together, they add up to a confusing barrage of inconsistent information. Between December 1982 and February 1983, several national papers did a peace camp 'feature', stressing the squalid conditions and the women's practical clothes.

Many articles do not go into details as to why the peace camp

is there but have plenty to say about the women. The descriptions of the camp and the quotes may or may not be accurate, but they are taken out of context and reported together with anecdotes, the writer's reactions and asides.

Journalists, photographers and editors act as a highly selective filter for information, and control how people and issues are presented to a wider public. Whatever is published or broadcast has enormous authority. Reporters are not superhuman. They cannot be in two places at once or, for example, see all the way round the nine-mile perimeter fence at Greenham. Yet they talk and write as if they do see and understand everything. As outside observers they usually have little information or understanding about how an action is organised or what those involved feel about it. They never admit this limitation even if they are aware of it. They take people's experience and ideas and recreate them in another context, screening out certain points and introducing others from different contexts. We do not speak directly to the audience but through screens, which vary somewhat from editor to editor. Something of what is said gets through – more or less coherently – but muddled up with other, often louder 'voices'.

Some reporters admire the women's commitment and imagination. Others are hostile but cannot ignore the women, so aim to neutralise and suppress what they are doing, by passing them off as well-meaning but deluded, childish, muddleheaded, ignorant of life's realities, reckless and irresponsible, or simply as communists. Some make out that the women, and the Western peace movement generally, are in the pay of the USSR and interweave their report with remarks about Moscow and the Kremlin.

Others claim that they are freaks, hippy layabouts, social misfits, living on social security, or living like gypsies. This serves two purposes. It allows men (and a few women) to express their hatred of independent women in clichés:

'strident feminists', 'burly lesbians' (The Sun, 14 December 1982),
'hefty ladies . . . a fairly gruesome bunch' (The Spectator, 1 January 1983),
'the harridans of Greenham Common' (The Spectator, 8 January 1983),
'Amazon waifs and strays' (letter to Newbury Weekly News, February 1982).

All of these remarks are also designed to alienate so-called 'ordinary' women and, of course, men. The message is clear: 'You, reader,

Tinkerbell is alive and well, living off lentil soup . . . and really believing that, if we all wish hard enough, nuclear bombs will just go away and everyone can live happily ever after

Daily Mail 13 January 1983

cold slippery mud had covered everything . . . their green dustbin bags wait for the weekly pick up smelling strongly.

What food supplies there are – a large hunk of cheese, several loaves of bread, dust-bins with cereal and dry food – lie scattered, rain-soaked and hap-hazard on make-shift tables.

The Times 10 December 1982

are not like this, so you will not want to know what these women are talking about.'

The photos chosen to illustrate newspaper articles reinforce the text. This raises an important dilemma. People want to express themselves without worrying about how they might be represented, but photos of women with, for example, very short hair, dungarees, 'unusual' clothes or painted faces, which some women like and which anyway are thought of as a personal matter, are used by unsympathetic editors as part of this stereotyping and undermining process.

News reporting of the arrests and trial of the 44 women who climbed on to the missile silo on New Year's Day devoted a lot of space to the 'emotional scenes' inside and outside the court – the dancing, singing, hugging, and crying. Emotional response is presented as something to gawp at, typically female, weak and irrational. Of course women were angry and upset as the magistrates and police got on with just-doing-their-job. Of course we want to encourage each other to confront the military insanity

going on all around us and upheld by these same magistrates and police. Those present describe how the authority of the court was completely overturned for them by the atmosphere of joyful defiance, despite the inevitability of the sentences.

Only The *Guardian* (3 January 1983) reported that the women risked charges under the Official Secrets Act. Only The *Morning Star* (16 February 1983) reminded readers that each cruise missile is 15 times as lethal as the bomb dropped on Hiroshima in 1945.

A second example of highly selective reporting occurred in accounts on 14 December 1982 of the mass blockade at Greenham on the previous day. The women's complete nonviolence was ignored entirely. Police violence was mentioned but with the suggestion that this was somehow forced on them by the women, rather than a deliberate choice. The police

> 'tried to cool the situation' (*Daily Express*),
> 'tried to preserve a delicate balance' (The *Guardian*),
> were 'caught in the crush' (*Daily Mirror*),
> were 'struggling' while they 'tried desperately to maintain a good humoured presence',
> they 'decided to avert a situation whereby hundreds of women might end up behind bars' (*Daily Telegraph*).

The press has a fixation about arrests. The *Daily Telegraph* even headlined its account of this blockade: 'Peace women fail to get arrested.' This emphasis is a gross and dangerous distortion because it glamourises dramatic actions and judges them by irrelevant standards. It completely overlooks whether those involved in an action feel it has succeeded in making its point, or even what that point is. It may also make some women feel that they have to get arrested to demonstrate their commitment. Many do not want to, and they are not weak or useless because of it.

Another kind of distortion is the habitual reference to leaders. Journalists like leaders and where there are no obvious leaders they create them – even to the extent of referring to 'a spokes*man* for the women . . .'! It is obviously much more convenient to deal with one or two people, especially if you can get them on the end of the telephone when you want them. Loose, non-hierarchical ways of organising are unfamiliar and it takes time and effort to talk to a range of people, sometimes genuinely impractical with tight deadlines. As one reporter exclaimed in frustration about the organisation of the actions on 12 and 13 December 1982: it's all so 'damned decentralised'. Reporters want concise, 'authoritative' statements,

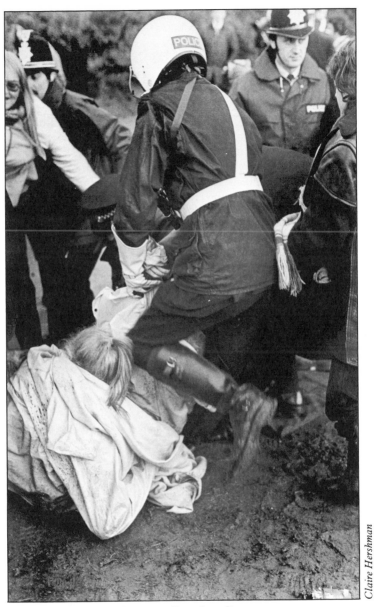

Nonviolent blockade of the base, Greenham Common, 13 December 1982

Claire Hershman

preferably with a minimum of trouble. Leaders are assumed to speak with authority and talking to them contributes to the reporter's 'omniscience'.

While all this is particularly true of the national media, it is not always the case in the local press and magazines with smaller circulations and a different political perspective. For many people, the local newspaper is the chief source of news. There is not the same pressure on space in local papers and it is generally much easier to get journalists to cover local groups and actions. Letters pages are one of the most popular items in local papers, and many women have used this as an opportunity to get their ideas across. This article from the *Chester Chronicle* is a good example of women using local media resources to publicise their group and advertise their ideas.

Peace has to be something today's women care about, whatever form the concern takes . . . in Chester there is now an effective Women for Peace Group which offers a channel for both concern and action . . .

Denise Aaron, mother of three young children, brought together 13 like-minded women in the sitting room of her home for a meeting in September 1981, and thus the Chester Women for Peace Group was born.

It has prospered. At the last count 300 newsletters went out and on 12 December, three coachloads went to join the day of protest at Greenham Common. And there are plans for a mammoth women's march from Chester to Greenham Common to arrive at the base for Hiroshima Day on 6 August.

Group meetings are now getting so large that there is a plan for splinter neighbourhood units, but everyone will still get together regularly for planning purposes – and the pleasure of seeing so many united in a cause.

There are no leaders, everything being done through co-operation. At meetings members always sit in a circle and one person (different each time) acts as 'facilitator', drawing up the agenda, making sure all runs smoothly, checking everyone who wants to have a say, and, in particular, drawing in newcomers.

The group is broad based . . . Members believe that, as women alone, they can achieve more, and securing their children's future is a common driving force.

Denise says that, being all women, they get emotional support from each other.

'We come along in the first place because we are worried sick about the nuclear arms race, and one of the first things we need is understanding, comfort and support from others who feel the same.'

'This is what gives us the solidarity to go out and face people who

are hostile to us, on the streets or at meetings or knocking on people's doors. It can be lonely out there.'

Members of the Chester group tend to do their own thing, ranging from leafletting houses to organising street theatre sessions on a peace theme. They fund-raise to finance their own efforts, and write letters all the time, to newspapers, MPs, councillors, civil defence planners, the prime minister, even, recently, Prince Charles.

They go out on the streets to talk to people and find that in the 15 months since the group was formed, there has been a switch in people's attitudes. People are much better informed, and they are concerned and ready to listen . . .

There are many local magazines that report women's actions in a more sympathetic manner than the national press, and anti-nuclear magazines like *Peace News* and *Sanity* give a lot of space to the women's peace network. Feminist publications like *Spare Rib* and *Outwrite* have carried many reports on Greenham and feminist views on nonviolence. The *New Statesman* has published various articles over the last few months on women's actions and the legal system and the peace camp.

Whatever the publication, all events at a particular time compete with each other for 'newsworthiness'. Even some 'hardened' press people found the embrace of the base on 12 December interesting and moving, but they were not interested when women handed out peace pies outside the Bank of England at lunchtime on 8 March, International Women's Day, though this generated constructive conversations about peace with passers-by. Nor did the press want to know about women from Greenham who had been brutally treated by the police at Comiso in Sicily, another site in Europe which is expected to receive cruise missiles in 1983. As these examples show, actions deemed to be of sufficient public interest must fulfil certain criteria. Of course this does not mean that actions which do not get reported at all are less valuable – the criteria certainly bear no relation to the strength and significance of action.

As well as journalists' accounts, there have been hundreds if not thousands of letters sent to editors of newspapers all over the country, giving information; putting personal points of view, both supportive and critical; discussing women's actions or the importance of nonviolence – all contributing to a continuing public debate, and often correcting or challenging earlier news reports or editorials.

I went to Greenham Common. As an individual I decided it was time I voiced my protest, expressed my opinion in a way that would be heard. This seemed to be the view expressed by all the women on our bus (and the two gentlemen who came along to look after the children). We shared a feeling of purpose, of hope, along with our fears of what cruise means to our children's future.

We asked which group people belonged to, and the overwhelming impression was that it was not a group they represented but themselves. There were Quakers, CND supporters, Roman Catholics, feminists, members of the Ecology Party, members of the Labour Party, Conservative women, actresses, students, grand-

mothers protesting for their grandchildren, and we two, Methodist women, holding hands round the camp.

This was not an 'organised' event; we were not exhorted to go, we only heard about it a week ago and it took some detective work to find out if there was anyone else going. We two were determined to go, even if it meant going on our own, each as an individual; this was the view expressed time and again, 'We would have come on our own if it was necessary.'

As it happened two coaches were booked from Barnstaple, women travelling in from villages all over the area. On the day we found that there were other coaches from Torrington, Bideford, Appledore, Holsworthy – all from an area traditionally slow to react.

We were all at Greenham Common from a personal belief, not because we had been pressurised into going, not necessarily because we are politically motivated, but because we believe that cruise missiles are an unholy and horrific weapon for anyone to contemplate using.

Margaret Bailey and Gill Weeks
Methodist Recorder, 23 December 1982

Your recent editorial and your answer to Patricia Pulham's letter both raise the tired old myth that the Peace Movement, in this case the Greenham women, are pro-Russian.

This is, if you'll excuse the phrase, a red herring. We are people (American, English, Chinese, yes, and Russian) and against nuclear weapons, whoever they belong to.

The reason why we seek to change the policy of our own country, rather than someone else's, is surely fairly obvious. We live in a democracy and are therefore responsible for our Government's actions.

In this case, our Government is forcing American-controlled missiles upon us and giving its support to American defence policy, so we have the right and, more than that, the responsibility as members of a free society to object to actions, which we deplore, being taken in our name.

The Russians have never claimed to be acting in our interests or by our mandate. Of course, we deplore Russian missiles and we are in no position to guarantee that they would not use them if we disarmed unilaterally, any more than the Government can prove that its policy does not make nuclear war more likely. We are necessarily dealing with conjecture.

One thing we can say, however. Our way is morally justifiable, the Government's is not. Blowing up or threatening to blow up innocent people is wrong, and I, for one, will not let anyone do such a thing in my name without protest.

Stephanie Bowgett
Chester Chronicle, 14 January 1983

BBC TV News carried an item (December 18) showing the good citizens of Newbury clearing up the 'rubbish' left at Greenham Common. This 'rubbish' comprised the symbols of love, hope, peace and life which I and 30,000 other women had attached to the wire fence around the base in opposition to the camp's message of hatred, despair, war, and death.

Among the items torn down was a photograph of my four daughters. It is because there are many who consider my children to be just so much rubbish that I shall continue to work for the abolition of the values and symbols of this war-crazed world.

Yours faithfully, Christine Garnier

The *Guardian*, 23 December 1982

If you decide you want to get an action publicised it is worthwhile spending some time thinking out the best ways of doing this and the pitfalls. It is often useful to write a press statement explaining the action, and for one or two women to take responsibility for making sure it is circulated and for talking to the press. The following notes from a workshop discussion may provide some useful starting points for discussions.

The vast majority of press reporters are just doing a job - getting a story. We can't rely on them to have any interest in supporting what we're doing or understanding things from our point of view. In fact it's quite often the reverse and they try to exploit what they see to be our weaknesses.

While we may want media coverage we don't just want to be passively on the receiving end of journalists' questions and comments, or simply objects of interest for photographers.

Being interviewed can be very isolating. You are singled out and under pressure to answer questions which may be irrelevant, undermining or patronising, or which misrepresent how you or others feel.

Some journalists adopt an aggressive style because they seem to think it goads people into saying what they really believe.

Usually when you're asked a question you feel some obligation to reply. It's very easy to get drawn into this, often without realising it, and to waste time talking about things you don't think are really important. Just because they ask a question you don't have to answer it if you don't want to. You can ignore it and just say what you wanted to say anyway, or turn the question round:'Oh, people don't really want to know ... what's important is when the government is going to see sense...' You can give a

joke answer if you think it's a silly question, but you can't trust reporters not to print it or broadcast it.

TV reporters may be friendly and supportive to get your confidence until the cameraman is ready, and then switch completely and ask difficult or hostile questions. For example, you're outside your town hall, protesting about the council's plan for so-called 'civil defence' and suddenly you're asked: 'Surely you don't think you're doing anything constructive by sitting here today. After all the council knows what it's doing/ You're just making people angry/wasting their time/making work for the police ...' People are used to seeing TV announcers and newsreaders who speak authoritatively from a prepared script. If you fumble for words, viewers may think that you don't really know why you're there. No one will know that you just weren't expecting the question.

Press photographers - almost always men - tend to give orders: 'move over there, love', 'turn round', 'look that way'. There's always a reason why they want you to do this and it's worth looking to see what or who you'll be standing next to if you do move over there. You don't have to move.

You can sometimes refuse to be photographed, but if you're involved in an action there often isn't a choice. However, you may be able to walk away/ turn your back on the camera/walk straight up to the camera so that you're too close and the photographer will only get a close-up of your coat buttons or your nose.

Journalists and photographers may callously exploit someone's vulnerability, for example, by picking on someone who is crying. You can distract their attention/send them on a wild goose chase/mess up the shot by getting in the way - walking between the camera and the shot.

Make it clear to journalists what you think of how their paper is reporting the issue.

We cannot rely on the established media to report systematically or accurately what we are doing, and so our own communication networks are absolutely vital:

- talking to people, writing personal letters
- producing leaflets, information sheets, newsletters and magazines
- putting up posters, leaving messages in library books or

doctors' waiting rooms, writing on walls
- organising meetings, discussion groups, film shows and gigs
- setting up peace groups committed to nonviolent direct action
- having telephone networks for passing information
- recording events and experiences with photos, sound recordings, film and video
- making songs, poems, plays.

These are all active processes: we pass on our ideas, sharing information and experience, encouraging and affirming each other, rather than being passive consumers of official 'truth'.

This is the thinking behind the chain letter for organising the actions of 12 and 13 December 1982. Women at the peace camp sent out letters to about 1,000 women. Each woman was asked to copy the letter and send it to 10 friends who would also copy it and sent it to 10 more, so everyone was part of the organising.

This was an inspiration for many women, giving them a chance to participate on their own terms. Responsibility was not in the hands of a central organising body, but focused on each woman responding to the invitation. In this way each woman took responsibility for publicising the event and making it a success. Women heard about the actions over a period of three months; they talked about it, made phone calls, wrote letters. The information was transmitted in a lateral way, changing as it moved from one to another, remaining a living communication. This process is diametrically opposed to more standard means of communication, where a static body of information is transmitted downwards. It is an attempt to reach the vast numbers of women untouched by other networks, partly by speaking in a different language and partly by using different channels. It seemed at the time as if we were plumbing older networks of talk and rumour, and rediscovering how efficient a means of communication they are. If the information strikes a chord, it is transmitted.

The success of the chain letter at informing many thousands of women about the actions was partly to do with the information being a starting point because duplicating it, thinking whom to send it to, phoning friends, are all active processes, they open the information and enable each individual to make a real contribution, which is likely to spread to assuming greater responsibility.

In October, I received a chain letter from Greenham Common women's peace camp. I had been to the camp several times but had not taken an active part for a few months. The letter came out of the blue. It told me about the action planned for 12 and 13 December, embracing and then closing the base. The women asked me to copy the letter and send it to 10 friends, the idea being that if every woman who received one did this, then the 10,000 women needed to encircle the base would arrive on 12 December. I didn't read so-called 'impartial' information in a newspaper. This was a personal communication addressed to me, requesting things of me, making it plain that *every* woman was included, was important. Not only did I copy the letter, but I spent a long time considering who to send it to. I didn't send it to women who I thought would hear about the action anyway, nor to women who would never go to such a demonstration. I sent letters to women I thought would be interested but had not become directly involved. I felt that the spur of a personal letter might spark off enthusiasm. As it turned out, several of these women were at Greenham on 12 December. Some had not been to a demonstration before. I am sure that everyone who received the letter must have gone through the same process, ensuring that women we knew heard about the action.

I was also asked to bring something to put on the perimeter fence: 'anything related to "real" life – as opposed to the unreal world that the military base represents'. When I first read this it did not strike me as important. As the time grew closer, I increasingly found myself wondering what to take. In the end I took a photograph of my mother and some poems. Sticking them on the fence was, to my surprise, the most moving experience of the weekend. I kept seeing my mother's face on the wire fence. I often think of every single one of the 30,000 women doing the same: carefully thinking what symbol they would leave at the base.

Alice Cook, April 1983

Despite its serious limitations, media coverage has been crucial in alerting people in this country to the danger of nuclear weapons, and by December 1982 a majority were actually against cruise missiles. This has been described as 'the Greenham factor', a media phrase which manages to both acknowledge and trivialise the influence of the peace camp. Ironically, if there *had* been a tele-

How we spin and thread ourselves together as women for this day — To make
it strong + effective··········· .

You are a spring and if you copy both sides
of this letter and send them to 10 other women,
who then do the same, who then do the same, etc.
we will become rivers that will flow together on Dec. 12th
and become an ocean of women's energy. Believe it
will work and it will work.

vised debate in September 1981 the peace camp might never have existed and far fewer people would have known anything about cruise missiles.

Over the months, women's actions have broken through a barrier of media silence, but press interest can be pressurising and seductive. It is important to continue to do things that capture people's imagination and do not play into the hands of press slurs or pressure to be arrested or imprisoned.

There are more than a dozen peace camps in Britain at present, outside military bases and weapons factories, but the media focus in on Greenham almost exclusively, at the expense of the others – another important aspect of editorial selection.

Greenham has not been singled out for particularly bad coverage by the media. All kinds of issues are trivialised, subjected to the cynicism and opportunism of journalists, and editorial control. But this issue is not simply good 'copy' for a few months of media treatment. It affects journalists personally just the same as everyone else.

Using the law

I do not feel I stand here today as a criminal.

I feel this court is dealing in trivia by making this charge against us, while those who are the real criminals (those who deal in our deaths) continue their conspiracy against humankind. We will continue to make a peaceful stand against them and continue to uphold our moral values which celebrate life.

We are all individuals whose responsibility it is to maintain and nurture life, something all of us can do together – with mutual support.

While we stand here the silos, which are intended to house the cruise missiles from December 1983, are still being constructed at Greenham Common. We all feel the urgency of this threat to our lives – and are determined not to remain silent.

As women we have been actively encouraged to be complacent, by sitting at home and revering men as our protectors: we now reject this role.

The law is concerned with the preservation of property. We are concerned with the preservation of all

life. How dare the government presume the right to kill others in our names?

Women's statement to Newbury Magistrates Court, 14 April 1982

The decision to site US cruise missiles at Greenham by December 1983 was taken by top NATO commanders in December 1979. There was no discussion in parliament, though a few British politicians knew about the decision and supported it. Our system of government is supposed to be open and democratic. There are 'proper channels' for making our views known: voting every four or five years, writing to MPs who are supposed to represent us, forming pressure groups to campaign over particular issues. Once government policy is decided – especially, as in the case of cruise missiles, way above the heads of most MPs – the 'proper channels' are virtually useless.

This has led the women involved in the peace movement into direct action and into possible conflict with some aspect of the law. In many people's minds, there is an important dividing line between legal means of influencing government and actions that break the law. However, whether a particular direct action is deemed illegal is in the hands of the authorities. There are laws to cover virtually any situation: for example, simply standing still on the pavement can be deemed an offence.

The authorities have tried to deal with the women at Greenham Common by attempting to evict them and, sometimes, by arresting women involved in various actions and charging them with relatively minor offences – obstructing the highway, obstructing a police officer, behaviour likely to cause a breach of the peace. In reserve are more intimidating charges which carry heavier fines or prison sentences, such as offences under the Official Secrets Act which could apply to actions on or around military bases. The authorities rely on precise, often very trivial, legal technicalities. What is really on trial, however, is our freedom of speech and freedom to express political opinion, a central principle of democratic government and, ironically, exactly what the government claims to be defending with nuclear weapons.

Many people know almost nothing about the law and the courts and this lack of knowledge may be one of the most intimidating aspects of direct action to begin with. In preparing for an

action, whether or not we will be breaking the law is an important consideration – what we can be arrested for and what the maximum penalties are. Women lawyers give legal advice which is usually included in a legal briefing for each action. This allows women to discuss the legal position beforehand and decide what part they want to play in the action. The following is an amended version of the legal briefing drawn up for the actions at Greenham on 12 and 13 December.

Offences for which you may be arrested

a) obstructing the highway; b) obstructing a police officer in the course of his duty; c) various public order charges, for example, breach of the peace; d) criminal damage; e) Official Secrets Act.

The first four are the offences most often used by police in enforcing order. They all carry the power of arrest and allow police to remove you from the action and possibly hold you in custody overnight. They must be heard in a magistrates' court.

In all cases we list the *maximum* penalties, but usually the penalty is a small fine or an order to be bound over to keep the peace. If you refuse to pay a fine or be bound over, you will be jailed.

a) *Obstructing the highway:* highway means any highway available to the general public, which need only be partially obstructed or obstructed by someone else because of your action. Max. penalty: £50 fine.

b) *Obstructing an officer:* useful to police when they cannot get you for anything else and almost impossible to argue with (arguing could itself constitute an offence). Max. penalty: £200 fine and/or one month in prison.

c) *Breach of the peace:* it is an offence to use 'threatening, abusive or insulting words or behaviour' either deliberately or which could cause a breach of the peace in any public place. You can be charged with this if it seems likely that a breach of the peace *might* happen. Max. penalty: 6 months in prison and/or £1,000 fine. Or the magistrate can be asked to *bind you over to keep the peace*. This will be for a specific time with the surety of a fixed sum.

d) *Criminal damage:* it is an offence to 'without lawful excuse deliberately destroy or damage property belonging to another'. Max. penalty if damage less than £200: 6 months and/or £1,000 fine. If more than £200 can be tried in crown court with max. penalty of 10 years, and/or large fine.

e) *Official Secrets Act:* this is mentioned simply to acquaint you with the remote possibility of it being used at some point in the next year against a few individuals to deter us from increasing activity. It covers 'prohibited places' which include military establishments, and UK Atomic Energy Authority establishments. There are several

sections, carrying different maximum sentences ranging from 14 years to life imprisonment.

By-laws
Infringement of by-laws can only be prosecuted in the magistrates' court and normally carries a maximum fine of £50. *There is no power of arrest.*

Getting arrested
Each group should have a *legal observer* with the names and phone numbers of members of the group. This woman should observe everything that happens, keep notes and be a witness in court; *stay* with her group and *not* get arrested; note numbers of arresting officers; get in touch with a solicitor; if arrested, hand over task to someone else.

If you are arrested you are usually warned first and given the chance to leave. If you decide to stay, call your name to the legal observer. You will be taken to a police station; asked your name, address and phone number, birth date and occupation; then searched. You may be questioned but you do not have to say anything. You do not have to have fingerprints or photographs taken. Once you are charged you will probably be released. If not, don't panic – a solicitor will have been contacted by your legal observer.

Efforts by Newbury District Council to evict the women's peace camp aimed to avoid the political dimensions of the campaign by concentrating on simple squatting charges. The Council's first attempt to get a possession order to reclaim the land was heard in the High Court in London in May 1982, when the judge ruled that the issue was not a political one, that the women had no right to camp on common land, and granted the possession order. However, it was clear that the Council's hope of quietly removing the peace camp from the public eye had come too late and in fact it backfired – support was growing fast. A demonstration outside the court, and the dozens of women who added their names to the list of defendants and filled the courtroom to overflowing all testified to this. Each one of the defendants who stood up to make a statement stressed that the issue was not camping but cruise missiles. Squatting cases are usually heard in closed court. The judge relied on this practice and refused access to the press so that none of these statements could be reported.

This move was made eight months after the peace camp was established. Presumably the Council had hoped that the peace camp would fold up by itself through the previous, bitterly cold winter. A strip of land alongside the main road near the airbase is

Ed Barber

After the second eviction, Newbury District
Council tipped tons of rubble on the site of
the peace camp, September 1982

not owned by the Council but by the Department of Transport. The Council removed some caravans and destroyed a large shelter, but the women neatly circumvented the effect of the possession order by moving the camp a few yards on to the Department of Transport land. Whereas various national newspapers carried reports of this court case and photographs of protesters outside the court being dragged away by police, the continuation of the peace camp went unreported. The same thing happened in September 1982 when the camp was evicted again, this time by the Department of Transport itself. Television reports showed caravans being towed away and the camp dismantled, but there was no coverage over the next few weeks to show that women were continuing to live in the open at Greenham, back on land belonging to the Council.

This time, however, the Council decided to enforce its by-laws much more strictly. Accordingly, women were not allowed to put up any 'structures' and had to live under plastic coverings, sleeping in vans or in small benders made from branches covered with plastic, and hidden in the woods. In effect, they have been forced by the Council to live in extremely primitive conditions.

Although still arguing over by-laws, Newbury Council's next move was more hard-hitting. They first revoked the deed allowing public access to the common land. The Council then applied for a second possession order, as well as injunctions against 21 named women, forbidding them to set foot on the common land for an unlimited period or to 'conspire with others' or incite others to go there. Again, by the time the possession order hearing came to court, several hundred women had added their names to the list of defendants, and while both the possession order and the injunctions were granted (though the incitement part was dropped), the groundswell of support and counter publicity meant that the attempt to dispose of the camp backfired once again. Indeed, women just moved their things back on to the strip of land belonging to the Department of Transport, as before.

The Council decided to revoke the deed allowing public access in order to ban the 21 women from the common, thus putting themselves in the ridiculous position of making it out of bounds to anyone at all, except the few people who live around the common and have long-standing commoners' rights. Many people were angry about ths tactic.

Sir – Mr Bryan Philpott [Newbury Councillor] said (The *Guardian*, Friday 25): 'We realise we have technically taken away the right of everyone to use the common, but I am sure most of the people would regard that as a small price to pay to get rid of the camp.'

What price democracy?

We who live in Newbury find ourselves the current focus of Europe on a crucial issue for mankind. Surely it is the very freedom which Mr Philpott is sacrificing which is the bone of contention between East and West?

Are we to set about crushing opponents' rights to express themselves by mass prohibition?

Mr Philpott makes a sweeping assumption of support for this move without having the courage to expose it to debate beforehand.

It has been said that when women are allowed to join hands round the Kremlin, the West will take the peace movement seriously. Women are no longer allowed to join hands around Greenham Common. Is this a step forward?

Yours sincerely, David Hawkey

The *Guardian*, 1 March 1983

On 12 May 1983, Newbury District Council evicted the part of the peace camp that was still on their land and impounded several cars, allegedly to defray their costs. When the women lay down in the road to try to stop them moving the vehicles away, they were forcibly removed by High Court bailiffs. Despite growing harassment from the authorities, the women at the peace camp have said time and time again that they do not intend to leave. Moreover, the 21 women affected by the High Court injunction have refused to let this ruling limit them over-much. It is undoubtedly a restriction on their freedom, but unlikely to affect the peace camp. Many of these women are now very active in other ways – talking to public meetings, CND groups, working through trade unions – and there are many others organising future actions. Newbury District Council is in the process of drafting new by-laws for Greenham Common. Amongst other things, they want to fence off sections of common land, presumably as another possible line of attack against the peace camp, and to 'regulate' assemblies.

Whatever one may think of the cause embraced by the women of the Greenham Common peace camp, it is plain that the authorities have made a fearful hash of dealing with them.

The women's cause thrives on publicity and attention. The actions of the authorities, particularly those of the Newbury District Council but also those of the Ministry of Defence and the police, have ensured that the camp has got great and growing exposure.

> They are like firemen trying to put out a fire by throwing petrol on it.
> The *Observer*, 13 March 1983

Just as the Council has tried to ignore the political implications of the peace camp, so the authorities, by not pressing charges or by charging women with relatively minor offences, are trying to deny that there is any threat from the women's actions. This tactic is a way of trying to incorporate and neutralise their effect, and it may well change again over the next few months. In the early 1960s, the leaders of the 'Committee of 100' were given prison sentences of up to 18 months under the Official Secrets Act when their campaign of direct action began to expand. This seems to be the thinking behind Newbury Council's decision to get injunctions against 21 women whom they presume to be ringleaders. But the experience of the past 18 months has shown that, whatever has happened to some individual women, there have always been many more ready to commit themselves.

Those arrested at the first blockade in March 1982 were charged with obstructing the highway, and faced small fines. Some women decided to pay the fine. Others refused and were given prison sentences of a week, in practice reduced to four or five days with remission for 'good behaviour'. All through the summer individual women served these sentences with very little publicity. It was left to local police to chase them up for non-payment, and so they were dealt with separately and sent to different prisons at different times. Apart from one woman's 'sponsored' prison sentence, little appeared in the press.

This altered in November 1982 with the case of 19 women arrested for going on to the base at Greenham and occupying the security box on 27 August. They had been charged with behaviour likely to cause a breach of the peace. By an accident of timetabling, which the authorities must have regretted later, the case of 12 women arrested on 5 October for attempting to stop construction work at Greenham was also heard the same week. This meant that on three consecutive days women were given prison sentences for refusing to agree to be bound over to keep the peace.

At the first of these cases various witnesses – including E. P. Thompson and the Bishop of Salisbury – testified that the women were engaged in keeping rather than breaching the peace. Whereas they were charged under legislation dating back to 1361, the women used the Genocide Act 1969 in their defence, arguing that it is the actions of the government that are illegal, in that they are

planning for genocide by agreeing to have cruise missiles in this country.

Article II of Genocide Convention
In the present Convention, genocide means any of the following acts committed with intent to destroy, in whole or in part, a national, ethnical, racial or religious group, as such:
(a) Killing members of the group;
(b) Causing serious bodily or mental harm to members of the group;
(c) Deliberately inflicting on the group conditions of life calculated to bring about its physical destruction in whole or in part;
(d) Imposing measures intended to prevent births within the group;
(e) Forcibly transferring children of the group to another group.

Women argue that they are justified in taking actions which may be seen as illegal, to counter the far greater illegality of nuclear weapons. The Genocide Act is an interesting piece of legislation – a virtually unenforceable law. While it complies with the international Genocide Convention, only the Attorney General can prosecute under it. As a member of the government, he is hardly likely to bring a case under this Act against other members of the government.

Being involved in a court case creates a lot of work, marshalling the various arguments and evidence, and preparing statements. Supportive and committed women lawyers have added immeasurably to women's confidence about all this. Women who have never before been involved with the law have found themselves dealing with the police and the courts: planning their defence, often defending themselves, making personal statements, questioning witnesses. This is possible because women are supporting each other and working together in a legal system designed to isolate people and induce feelings of guilt.

There is always a risk in hiring lawyers that everyone gets bogged down in obscure legal points. Lawyers are trained to win cases, by fair means or foul, rather than to assist their clients to say what they think is important. Women don't say what they want in that atmosphere, or it is lost in a conspiracy of professional courtroom workers.

However, the Greenham women's cases followed almost none of the patterns of the usual magistrates' court case. The first big court case was the trial on 15 November of the women who invaded the base at Greenham on 27 August. There were three lawyers (me, Liz and Izzie) involved in preparing the case

with women who had been arrested for breach of the peace. When we met the women, we were almost washed away by the huge flood of information, ideas and argument that they wanted to put over in court. Whatever the police wanted to talk about in court, it was plainly our job to put the focus of the hearing on to the issue of cruise missiles, disarmament and protest. None of the Greenham women seemed to have illusions about the courts – they don't offer justice – or about lawyers, who can't work miracles. What we were asked to do was create a framework which would enable women and their witnesses to testify as to their own knowledge and experience of the nuclear issue.

In the end, listening to the women from Greenham talking, it was plain that the emphasis of the case would have to be on the defence. So often a court case revolves around denying what the prosecution say. In a series of meetings we agreed that we were not really interested in what the prosecution would say. We would concentrate on putting forward the real reasons that led women to leave their jobs, homes, families and cross the physical and psychological barriers that keep people out of USAF bases in this country. To do this we designed a series of legal arguments about the right and duty of all of us to prevent our own government and the US government from breaking the terms of the Genocide Act 1969 (an Act of Parliament that hardly anyone had heard about before).

I had done cases with many other demonstrators before, but never anything quite like this. It wasn't that the Greenham women didn't care if they were convicted, because they did worry a lot. It was more that the issue of cruise missiles was so important that it overrode every other concern. It was something that so desperately had to be said and heard that nothing else seemed at all important. We found we were working on issues far wider than a lawyer would usually consider, instead of having to chop everything up into little bits to fit in with the court's preconceptions.

I think courtrooms are frightening places at the best of times. My experience of that is particularly as a woman working in the male-dominated legal profession. Women are treated badly by the courts – not openly, but in all the male assumptions about how business in court should be conducted. It is so easy and comfortable for men to assume and exercise power and superiority over women, and given that courts are all to do with

the legitimate exercise of power, women tend to come off very badly. There are elaborate codes of behaviour in court that women are not at home in. There are special ways of being polite (courtesy) and of being rude (sarcasm and bullying) that are almost uniquely male. No one smiles very much. For women to join in, it usually means joining on men's terms. I find it very alien, and I suspect that most women lawyers really feel that too.

The triumph was that Greenham women cut through all that. They gave all the wrong responses. They laughed, cheered and clapped. They didn't take half of it seriously. I know most of the women were scared before they spoke, but in the end some things had to be said, which overcame the fear. That applied to the lawyers too, because we were very scared before the first hearing. We didn't know whether the court would let us use the Genocide Act arguments or call the witnesses who were coming along. We had no idea if we'd be thrown out of court within an hour or so of starting.

What did happen, once we'd got started in November, February and at other trials since, has changed all my feelings about courts. We took control of that environment away from the men, however briefly. It didn't mean that arguments were just put in expressive, emotional, feeling ways, though that was unusual enough. It was also seeing women make the court listen to arguments that were articulate, intellectually coherent and historically wise. Women did it by poems, by singing, and some cried while they spoke. Even policewomen were moved to tears. Everywhere there were flowers. Courtrooms hardly frighten me at all now.

But then the whole focus of my fears in life has shifted. Why should courtrooms worry anyone while the threat of utter destruction hangs over us? I sat through the 15 February case in Newbury when women scientists backed up our own knowledge with the terrifying implications of their research. I couldn't believe, then, that the magistrates would not simply step down from their table and join us. I have moved from merely being 'against the bomb' but not believing it could be changed, to joining Greenham women in stopping it.
Jane Hickman, May 1983

In the second of these cases in November, women were also charged with behaviour likely to cause a breach of the peace by

obstructing construction workers attempting to lay sewer pipes outside the main gate of the base on 5 October by lying in the trenches, weaving woollen webs across them, and lying down in front of bulldozers. Several women presenting their own defence questioned construction workers, who finally admitted that the women's behaviour would not have led to any violence. Others asked, 'Who is really breaching the peace?' All these women, several of whom appeared in both cases, were found guilty and given the choice of being bound over to keep the peace for one year or going to prison for 14 days. As they refused to give assurances of 'good' behaviour, 23 of them were sent to prison. While they were split into smaller groups and sent to different prisons, they were not isolated as women had been in the summer.

This is not to say that those who have served prison sentences did not find it alienating and frightening. Many women have been badly treated in prison and in police cells and would think hard before putting themselves in that position again. All have gained strength as a result, however, and pass this on to others. What is intended as a humiliating and punishing system has become an experience from which women learn and gain power, both for themselves and for others. The many thousands of women who have not put themselves in this position see that there is the support to deal with the legal system without being rendered completely powerless in the process.

On New Year's Day 1983, 44 women were arrested and also charged with breach of the peace when they went over the fence at Greenham and climbed on to a missile silo still under construction. Thirty-six of these women refused to be bound over to keep the peace and were also sentenced to 14 days in prison in February. In this case it was decided to call women expert witnesses: Dr Rosalie Bertell from Canada who gave evidence about the far-reaching and long-term effects of low-level radiation; and Dr Alice Stewart, an epidemiologist, who has studied deaths from US atomic tests in the Pacific.

The action of closing the base on 13 December 1982 proved there are thousands of women willing to take this kind of direct action. As a result, the tactics of the police and courts have changed at least for the time being. Magistrates now seem to have decided to make any punishment as light as possible, if the charges cannot be dismissed entirely, in an attempt to damp down further publicity

Meeting women out of Holloway, March 1983

and support for the women. In some cases confused or contradictory police evidence has also made it impossible to uphold the
charges. Women went on to the base at Greenham many times
between New Year's Day and Easter 1983, though not on to the
silos. Most of them were not charged at all. Sometimes they were
taken to the police station and later released. On other occasions
they were merely removed from the base. The group who lay down
in Downing Street in February while the US Vice-President,
George Bush, dined with Margaret Thatcher, received conditional
discharges after having been charged with obstructing the highway.

There is an important element of discretion for the police and
the courts concerning what people are charged with and what
punishments they get. While there may be legal precedents as
guidelines, this area of discretion makes it possible for the authori-

ties to vary their responses to the women's actions according to what seems to be in their best overall interests – even if this sometimes means not charging women who flagrantly break the law. Although we are not suggesting that the police and courts simply act on government 'instructions', this suggests co-ordination between them.

It is interesting that the law and the established media, both neutralising the women's action in their different ways, sometimes work together and sometimes against each other. Journalists are invariably angry when they are not allowed into court. Their interest in some of the actions and their reporting of arrests and imprisonment has done a lot to fuel the whole campaign, which in turn has resulted in this apparently more lenient approach by the police and the courts, as they try to minimise opportunities for further publicity. At the same time the media also support the workings of the law – for example, by not reporting the women's most challenging court statements, or, in their reports of the first two evictions, by omitting to mention that the women stayed on.

Reliance on petty by-laws concerning property and land ownership is one way in which the authorities refuse to acknowledge the political nature of the women's peace camp. By contrast, the women have used the courts and legal proceedings to their advantage, refusing to be sucked in to what they think of as irrelevant discussions.

Something that rarely reaches the newspapers is the atmosphere of these court cases. We hear much about 'tears' and 'emotional scenes' but little about the manner in which women choose to conduct their defence. At the injunction and possession order hearings in March 1983, for example, hundreds of women gathered outside the court. The court room was full of defendants, so many they had difficulty fitting in. The women refused to be intimidated by legal niceties, thus making the rigid, authoritarian principles which guide court procedure simply ridiculous. Each woman has the opportunity of justifying her actions to the court and uses this to make a personal statement. These statements are an integral part of the proceedings. Woman after woman gets up to explain what her action means for her, recounting dreams, putting direct questions to the magistrates, telling personal histories and discussing personal priorities. These statements allow individual women to put their case on their own terms to the court and potentially the public.

When we lay down in the sewer pipe trenches, we took an action to make the men fully aware of what they are doing. The men found it difficult to look at us because they understood what we were trying to achieve. They don't want a nuclear war to happen, but because they have no alternative, we are forcing them to work at the base . . . We can be sent to prison, treated like criminals, because we do not want to see our families or any other individual on this planet obliterated by nuclear devastation.
Helen John, 17 November 1982

Time is running out. People have to realise and face the drastic situation . . . British people and people all over the world have been protesting legally for 40 years and it hasn't worked. Britain's economy is falling to pieces because of nuclear weapons. We still have more per square mile than any other European country. Cruise missiles are the limit – the last straw. They are illegal. They contravene international law.
Charlotte Kiss, 17 November 1982

In February, three women were arrested for blockading an entrance to the base at Greenham. They were charged with obstruction and faced a small fine. In order to make their statements public, however, and to take part in public discussions about nuclear weapons, they decided not to appear in court to be judged by the magistrates, but to hold a public meeting instead. They publicised their reasons in a letter to The *Guardian* (11 March 1983):

Sir – The *Guardian* reported (4 March) the trial of women at Newbury Magistrates' Court charged with wilful obstruction at Greenham Common.

We did not appear in court – we preferred to present our case to an open meeting that day at the Mound in Edinburgh – for the following reasons:

On 15 February, 44 women appeared at Newbury, charged with breach of the peace. They had been arrested for singing and

dancing on the silos being built to house cruise missiles at Greenham Common.

They were found guilty, and 39 of the women have since served 14 days in Holloway for refusing to be bound over. At their trial the women presented a mass of evidence justifying their actions by proving that the introduction of cruise missiles is a criminal step towards genocide.

We believe that if their case had been decided by public opinion, their action would not have been condemned as a crime, but supported as a valid and urgent protest against the crimes being carried out in our names, but without our consent, at Greenham Common, military bases, and nuclear research centres throughout the world.

The courts, in trying and condemning people arrested for protesting against nuclear weapons, are trying and condemning the validity of direct action, that is, our right to be involved in the decisions which affect our lives when we are denied representation; and the validity of our arguments, that is, whether nuclear weapons are necessary or acceptable in our society.

We believe these issues are beyond the jurisdiction of the courts.

At the trial of the 44 women, three magistrates assumed the responsibility of public judgement, but passed verdicts unrepresentative of public opinion. Evidence presented to the court could not be reported to the public outside.

We were arrested, with the 14 other women who appeared in court, for blockading traffic entering the base at Greenham Common during action in support of the 44 women on trial. We were charged with 'wilfully obstructing the highway without lawful authority or excuse'.

In law, the desire to prevent the negligent destruction of our world as we know it is insufficient excuse for obstructing traffic. In law, we have no alternative but to plead guilty to the offence as charged. In law, our case is decided even before our trial and, unlike the 44 women, we would be given no opportunity to offer evidence in our defence, only in our mitigation, thus admitting our guilt.

We do not accept that we are guilty of any crime, nor do we accept that a magistrates' court is the appropriate place to judge our actions.

The Edinburgh meeting – having heard our statements and

evidence from others against nuclear weapons – found us not guilty of any crime.
Yours sincerely,
Shara Hanna, Louise Robertson, Jenny England,
Faslane Peace Camp, Argyll

These women were arrested again a few days after this, however, and taken to Newbury Magistrates' Court. They were given a small fine for the obstruction but sentenced to 14 days imprisonment for failing to appear in court when summonsed. The usual punishment for failing to appear is a £5 to £10 fine. This is a telling example of the importance of the court's discretion. By contrast, charges were quietly dropped against two of the 44 women involved in the silo action who did not turn up in court – the only difference being that they did not publicise the fact.

Despite the vast body of law at their disposal and their access to the media, the authorities have so far completely failed to intimidate the women or to silence them. It is difficult to speculate on how they will respond as the campaign continues to grow.

What are you doing to keep the peace? The power you are using is supporting nuclear weapons. It supports binding women's voices, binding our minds and bodies in prison so our voices cannot be heard. So our warning of Death is being repressed. But we cannot be silenced. And I cannot be bound over. I am asking you to keep the peace. We are not on trial. You are.
Katrina Howse, 17 November 1982, addressing Newbury magistrates.

125

Ending

The symbol most closely connected with the women's peace movement is the weaving of webs. Each link in a web is fragile, but woven together creates a strong and coherent whole. A web with few links is weak and can be broken, but the more threads it is composed of, the greater its strength. It makes a very good analogy for the way in which women have rejuvenated the peace movement. By connections made through many diverse channels, a widespread network has grown up of women committed to working for peace. Greenham Common women's peace camp has been one thread in the formation of this network, showing the clear-sightedness and determination that so many women feel over the issue of nuclear weapons.

Women at the 1981 Women's Pentagon Action wove webs around the doors of the Pentagon, symbolically closing them, and this activity has since been used elsewhere. It has been taken up by women partly because it sets up such clear opposition. Police, for example, are trained to deal with force and aggression, not to extricate themselves from woollen webs. Thus, the confrontation that develops is very direct yet nonviolent and on women's terms. Images of gates shut with wool rather than iron bolts, and women being lifted out of webs are also graphic illustrations of polarised

philosophies: those planning nuclear destruction, and those determined to preserve life.

To oppose nuclear weapons requires a fundamental change in our attitude to life. Clarity of purpose and utter opposition is the only chance to reverse the threat that hangs over all our lives.

What we want to change is immense. It's not just getting rid of nuclear weapons, it's getting rid of the whole structure that created the possibility of nuclear weapons in the first place. If we don't use imagination nothing will change. Without change we will destroy the planet. It's as simple as that.
Lesley Boulton, June 1982

The way things are organised is neither natural nor inevitable, but created by people. People have a wealth of skill, intelligence, creativity and wisdom. We could be devising ways of using and distributing the earth's vast resouces so that no one starves or lives in abject poverty, making socially useful things that people need – a society which is life-affirming in all its aspects.

For more information:

Books

Joel Kovel, *Against the State of Nuclear Terror*, Pan 1983.
Paul Rogers, Malcolm Dando and Peter Van Den Nungen, *As Lambs to the Slaughter: The Facts about Nuclear War*, Arrow 1981.
Gwyn Prins (ed.), *Defended to Death*, Penguin 1983.
Jonathan Schell, *The Fate of the Earth*, Picador 1982.
Nicholas Humphrey, *Four Minutes to Midnight: The Bronowski Memorial Lecture*, BBC Publications 1981.
The Greenham Factor, Greenham Print Prop 1983.
Susan Koen and Nina Swaim, *A Handbook for Women on the Nuclear Mentality*, Women's Action for Nuclear Disarmament 1980.
John Hersey, *Hiroshima*, Penguin 1946.
Lynne Jones (ed.), *Keeping the Peace*, The Women's Press 1983.
J. Humphrey, Dr M. Hartog, Dr H. Middleton, *The Medical Consequences of Nuclear Weapons*, Medical Campaign against Nuclear Weapons 1981.
Dr Helen Caldicott, *Nuclear Madness*, Bantam 1980.
Feminists against nuclear power, *Nuclear Resisters*, Publications Distribution Co-operative 1981.
Peace News, fortnightly magazine, 8 Elm Avenue, Nottingham 3.
Piecing It Together, Feminism and nonviolence study group 1983.
Pam McAllister (ed.), *Reweaving the Web of Life: Feminism and Nonviolence*, New Society Publishers 1982.
Raymond Briggs, *When the Wind Blows*, Hamish Hamilton 1982.

Films and videos

Critical Mass, 40 mins, videotape of talks by Dr Helen Caldicott; and *If you love this planet*, 25 mins, 16 mm film of Dr Helen Caldicott, both distributed by Concord Films Council, 201 Felixstowe Road, Ipswich, Suffolk IP3 6BJ. Concord Films Council has over 200 films about militarism, noviolence, nuclear weapons, the arms race, etc. available for hire.
America: from Hitler to MX, 90 mins, 16 mm film and video about the arms industries in the US. The Other Cinema, 79 Wardour Street, London W1.
Commonsense: Actions 1982, 40 mins, Super 8 film and video of women's nonviolent direct action, London Greenham office, see below.

Addresses

Women's Peace Alliance, Box 240, Peace News, 8 Elm Avenue, Nottingham 3.
Women's Peace Camp, USAF/RAF Greenham Common, Newbury, Berkshire.
Women for Life on Earth, 2 St Edmunds Cottages, Bove Town, Glastonbury, Somerset.
Women Oppose Nuclear Threat, Box 600, Peace News, 8 Elm Avenue, Nottingham 3.
London Greenham Office, 5 Leonard Street, London EC2.
Campaign for Nuclear Disarmament, 11 Goodwin Street, London N4.

First published in 1983 by Pluto Press Limited,
The Works, 105A Torriano Avenue, London NW5 2RX
and simultaneously in the USA by South End Press,
302 Columbus Avenue, Boston, Massachusetts 02116

Second impression 1984

Typeset by Wayside Graphics, Clevedon, Avon
Printed in Great Britain by Photobooks (Bristol) Limited
Bound by W.H. Ware & Sons, Tweed Road,
Clevedon, Avon

Cover illustration by Saša Marinkov
Designed by Kate Hepburn

ISBN 0-89608-199-0

Greenham
Women
Everywhere

Dreams, Ideas and Actions from the Women's Peace Movement

Alice Cook & Gwyn Kirk

South End Press

Foreword

THE NATIONAL CONFERENCE ON SOCIAL WELFARE in Cleveland, from its opening session to the closing luncheon, embraced the theme "Caring Communities: Responsible Actions for the Eighties." "Caring" became more than the commitment to extend help to persons in need but also became a commitment to create "caring communities" where we live or in the organizations in which we work. The Cleveland Sponsoring Committee demonstrated this theme in the opening reception at the Arcade and through the many amenities and educational tours arranged for meetings during the week.

Patricia Roberts Harris, Secretary of the U.S. Department of Health and Human Services, the keynote speaker, portrayed the present record of the current administration and made projections for the next decade. In the following general session Marian Wright Edelman of the Children's Defense Fund presented a vigorous challenge that the rollback of programs and services for children must be reversed by becoming involved in the struggle to save vital programs.

Gar Alperovitz helped the Conference gain a perspective on the economic issues of inflation, energy costs, and the effort to balance the federal budget. He suggested that new economic perspectives can address the fiscal problems while placing priority on human needs. These and many other stimulating presentations made this Forum outstanding. The new format of fewer workshops and symposiums was received positively by speakers and participants alike.

Appreciation is extended to the Editorial Committee members for their work that involved extensive reading, commenting, rereading, and commitment to decide cooperatively on the contents of this volume. Special thanks go to members who provided extensive editing of major papers which the committee included but felt needed revisions, primarily in length. The Editorial Committee was pleased to be able to serve the interests of the many members of NCSW, particularly those who were able to attend and contribute to this Annual Forum.

The members of the Editorial Committee were: Bernice Catherine Harper (Chairperson-elect), Medical Advisor, U.S. Department of Health and Human Services; Carl Schoenberg, Editor, *Child Welfare;* Charlotte Nusberg, Editor/Program Specialist, National Association of Retired Teachers/American Association of Retired Persons; William Ray, Program Analyst, U.S. Department of Health and Human Services; Jane Collins (Program Committee representative), Denver Department of Health and Hospitals; Ronald A. Feldman, Professor, George Warren Brown School of Social Work, Washington University, St. Louis. We are indebted to the able staff assistance of Maureen Herman, NCSW, and the editorial guidance of Kathleen McCarthy of Columbia University Press.

We hope you will enjoy reading this volume and that it properly reflects the theme of "Caring Communities: Responsible Action for the Eighties." May the ideas and challenges aid us all as we approach this new decade of work and commitment to the social welfare needs of our nation.

H. FREDERICK BROWN
Chairman, Editorial Committee

National Conference on Social Welfare Distinguished Service Awards

THE NATIONAL CONFERENCE on Social Welfare Distinguished Service Awards for 1980 were awarded to the following:

MR. JUSTICE WILLIAM O. DOUGLAS who, in his long and distinguished career as an Associate Justice of the Supreme Court of the United States, contributed significantly toward ensuring the protection and well-being of all citizens; and who, as a student, teacher, author, and traveler demonstrated and communicated his love and appreciation for the richness and diversity found in the world and its people.

DOUGLAS A. FRASER who, in addition to his successful career as a leader in the union movement, has been a vigorous and consistent advocate and spokesman for seeking ways to meet the social and economic needs of the poor and neglected; and, who, as President of UAW, is providing unique and admirable national leadership in focusing attention on the need for realistic policies and programs required to advance the health and welfare of our society.

ACCEPTANCES

REMARKS BY SENATOR HOWARD M. METZENBAUM (OHIO)

I feel very privileged to be here this evening to accept, at the request of Cathy Douglas, this Distinguished Service Award on behalf of Bill Douglas. Bill Douglas was more than a jurist. He was concerned about the quality of life of all people, whether they were Native Americans, black Americans, or Hispanic Americans. I know if he were in my place he would not let the opportunity go by to say at least a word about the pressing problems facing all of us.

I have just come back from a week in the Senate and have seen what is happening to all Americans. I saw the Senate Budget Committee deliberate on the issues facing the people that you serve and the people about whom we are all concerned. I saw that this nation has moved a long distance away from its objectives of yesteryear. I saw that the President came to Congress with a budget that provided for practically no increases for human services needs and about $8 billion in increases for defense spending. Then I saw a senator propose an additional $7 billion on top of that for defense spending. I realized what was happening: the programs for youth unemployment, nutrition, child health, employment opportunities for adults, CETA, and food stamps were being cut across the board by one percent. Let the poor fend for themselves. Let the elderly figure out their own problems. Let the children of America and the pregnant mothers who cannot get adequate care worry about it. Why should we? This is the attitude the Senate has taken.

As I sat here listening to Secretary Harris, I thought how appropriate it is that this evening I stand here on behalf of Justice Douglas, because he was concerned not only about our national security, but our domestic security as well. And it is the domestic security which has been so impoverished in the actions of the Senate.

I am here tonight because Justice Douglas was one of the very few people in whom I truly believed and trusted. He was far more than a great legal scholar and jurist. He truly felt for the poor of this country. He truly had compassion for the elderly and minorities of all kinds. He understood the need and right of all people for legal services on an equal basis. Few people are aware of this. I think Justice Douglas will be remembered by posterity in so many ways that I could not possibly name all of them for you, but I think he said one thing, "Man is strong only when man is free." Bill Douglas loved liberty. Bill Douglas loved America, and felt for and loved the people—the smallest to the largest. I cannot think of anybody that you could have selected more appropriately for this group, this National Conference on Social Welfare. I wish he were here, but since he cannot be I consider it an honor and privilege to accept this award on his behalf.

REMARKS BY MELVIN A. GLASSER

Douglas Fraser was pleased and proud to be notified that he was to receive the National Conference Distinguished Service Award. He asked me to convey to you his appreciation and his sincere regret that a long-standing commitment to make an address in another city prevents him from being with us tonight. But I must express my personal satisfaction at the deserved recognition the National Conference on Social Welfare is giving Doug Fraser and the pleasure I have to receive it in his behalf.

A year ago President Fraser addressed this Forum. His remarks then were directed toward maintaining the priority of human worth in the midst of pressures from a disastrously inflationary economy.

The situation has worsened. Perhaps not since the 1930s has the American dream of a secure and dignified life for all individuals been so threatened. We now suffer the twin threats of inflation and unemployment. Whether one characterizes this as a recession or a depression, we are in trouble, and I suggest to you that at a time of belt-tightening and sacrifice, disproportionate demands are being made of the aged, the poor, the ethnic minorities, the low-income workers, and other disadvantaged groups in this society. Proposed solutions to social problems are more and more expressed in terms of money and sacrifice—money from

MELVIN A. GLASSER is Director, Social Security Department, International Union, United Auto Workers.

those in need and sacrifice by those with little or nothing left to give.

President Fraser's emphasis on maintaining the sanctity of human values during times of rapid and complex social change must be underscored. In the absence of such a commitment, the prevalent view of "economic reality," wittingly or otherwise, will result in new deprivations for individuals and groups with the greatest needs.

Few would question that it will take sacrifice to bring America's economy back on course. The point, however, is that sacrifice must be apportioned on the basis of the ability to contribute, not on the basis of the vulnerability and the political powerlessness of large numbers of Americans.

NATIONAL CONFERENCE ON SOCIAL WELFARE DISTINGUISHED SERVICE AWARDS, 1955–1980

1955 EDITH M. BAKER, Washington, D.C.
FEDELE F. FAURI, Ann Arbor, Mich.
ELIZABETH WICKENDEN, New York

1956 TIAC (Temporary Inter-Association Council) PLANNING COMMITTEE, New York

1957 THE REVEREND MARTIN LUTHER KING, JR., Montgomery, Ala.
WILBUR J. COHEN, Ann Arbor, Mich.

1958 THE HONORABLE JOHN E. FOGARTY, R.I.
LEONARD W. MAYO, New York

1959 ELISABETH SHIRLEY ENOCHS, Washington, D.C.
OLLIE A. RANDALL, New York

1960 LOULA DUNN, Chicago
RALPH BLANCHARD, New York
HELEN HALL, New York

1961 THE HONORABLE AIME J. FORAND, R.I.

1962 JOSEPH P. ANDERSON, New York
THE ATLANTA *Constitution*, Ralph McGill and Jack Nelson, Atlanta, Ga.
CHARLOTTE TOWLE, Chicago

1963 HARRIET M. BARTLETT, Cambridge, Mass.
ERNEST JOHN BOHN, Cleveland
FLORENCE G. HELLER, Glencoe, Ill.
Special Award: Television Documentary, "The Battle of Newburgh," IRVING GITLIN and the NATIONAL BROADCASTING COMPANY, New York

Special Citation (Posthumous): ANNA ELEANOR ROOSEVELT, "First Lady of the World"

1964 DR. ROBERT M. FELIX, Bethesda, Md.
Special Citation (Posthumous): JOHN FITZGERALD KENNEDY, "Man of Destiny"

1965 JAMES V. BENNETT, Washington, D.C.
SIDNEY HOLLANDER, Baltimore
CORA KASIUS, New York

1966 REPRESENTATIVE WILBUR D. MILLS, Ark.

1967 THE HONORABLE HUBERT H. HUMPHREY, Washington, D.C.
PLANNED PARENTHOOD—WORLD POPULATION
Special Awards (Posthumous):
HOWARD F. GUSTAFSON, Indianapolis
RUTH M. WILLIAMS, New York

1968 LOMA MOYER ALLEN, Rochester, N.Y.
KENNETH BANCROFT CLARK, New York

1969 THE HONORABLE ELMER L. ANDERSEN, St. Paul, Minn.
HARRY L. LURIE, New York
IDA C. MERRIAM, Washington, D.C.

1970 No award

1971 SAM S. GRAIS, St. Paul, Minn.
DOROTHY I. HEIGHT, New York

1972 WHITNEY M. YOUNG, JR. *(Posthumous)*

1973 WINSLOW CARLTON, New York
THE HONORABLE JAMES CHARLES EVERS, Fayette, Miss.
JOE R. HOFFER, Columbus, Ohio
NATIONAL COUNCIL OF JEWISH WOMEN, New York

1974 ASSOCIATION OF AMERICAN INDIAN SOCIAL WORKERS

1975 MITCHELL I. GINSBERG, New York

1976 BERTRAM S. BROWN, M.D., Rockville, Md.
THE HONORABLE BARBARA JORDAN, Washington, D.C.
THE HONORABLE WALTER F. MONDALE, Washington, D.C.
WILLIAM A. MORRILL, Washington, D.C.

1977 ROY WILKINS, New York

1978 COY EKLUND, New York
VERNON E. JORDAN, JR., New York
CYNTHIA C. WEDEL, Washington, D.C.

1979 JAMES R. DUMPSON, New York
GISELA KONOPKA, Minneapolis
NORMAN V. LOURIE, Harrisburg, Pa.
GEORGE M. NISHINAKA, Los Angeles

1980 *Special Citation (Posthumous)*: JUSTICE WILLIAM O. DOUGLAS
DOUGLAS A. FRASER

Greetings to the Conference from President Jimmy Carter

I AM pleased to greet the delegates at the Annual Forum of the National Conference on Social Welfare.

During the course of your sessions, Secretary Harris and others will explain the special steps my administration has taken to provide more effective social services for the aged and the poor, the neglected and the handicapped. Current economic problems may alter our strategy, but our goals and commitment remain stronger than ever. The difficult times we live in call upon us to make the best use of all of our resources in focusing national concern on our fellow citizens in need.

You have my sincere encouragement and best wishes as you explore the critical social welfare issues of today. No challenge could be greater than that of offering all Americans a healthy and productive life, free from poverty and dependency: a life of hope and opportunity. Your resourcefulness and dedication are vitally needed in helping our nation meet this challenge, and I trust that these meetings will do much to advance the goals we share.

Contents

xvi   *Contents*

Caring Communities for the Eighties

PATRICIA ROBERTS HARRIS

PRESIDENT CARTER'S personal commitment to the mission of the new Department of Health and Human Services was confirmed when he spoke at ceremonies inaugurating the department that came into being on May 4, 1980. That day marked the end of a chapter entitled "Health, Education, and Welfare" and immediately began another with a new name, a new seal, and a new flag. However, the significance of the change lies not in the name or the transfer of people and programs, but in our department's rededication to a special mission of service to our country's most vulnerable citizens.

The creation of the Department of Health and Human Services gives us an opportunity to define its mission and to clarify our goals. We are now able to devote all our time and energy to developing programs targeted directly to health and human service needs. In doing so, we will administer a budget in excess of $225 billion.

In a century of service, NCSW has sought to respond to individual Americans in need. It has consistently led the nation to accept fundamental responsibilities for aid to those who cannot meet their needs without help. It has served through the terms of eighteen American presidents, two world wars, countless recessions, and the great depression. It has seen America change dramatically since 1873, but through all those years it has kept its eyes on the goal: the

PATRICIA ROBERTS HARRIS is Secretary of Health and Human Services, Washington, D.C.

establishment of a society which places social and economic justice at the top of the national agenda.

With that history, it comes as no surprise that the 1980 Annual Forum theme proposes new strategies for the 1980s. The Conference is preoccupied with talk of "limited resources," because its members know that our country's resources are still considerable and because they want to use those resources to maximum advantage to serve those with the greatest need. In choosing the theme "Caring Communities: Responsible Action for the Eighties," for the Annual Forum, NCSW has looked in a direction that could very well set a national priority in the next decade.

No one can doubt the need for a broad, national commitment of resources to solve the problems which beset the sick, the aged, the infirm, and the young in this country. What we must all recognize, however, is that permanent solutions to problems such as poverty, inadequate health care, domestic violence, and long-term needs of older Americans and the handicapped will come only when substantial numbers of people in communities all across the country are personally involved, committed to, and supportive of, the solutions to these problems. Caring communities are the key to the progress we will make in the 1980s, just as they have traditionally helped the nation move forward throughout its history.

In the earliest colonial times, our ancestors established communities which accepted responsibility for the welfare of those too young or too aged or too infirm to care for themselves. More than a century and a half ago, the young French nobleman de Tocqueville toured the fledgling republic and noted the spontaneous generosity with which Americans hastened to aid their neighbors in distress.

That tradition even characterized communities in transition. As settlers moved West, they drew up contracts to govern their wagon trains. In each one of those social contracts the group pledged to help individuals and families who encountered problems along the way.

Americans from the start have been motivated by a sense of community which implicitly recognizes that the group will survive and prosper only when each member is involved and contributing. In a vast new nation where human resources were scarce, we instinctively understood the meaning of social interdependence, that we could not afford to squander the productive potential of any individual.

A more diverse and complex nation gradually institutionalized the private and government response to those in greatest need, and organizations like the NCSW helped chart that course. The people of this nation built permanent institutions to respond to the needs of our most vulnerable citizens: the sick, the orphaned children, the destitute aged. In the 1930s, when the depression, in President Roosevelt's words, left "a third of the nation ill-housed, ill-clad, and ill-nourished," this country began to marshal its resources by instituting federal programs designed to restore the economic health of the nation.

In the years since Franklin Roosevelt's time we have broadened the federal commitment. The new Department of Health and Human Services today administers a variety of programs which have helped to transform the nation. Programs such as Social Security, Medicare, Medicaid, Aid to Families with Dependent Children, Supplemental Security Income, and Head Start have dramatically reduced poverty and its consequences in our country. The work of the Public Health Service, the National Institutes of Health, the Center for Disease Control, and other health and human services agencies has contributed to better health for all Americans through research and improved delivery of care. These accomplishments have complemented the ongoing efforts of those in the private and voluntary sectors, working in communities across the country. In the 1980s we must strengthen that partnership.

I am concerned that we in the federal government do all we can to strengthen new and traditional support groups in our neighborhoods and communities.

While I was Secretary of the Department of Housing and Urban Development, that department worked to develop greater emphasis on community development. We recognized the need for a new direction in federal policy, and we established new goals and strategies—targeting resources on neighborhoods, envisioning communities better prepared to chart their own course.

We developed a comprehensive, national, urban policy which involved components from the arts to mass transit, from employment to business tax credits, and underlying all our programs was a concern for stronger communities. Our efforts resulted in new programs such as the urban development action program, and reorientation and revitalization of programs such as community development block grants, insured and assisted housing, and neighborhood self-help grants. We emphasized those programs because we believe that local communities are in the best position to identify local priorities. Active grass-roots participation in the development and implementation of federally supported programs leads to a more lasting commitment to the goals of those programs.

I intend to establish a similar spirit of partnership at the Department of Health and Human Services because our programs will continue to be supported only if they are accepted as part of the process of meeting real needs at the state and local level.

The problems we face—poverty, ill health, discrimination, and their consequences—pose difficult challenges. But we have made remarkable progress, and we are encouraged by what already has been accomplished. A smaller percentage of our people is poor today than ever before. The health of the American people has never been better. Opportunities for women and minorities have vastly increased in the last two decades. But we have not yet completed our task. There are still Americans in desperate need for whom the great depression is not a faded memory, but a continuing reality.

The statistics tell part of the story. America's poor number 25 million—one child in six and one elderly person in seven. Literally tens of millions of the poor and others in our prosperous country lack either access to health care or the financial resources to pay for such care. Despite our progress, discrimination on the basis of race, age, and sex is still prevalent.

The statistics tell only part of the story. They cannot describe adequately the meaning of such deprivation to an individual or a family. It means living without a job. It means undernourishment. It means inadequate housing. It means recurring, debilitating illness. It means little or no opportunity for higher education or for job advancement. In short, it means a dying dream and a decay of the spirit which affects first individuals and then the community.

If we are to become a nation of caring communities, conditions of poverty and other deprivations are not acceptable. Therefore, the challenges to responsible action in the 1980s are many.

We must guarantee to every child the right to normal development, to good nutrition, and to adequate medical attention.

We must guarantee to every family the right to economic security, to freedom from fear of the cost of health care.

We must guarantee to those who are handicapped an opportunity to lead productive lives, lives free from despair.

We must guarantee to every older citizen the right to a secure future, to adequate health care and expanded opportunities.

And we must build for all our people—men and women of every race, age, and background—a society which values character and treats all people fairly.

Achieving these goals will require a continuing commitment on the part of the federal government, a commitment to steady and secure funding for our most essential human services programs. President Carter has demonstrated that this administration can be trusted to preserve these programs.

Reaching our goals will also require new programs, ini-

tiatives designed to reduce poverty and improve health care.
This administration has offered new programs to move us
forward—welfare reform, the child health assurance program, and the national health plan. Those proposals have
not been abandoned, and with the help of the social welfare
profession they can be enacted by the Congress and signed
into law.

Finally, to reach those goals we will need to build a new
coalition in this country, an assertive majority which holds
the nation accountable for maintaining the traditions of a
supportive community life. People in all walks of life must
become involved in their neighborhoods, their communities, and the political arena—involved and active in seeking
to help the most vulnerable of our people achieve what they
really want: a fair chance for a productive life free of poverty, ill health, and dependency.

Dostoevski once observed that neither individuals nor nations can exist without a sublime idea. This nation was
founded on just such an idea, that we could build a new
society which is free, humane, and just. We must work together to seek that goal for our nation. We must work together to build not only caring communities, but also a caring nation.

In the 1980s the Department of Health and Human Services will work to meet that challenge with all the talent and
energy and resources we can muster. Our mission is not a
destination but a journey, and we will travel the road together with social workers and all committed people in a
spirit of partnership in service to this country.

Who's for Children?

MARIAN WRIGHT EDELMAN

CHILDREN ARE the easiest people in America to
ignore. They do not vote, lobby, or make campaign contributions. Changing demography is producing more childless
couples, fewer children, later childbearing, and an increasingly aging population. Inflation, unemployment, and uncertainty about the future have fueled fear and selfish instincts. Calls for preventive services like child care to
strengthen families for parents who work, are single, teen-
aged, or simply cannot cope, are immediately attacked by
purportedly profamily forces. Fragmented programs and
program constituencies respond to children's needs in
pieces rather than as a whole. Competition for scarce resources has been exacerbated by an administration and
Congress whose "bone politics" have pitted human services
proponents against each other rather than against the political untouchables which are the real budget breakers. "Families and children overboard, pork barrels and soldiers in
the lifeboats" could be the slogan for the current budget-
balancing exercise that everyone agrees will affect inflation
by less than one percent over three years. The $3 billion oil
depletion allowance and a nearly $2 billion tax write-off for
intangible oil drilling and development expenses are untouched while a maximum $266 million authorization to
keep children from being unnecessarily removed from their
homes and to help them gain a new family through adoption is attacked on the grounds it is an "uncontrollable" en-

MARIAN WRIGHT EDELMAN is President, Children's Defense Fund, Washington, D.C.
Reprinted by permission of Children's Defense Fund.

titlement and will be too costly. Those of us who advocate
for homeless children now have to battle the appropriations
process annually if we are to get these half million vulnerable children out of long-term and expensive institutions,
group and foster care, and give them the permanent families we all profess to agree they should have—even those
who voted against the appropriation. Confusion about national priorities continues as the defense budget remains
virtually sacrosanct while children, the future bearers and
defenders of our national values, institutions as well as
arms, are squeezed and neglected. Child nutrition and preventive child health services are deemed too expensive but
not the development of the MX missile which costs so much
more.

It is not just the absence of a strong constituency that
makes it costly to vote or act against children that causes
their needs to go unmet. It is also the hypocrisy of public
and private sector leaders who mouth profamily and pro-
children values while ignoring or working against children
and families unless it suits their personal political needs to
do otherwise. Still rejected is the notion of shared responsibility for the nation's future. Amidst protestations of "who
can be against children?" too few people are *for* children
when it really matters. As a result, under the guise of
budget balancing and controlling federal spending, protecting families against government intrusion, right-to-life rhetoric (which often seems to wane once children are born),
administrative convenience, and countless other seemingly
worthy reasons, millions of children are denied families,
health care, and education. Not only are children hurt, but
taxpayers are victimized by burdensome remedial measures
which are the fruits of our continuing failure to invest in
our children when it really matters most: before they get
sick, drop out of school, or get into trouble.

Let me share a few facts about the needs of children today:

Over 17 percent of our children—10 million—are poor,
making them the poorest of any group in America, includ-

ing the elderly. The younger children are, the more likely they are to be poor. In 1979 one in every six preschoolers lived in a family at or below the poverty line. The consequences to children of poverty are great. Poor children's chances of dying in their first year of life are two-thirds greater than those of children living above the poverty level. Poor children are four times more likely to be in fair to poor health than middle-class children, but only half as likely to have seen a doctor in the past year.

One million American children are not enrolled in school. Some 13 percent of all seventeen-year-olds are functionally illiterate.

America's children die at birth in greater numbers than children in fourteen other countries. One in sixty-five American infants dies each year. One in forty-three nonwhite infants dies each year.

Millions of American children are growing up in poor health. One in seven—or 10 million—children gets virtually no health care whatsoever. They never have the regular checkups that parents naturally want for their children.

One in three American children, or almost 18 million, have never been to a dentist.

Seven out of ten mothers under fifteen years of age receive no prenatal care in the first three months of pregnancy; over one fifth receive no prenatal care at all, or not until the end of the pregnancy. Almost 10 percent of all black mothers receive no prenatal care at all or none until the final trimester.

Only about one sixth of our poorest children—those eligible for Medicaid—get the services of the Early and Periodic Screening, Diagnosis and Treatment (EPSDT) program to which they are entitled. When they do get screened, 40 percent of their detected problems go untreated. That is why we are trying to pass a child health assurance program in 1980.

The majority of American parents do not have health insurance coverage to pay for crucial services.

Seventy-five percent of our children are covered through

private insurance for hospitalization, but less than 30 percent are covered for out-of-hospital visits to physicians.

Only 14 percent of group insurance plans cover children's eyeglasses; 9 percent, preventive care (checkups, for example); and 32 percent, children's dental care.

More than half of private insurance plans exclude prenatal care; 45 percent, postnatal care; and 90 percent, family planning. Under the Medicaid program, nineteen states do not cover maternity care during a woman's first pregnancy.

Over half a million children in this country live in out-of-home care, and many will grow up there. Over 100,000 of these children have been in care six years or longer. Tens of thousands are placed inappropriately without attention to their individual special needs. They are forgotten about. No plans are made to provide permanence for them.

Adolescent women accounted for 17.2 percent of all U.S. births, or one in six, in 1977. That accounts for 570,000 children born to single teen-agers.

In 1980:

There will be an estimated 23.3 million preschool children in the United States, an increase of 36 percent. An estimated 10.5 million of these children will have mothers in the labor force—a 63 percent increase.

An estimated one million more day care homes will be needed by 1990, and an additional 1.6 million child care workers will be needed, a two-thirds increase.

Although over-all fertility among adolescents is decreasing, trends show an increase in the number of out-of-wedlock births among this group.

We know that these statistics mean there will be more children born at risk in the 1980s. There will be more families who will be undergoing economic, psychological, and emotional stress in the 1980s. There will be more families undergoing crises and coming apart at the seams in the 1980s. Therefore, there will be more children in the 1980s who will need the support of their relatives, their churches,

their community, and state and federal governments to protect them so that they can grow up strong and healthy.

But ironically the 1980s will also be a decade of considerable economic and political pressure not to provide the
supports—both in terms of income and of social services—
that these children and families need. The financial and political pressures I referred to will militate for doing less to
meet the needs of children. These pressures are com-
pounded by a series of myths which contribute to a public
atmosphere which makes progress of children's issues difficult. Help is needed from the social work profession to
combat these myths:

Myth 1: Only other people's children have problems. Many people think school violence, drug and alcohol abuse, and teen-
age pregnancy are problems only of the inner cities, of the
poor, of blacks, and of the non-English-speaking. But they
are also the problems of the suburbs, of the middle class,
and of the white majority. Similarly, handicapping conditions do not strike one race or social class to the exclusion
of others, though minority and poor children suffer disproportionately.

Moreover, all our children will be touched by these problems in the years to come. It is all our children who will
have to foot the Social Security bill for a larger aging population. That will be hard enough without the burden of a
large number of dependent, unproductive peers. It is in
everyone's self-interest, therefore, not to ignore the needs
of other people's children.

*Myth 2: Families are self-sufficient; they should take care of their
own children.* Many of us picture the typical American family
as two parents—a working father and a mother who stays at
home—and two normal children. This nuclear family, we
believe, should be able to care for all its children's needs.
But in this day and age, no family is totally self-sufficient.
All need help from time to time raising their children,
whether it involves the services of doctors, teachers, house-
keepers, or baby-sitters, or temporary aid such as unem-

ployment compensation or student loans. Only one out of every seventeen families today is the "typical American family." The other sixteen, or 94 percent of all American families, may need some form of day care (while one or both parents are working), special help for handicapped children, job training, or temporary homemaker services. To deny this reality is to deny necessary services to children. In 1979 there were approximately 10.8 million children in the United States in single-parent families. This was 18.4 percent of all children in the country, or almost one in every five. Between 1970 and 1978, the number of families headed by unmarried women increased by 48 percent. Between 1970 and 1978, the number of families headed by unmarried men increased by 29 percent.

Myth 3: No one should take responsibility for children except their parents. All of us agree that parents have the primary responsibility for their children's upbringing. But does no one else have any responsibility? Yet when children cannot read or are not healthy, education and health professionals point their fingers at each other or blame parents. There has been too much buck-passing and not enough effort by those whose services affect children and families to seek constructive solutions to children's problems. Public and private groups must work together in every community to strengthen parental roles and to develop public policies that fit the diversity of American family life today.

Myth 4: Helping children whose families cannot fully provide for them condones and rewards failure and erodes American family values. Many of us turn our backs on suffering children because of what we believe their parents "should" be doing. For years, welfare reform has eluded us because we do not want to support "lazy parents." Yet we often do not make jobs available to them. Yet by failing to achieve welfare reform, we have penalized children, who are two thirds of all AFDC recipients, and contributed to family breakup. Similarly, we may not like the fact that 600,000 babies are born to teen-age mothers each year, but whom are we hurting by denying these mothers services? Their babies and ourselves. Common sense and our pocketbooks dictate that teen-agers should receive adequate counseling before pregnancy occurs. Common sense and preventive strategies also dictate that once they are pregnant, teen-agers should get help in deciding whether to have their babies. Prenatal care, social supports, education, and opportunities for skill development should be available to those who do decide to bear their children.

Myth 5: Child advocates want the government to take control over families' and children's lives. This is a red herring that thinking people must reject. None of us favors government intrusion into family life. None of us wants the government to dictate the values by which our children are raised or to undermine the integrity of the family.

The issue is not whether government interferes; it already does. Government policies and programs already affect family life, often badly. Our job is to make sure that governmental actions help, not hurt, children and strengthen, not weaken, families.

Myth 6: Meeting children's needs and protecting their rights will divide families and pit parents and children against each other. The best way to help 98 percent of our children is to help their families. Too many who preach family togetherness with great fervor oppose specific reforms that would strengthen the parents' voice and enhance their capacity to meet children's needs. We all must work to increase the confidence, power, and ability of parents to act effectively for children.

Myth 7: Providing needed services is too expensive. We all must help Americans understand that most services to children and families are preventive, relatively inexpensive, and good investments. The issue is what we as a nation value and are willing to pay for. Can a nation that will spend an estimated $21.3 billion on tobacco products in 1980 afford preventive health services for every child? Of course it can. Can Americans, who spent $26 billion in 1976 for the personal consumption of alcohol, afford to reform the child welfare system to insure that homeless children have permanent families? Of course we can. More important, we cannot afford not to.

Myth 8: Children's issues should be above the political process. The political process is the established route for change in this country. Why should children's issues be treated differently from other important issues? Almost every interest other than children has greater visibility in Congress, in the state legislatures, and in city councils. Adults must vote to change policies affecting children, just as we vote to change other policies. We must stand up to those who are using our tax dollars for causes less important than children and families and who are cutting expenditures for libraries, schools, health care, day care, and other services crucial to our children's well-being.

There are two areas in particular where professionals working on behalf of children can offer immediate help. First, a major new law, the Adoption Assistance and Child Welfare Act of 1980, among other things, offers hope for the hundreds of thousands of children without homes in this country. The Act amends the two major federal child welfare programs, the Title IV-B Child Welfare Services Program and the AFDC-Foster Care Program, and redirects current federal fiscal incentives away from out-of-home care and toward alternatives to placement. It sets a framework within which we can all work to provide permanence for these most vulnerable of our children. States will be encouraged to provide services to prevent initial placements in care and to reunify children and their families. Federal reimbursement for adoption subsidies will be available to assist in the adoption of children with special needs—mental, emotional, and physical handicaps for example. Further, protections will be put in place to insure that children enter care only when necessary, are placed appropriately, provided quality care, reviewed periodically, and provided permanence in a timely fashion.

In the 1980s we must work together to insure implementation of these federal reforms and to encourage similar reforms in each of our states. We must encourage the development of preventive service programs that will support families in more creative and helpful ways than has been done in the past. This means further development of home-based services for children with handicapping conditions, increased efforts to train foster parents to aid in strengthening natural parent-child bonds, further exploration of methods for utilizing informal social networks in the servicing of families, and expansion of advocacy and brokering skills in packaging services for children and families. Dollars must be redirected toward these alternatives to out-of-home placement, and dollars saved as children leave care must be used to increase and improve services.

Second, after more than five years of noncompliance we now have new day care standards. On March 12, 1980, HEW Secretary Patricia Harris signed final federal regulations governing the quality of child care for some 900,000 children in programs receiving Title XX, Title IV-B, and Work Incentive (WIN) funds. In so doing, she ended a five-year hiatus during which the staffing requirements for day care facilities were in abeyance, and groups from every end of the political spectrum vied to alter the final regulations.

The regulations walk a thin line between providing needed services and not increasing costs. A set of guidelines will be drafted, fleshing out what the department means by the bare bones of the regulations. They will give examples (though none of them will be mandatory) of how facilities and states can comply with the regulations.

In May, the Department of Health and Human Services (HHS) regional staff, state agency officials, and others were shown the guidelines, and the process of working out the details of implementation began. We urge social workers to participate in finalizing the guidelines and to work with state administrators and regional HHS officials on the details of implementing the standards and enforcing them.

The challenge for the 1980s is a big one. The litany of statistics with which I began outlined the plight of families and children in this country at the end of the last decade. We must work now to change those sad facts.

I have cited two things that can be focused on immediately. But real change will only result from a lot of hard work by many of us in a number of arenas. In the professional arena we must look hard at our customary ways of "helping" families—to uncover lurking biases, vestiges of those eight myths. We must become fiscally hard-nosed, and insure the most cost-effective use of our service dollars. We must also become more willing to hold ourselves accountable for the level, quality, and responsiveness of services provided; to monitor, or be willing to be monitored, in order to insure compliance with emerging professional and legislative expectations. We must also all work in the political arena to convince elected and appointed officials that there is a constituency out there that supports decent income levels for poor families, decent health care for children, and quality child care. More of us must join together in a network for children and work both within states and nationally to become a strong voice for positive policies for children.

COMMENTARY: MEN, WOMEN, AND CHILDREN FIRST

SHIRLEY JENKINS

IF I HAD to make not a "new year" but a "new decade" resolution for the field of social work, it would be to try to develop services to meet needs rather than the other way around. At present, we give priority to those needs that fit our existing service patterns. This holds for

SHIRLEY JENKINS is Professor, Columbia University, New York.

many fields of practice, and is particularly relevant for programs affecting women and children.

Titmuss, the British authority on social administration, warned us of the dangers of a selective approach, and stressed the desirability of universal services available to all.[1] That argument has bogged down in recent years in the face of restrictive budgets and austere social welfare spending. So the approach has been to husband scarce resources, and spend only for specific defined needs, crisis programs, and politically popular causes. It is no accident that the new edition of the National Association of Social Workers review of five years of social service research, which includes two chapters on children, deals only with adoptions, foster care, and children's institutions.[2] We are a long way from working for the welfare of all children—we are still trapped in the formal agency system defined as Child Welfare, capital *C* and capital *W*.

Categorical services are a necessary part of the service spectrum. My concern, however, is that the categorical delivery of services has led to a categorical conceptualization of problems, so that they fit into the tables of organization which describe our agency structures, and agency structure itself often follows government funding. Each of our categorical service solutions, however, tends to develop its own problems, and will continue to do so until we define services in relation to broad human needs rather than funding or structure.

The medical profession has a word for treatment-induced diseases: iotrogenic. One may go to a doctor or to a hospital with one complaint; that is cured, but the patient may then leave with some new and perhaps more serious disease. We need to recognize that the field of social welfare also has treatment-induced problems. We must try to understand their etiology and minimize their impact.

[1] Richard M. Titmuss, *Commitment to Welfare* (New York: Pantheon Books, 1968), pp. 113–23.
[2] Henry S. Maas, ed., *Social Service Research: Review of Studies* (New York: National Association of Social Workers, 1979).

Children's institutions provide care and shelter, but they can create problems of deprivation and alienation. Adoption provides legal protection and permanence, but does not guarantee identity or that, years later, the adoptee will not want above all to search for the biological parents. Protective services alert families and communities to the dangers of child abuse, but they may also carry stigma and divert workers from underlying family needs. So much of our public social services are part and parcel of our mechanisms for social control that they are hardly congruent with a social work ideology based on voluntary help-seeking behavior on the part of clients.

On the other hand, when attempts are made to achieve a broader vision, too often we are ideologically satisfied, but practically deprived. The work of the Carnegie Council on Children and Kenneth Keniston, *All Our Children,* is a case in point.[3] In discussing the demise of the Council, the New York *Times* cited various opinions of its work. One stated that the organization was "important ideologically but not politically"; another said it was "a great national vision with no place to go."[4] Must we choose between the social policy visionary and the categorical program specialist?

What Marian Wright Edelman has done is to suggest a way to go: vision and breadth with regard to basic universal needs, accompanied by specific categorical program proposals for immediate implementation. She has also laid to rest some dysfunctional myths, such as that we need not concern ourselves about other people's children. This is an important idea, one that has been stated before but needs reinforcement.

In 1899 John Dewey wrote: "What the best and wisest parent wants for his own child, that must the community want for all its children."[5] In commenting, Grace Abbott in 1938 wrote that in its provision for children in need of spe-

[3] Kenneth Keniston and the Carnegie Council on Children, *All Our Children* (New York: Harcourt Brace Jovanovich, 1977).
[4] New York *Times,* March 2, 1980.
[5] John Dewey, *The School and Society* (Chicago: University of Chicago Press, 1899), p. 3.

cial care the state has not acted on Dewey's theory. "Reluctant to undertake a clear duty," she said, "the legislators instead have sought to provide the cheapest possible care, and the lawmakers have been slow to recognize that this not only violated sound humanitarian tenets but was in the long run very costly economy."[6] Well, the 1980s are the long run of Abbott's 1930s, and the Edelman paper continues the argument put forth in *The Child and the State*.

We cannot have any illusions that the programs and policies that Edelman suggests will be easily achievable, in either this or the next administration. The worsening economy, the growing strength of the military establishment, the problematic political leadership, and the sharpening conflicts on the international scene all combine to push action for women and children even lower than usual on the national agenda.

But social workers have their own agendas and their own priorities, and Marian Wright Edelman has specified what they are. However, I shall add just one more item to the inventory of needs of women and children. With some hesitation, but much conviction, I suggest that women and children need men. Not as bosses, chauvinists, authority figures, or sexists, but as partners, colleagues, friends, allies in political struggles, brothers in the work place, husbands, lovers, and perhaps most important, as fathers and grandfathers for our children, sharing in their care and rearing. The need is mutual, and the benefits of a new equality between men and women will redound to all.

Marian Wright Edelman has correctly said that the current slogan appears to be "Women and children last." I am not proposing a return to the earlier version. Instead, we should try to build better universal services which are sounder and more seaworthy, so that we can put an end to our prevailing system of social service triage and all of us, men, women, and children, can survive in the difficult years that lie ahead.

[6] Grace Abbott, *The Child and the State* (Chicago: University of Chicago Press, 1938), Vol. II.

The Personal Challenge of the Economic Crisis

GAR ALPEROVITZ

Many lay people who are asked to reflect on economic issues simply go to sleep. The first thing they think is: "I don't know anything about economics; it is something only experts understand. . . . Probably affects me directly and indirectly but it's too complex. I can't take much time to learn about it. Maybe I'll go hear this lecture this morning; and then go back to business as usual. . . ."

Now, I have a professional bias: I tend to think that economics is worth thinking about. I attempt to discount for my bias. However, in all honesty I believe that those who choose to regard the economic problems facing the American political-economic system in the 1980s as a side issue they can worry about later (or simply "go hear a lecture about")—at least those who care about equity and social justice—are a major part of the problem; they are certainly not part of the solution.

I know no way to understand what has happened in the spring of 1980 in Miami (and what I think will happen in other cities in 1980 and many years in this decade) without understanding not only the racial and discrimination aspects of the problem, but the extraordinary economic difficulties of people who are either unemployed or must cope with staggering double-digit inflation rates—or must deal with both problems at the same time that the meager social services available to them are already being cut back. This

Excerpts from Transcript of Informal Remarks by GAR ALPEROVITZ, Codirector, National Center for Economic Alternatives, Washington, D.C.

is how the context in which we live is shaping up. We need to get a handle on what is wrong with our economic system and what we are doing about it. Unless we confront the central economic issues directly, I think the difficulties that face most people day to day will increase; the small positive steps we take will be like trying to go up on an escalator—when the escalator is going down.

So I am going to ask you to stretch a bit intellectually and politically. I have a feeling that some of us will be willing to stretch, and some will not. Economic issues are not easy to contend with; they are just *central.* My comments, therefore, are directed mainly to the people who are seriously worried about the fundamental economic problems of the 1980s. Those who care to deal with economic issues—to stretch beyond the usual rush of day-to-day problems—could make an extraordinary contribution.

It may even be a critical contribution. As we go deeper into more difficult economic times we will see more violence, and with that, repression: the 1980s may offer a choice between democracy and equity on the one hand and a very ugly scenario for the future on the other . . .

One of the triumphant themes in economics these days is concerned with what I would call the illusory theory of inflation which governs the premise upon which most of the programs we deal with stand. For instance, we have all been told that cutting the federal budget is absolutely essential to dealing with inflation. So long as that idea persists, so long as that is the ground we stand on politically and socially, so long as we believe that theory, many of the most fundamental social programs we deal with will be continually cut back. The pressures on limited resources will move funds increasingly to other interests away from helping those least able to defend themselves. The United States is now projecting a one trillion dollar military budget in the next five years. If we believe that cutting the budget is necessary to solving inflation, it is obvious whose budget will be cut.

It is well known—the Congressional Budget Office and

many others have studied this extensively—that even a $25 billion cut in the federal budget would at best take from two tenths to four tenths of one percent off our double-digit inflation rates. (Most of the studies, however, say it would be less than that—one tenth, perhaps.) Despite a great deal of public rhetoric, budget cutting will not significantly affect our inflation. In fact, I know of no high-level economist in the United States government who believes that cutting the budget will *significantly* alter the inflation rate. Why is this so? First, it is because we have a gigantic economy, roughly $2.5 trillion in the gross national product. Secondly, even with the 3.6 percent inflation rate when Gerald Ford was President, we had a massive deficit. It is understood in country after country elsewhere around the world that major deficits can occur with low inflation, with high inflation, even with no inflation. It all depends on what is going on elsewhere in the economy.

But we have been taught politically to believe that the federal budget must be in balance, and this idea sets the context for not only budget cutting but tax cutting. At the local level this affects both the services and the salaries of public servants. Many people who should be attracted to expanded service programs are in practice eliminated by this mythology. The doctrine even affects the poor and the unemployed, who often believe that *they* are the cause of inflation. They then, consciously or subconsciously, become silent partners in believing that budgets must be cut or else the country cannot get on with solving its difficulties.

Again, those who care about the problem must confront the need, first, to *understand,* "to stretch a little," and then to begin to educate others. Political-educational activity can begin to discredit these myths. They are myths that have been well-paid for, well-financed, so that after ten years of increasing propaganda (often by extremely conservative groups), we have come to believe them.

One of the ways to begin to stretch beyond the day-to-day difficulties, to examine the larger context—and I strongly urge this as an economist—is to trust our own experience more. We must be acutely aware of what, in fact, happens when we pay for our groceries, when we pay heating bills, medical charges, housing costs. In fact, those four areas— food, basic energy (heating oil, essential gasoline), health care, shelter—constitute some 60 percent to 70 percent of the average family budget. They are necessities; they cannot be postponed. They are 90 percent of the spending of the bottom 30 percent of the income distribution. According to a presidential commission, they are roughly 120 percent of the income of the bottom 10 percent of society. (How can these items constitute 120 percent? Some people borrow to pay for the groceries. Others, the elderly, finance and refinance homes they may have worked all their lives for. Sadly, others steal to feed their children.)

From our own experience we know personally that the causes of inflation in each of these areas have little to do with the national budget. Consider the obvious, extraordinarily simple fact that energy prices in the first quarter of 1980 went up 64.8 percent. Will cutting the budget change Exxon's record profit rates? Will it alter food prices? Will it do anything about medical bills?

Again, as an initial step common sense is often more powerful than the arcane economic theories we are taught. If we consider the necessities we will very quickly see that the main sources of inflation are, instance by instance, special to each area of spending. Unless the power of very powerful groups, such as the oil companies, is challenged directly, there will *not* be a solution to inflation—and certainly cutting the budget will not be a solution.

Economics is much simpler in its basic outlines than it is in some of its theoretical aspects. To be sure, there are technical problems that we must solve once the value choices are set. But we must start, I believe, with awareness from ordinary experience that certain things matter more than others. And that public policy to stabilize the prices of the self-evident necessities of life would, as one might expect, first have to attack powerful interests rather than cut budgets that affect the weakest members of society. This is only one example, but there is a substantial literature on what is called "sectoral" economics.

To take up another sector briefly, if we tighten the money supply or raise interest rates to control inflation, the cost of housing mortgages and rent will go *up*, not down. Very few families—only the top 3 percent or 4 percent—can now afford a new home in 1980.

Another issue has to do with the idea that creating a massive recession will control inflation. Now again, will a recession change Exxon's prices? Common sense is pretty clear on that point. It is also reinforced by a variety of studies. The late Arthur Okun, chairman of the Council of Economic Advisors under President Johnson, reviewed the technical literature. If we want to control an inflation that starts in energy prices, powerful banking groups involved in interest rates, housing speculation, and real estate development—if we want to control *this* kind of inflation by creating a recession we must be prepared to throw a million people out of work (and keep them out of work for roughly two years running) in order to knock one percentage point off inflation.

Recessions are extraordinarily costly. In the spring of 1980 we experienced an 18 percent inflation rate. If we want to control inflation by means of a recession, we had better be prepared for a lot of Miamis.

I am suggesting that unless we can change the context in which we think about economics—personally, each one of us—and then begin to build a different way of thinking about our economic system through this decade, we will be in increasing trouble. We need just the opposite of a planned recession. Moreover, unless we can get on a full-employment, high-growth track, the amount of money available for unemployment insurance, Social Security contributions, and so on, also will decline.

There is a great deal of discussion these days about Social

Security financing. Most of it emphasizes the fact that there is going to be a change in the relationship of the population cohorts, with fewer people paying *in,* more taking money *out.* But if we had had decent levels of full employment over the last five to six years, we would have had from $25 billion to $40 billion more in tax receipts for Social Security. *This* is the core of the matter. The only way to deal with the fundamentals is to have a working economy which produces the tax receipts we need to deal with the problems.

This puts the larger economic issue to us in a very sharp way. Are we prepared to take part in beginning to break through some of the myths and then to move toward a different political-economic strategy? Or are we willing to sit by and allow the old illusions to continue to dominate the situations we work in day to day?

I am a long-term, prudent optimist, but I have no illusions that in the near future we are going to face an easy situation in the United States. I think times may get rather ugly; they may get worse before they get better. Whether they get better, however, depends upon whether we are able to stand back and recognize the most obvious simple fact that this is the wealthiest country in the history of the world, bar none. And therefore, quite simply, we ought to be able to provide for all our people in a decent manner.

Tolstoy used to say: "If you can't explain it to an ordinary peasant, that's *your* problem, not his." Self-evidently, this is the wealthiest country in the history of the world. Self-evidently, if we cannot get on a positive economic tract that is our problem, not the fault of the fundamentals.

The Japanese are three times as dependent on foreign energy sources as we are. We have a tremendous amount of energy by comparison. Yet they have not had massive unemployment; their mid-1980 inflation rate is in the 6 percent range; they have not had a recession; they are growing at a rate of 6 percent. Their productivity in manufacturing is in the 8 percent to 10 percent range while ours is going downhill. In the light of such obvious facts, blaming all our difficulties on the oil crisis is an illusion: The real question is whether we manage our economic affairs intelligently.

The choice we face in the 1980s, I believe, is whether we meet the challenge of getting on a positive economic track in this country or whether we go down the track of cutting the national budget, creating recessions, increasing military spending—the track which sparked Miami's violence and repression.

Can we move forward positively rather than negatively? This is not a problem simply for economists. It is *our* problem even if we do not want to study economics. To the extent that we ignore our strengths, to the extent we are unwilling to rise to the challenge, to the extent we do not use opportunities day to day to stretch out of the context of specific programs to begin reeducation, to the extent that we say, "I really don't have time this week"—to that extent, *we,* I believe, are the central difficulty.

Who else is going to do it?

Another way to approach the general issue is simply to ask what is important. It becomes rather obvious what the major goals of economic policy ought to be. If we are interested in inflation, we must first look to the basic items that matter most to most families, and that means developing policies which allow us to get ahead with direct programs to achieve stability in the price of the necessities without having to create a recession. This means, for example, programs to restrict gas guzzlers and provide more insulation while at the same time controlling basic energy prices and profits; or setting up programs to expand the supply of housing rather than restrict it.

Let us also review our approach to employment. If we are interested in what is happening in the local community, we should have to focus directly on community economic health. We are in a period when unemployment is devastating local communities. As a progressive economist, I am interested in full employment. But I do not know anybody other than a few economists and a few of my progressive political friends who really care about the abstraction "full employment." It is a general, statistical idea. What people want are *jobs, here* and *now.* And this is very different: so long as we allow the general, statistical idea to dominate our thinking, we will build up the Houstons to 2 percent or one percent full employment—and destroy the Youngstowns and Detroits to 8 percent and 9 percent and 12 percent unemployment.

In 1979 the League of Cities adopted as its national goal "community full employment": 4 percent by 1983 for each specific community of the nation. The point is that we must add up *to* national full employment rather than subtract down to community instability.

Again, beginning with local needs—and the obvious issues of a local community—and saying that public policy ought to provide productive jobs, here, now, for each American community is understandable. It meets the requirements of conserving cities that are less energy wasteful (particularly in the Northeast and Midwest), of conserving the local tax base, and of providing stability for small-business people and taxpayers. If we can stabilize local economies, we can also get at one part of the taxpayers' crisis that is undermining social service and at "pockets of poverty" and unemployment. The concept also allows a value criterion—community—to govern a variety of programs that we are going to need in the economy.

The notion that stability in the necessities of life *as a value* is important meets the test of everyday experience; it also sets a different paradigm for economic policy. Similarly, the idea that the health of local communities ought to be a priority of public policy begins with local experience and common sense; it also offers a value structure, a way of looking to the things that matter most to guide the technicians. Both say: "If we are going to go forward, *these* things matter first and foremost."

Without going too deeply into the economics of it, it is clear that if we put such ideas together there are some ob-

vious logical connections. We are in a situation of tremendous housing shortages; we are in a situation of great unemployment. Expanding the housing supply also reduces
inflation. It simultaneously produces jobs, locally.

We are in a staggering energy crisis. We need solar equipment, we need insulation, we need mass transit, we need
railroads, we need biomass conversion. Self-evidently, these
things require people to do the work and fill the jobs, locally. And this produces low-cost energy, compared with
OPEC prices.

Policies which achieve such an integration begin to tell us
what our over-all priorities ought to be: to meet local needs,
to provide jobs, and (in my view as an economist) to provide
the economic stimulus to secure higher economic growth
rates and with an efficient economy. The elements of a coherent, positive economic plan can be derived from the
most basic issues we face.

The things that are most important—rather than the difficult but secondary technical problems—are not impossible
to understand. Nor are they difficult to explain to our fellow citizens both locally and in Washington.

I commented at the outset that *we* are part of the problem
to the extent that we refuse to stretch. I mean that rather
personally, too. I live in Washington, I do research, write
books, testify before Congress. But the real issue is to
stretch out of that context and to ask myself: Am I willing
to spend one hour a week on something *else*? That is a nasty
question. One hour a week seems like absolutely nothing.
In reality, people do *not* do it. Am I willing to spend one
hour a week changing my day-to-day pattern in order to
address *the central issue* rather than my current priorities ex-
pending my budgeted time?

We should all ask ourselves that question: Are we willing
to get on with learning something about the overriding economic crisis? Are we willing to look concretely into what
might be done in the neighborhood, our community, the

state, our educational institutions, to begin to have a broader vision of some of these issues?

Are we willing to allocate a *half* hour to begin to reach out in a new direction that is slightly beyond what we *have* been doing? It is a very nasty question, and I have no illusions about how many people in American society are prepared to stretch. If we are not, I think we will witness the results of our own sins of omission.

And during the 1980s—as the economic situation worsens, and as we are content with moving by small steps up a down escalator even as the budget cutting slows our capacity to move up even one step—if we are content to look the other way and avoid the economic crisis, if this is our posture, then we truly *are* a part of the problem. Perhaps the worst part, because we have knowledge and thus can act otherwise than as we do act.

On the other hand, those who care to think positively about the decade and our emerging history know that this is an extraordinary nation. It is extraordinary in its wealth of material resources, in its resources of land and water, in its people, in its technical skills and its scientific know-how. It truly could be a bountiful, positive, exciting nation. We are so much encompassed by the pessimism of the day that we forget our birthright.

So, in a different sense, were we seriously to stretch a bit we might find not only the solution to the pressing and dangerous crisis of the economy in the 1980s. We might even find ourselves participating, steadily, soberly, prudently, seriously, in the careful expansion over this decade of a great social movement that might just possibly begin to see the future of the country in its positive breadth, indeed, as an experiment, a great challenge, as an opportunity. In dreary times the idea of hope is very threatening. We do not like to think of the challenge that our true potential presents. It is more easily left in the corner as we continue with business as usual.

But the 1980s will not be business as usual. They cannot be. We live in a new economic era. The personal challenge will be either to participate, as a quiet witness, in the dissolution or to begin that stretching process that allows each of us, together, to deal with the central issues facing our society in these brief, quarrelsome years that are the staging ground of the twenty-first century.

RESPONSE

MELVIN A. GLASSER

THE SOCIAL CONSEQUENCES of the present economic malaise will be vast and long-lived. It is, therefore, essential that we develop an agenda for change and participate fully in the public debate on the future of our nation's social programs. The need for collective political action in order to implement this agenda for change is apparent; the remaining question is: how will our collective energies be channeled? In his essay "The Idler," Samuel Johnson wrote: "To do nothing every man is ashamed and to do much, almost every man is unwilling or afraid. Innumerable expedients have therefore been invented to produce motion without labor and employment without solicitude."

As Gar Alperovitz points out, our situation today demands the identification of that aimless motion; the setting of social priorities; the identification and rejection of political expedience; and the adoption of programs of substance, focusing on community change, employment, and housing which will enable us to begin to deal with the over-all economic problems that we face. Regrettably, the public debate on our economic problems seldom includes this kind of social vision of constructive change.

MELVIN A. GLASSER is Director, Social Security Department, International Union, United Auto Workers, Detroit.

The principal hallmark of the present inflation-control programs is balancing the federal budget. It is a device of the kind that the late economist Arthur Okun termed "muddle-through economics." It has little to do with changing things; and yet more rhetoric is being advanced in this sphere than in almost any other.

But the political process distorts even the balanced budget approach. The special-interest groups protect their turf. Appropriate taxation of the scandalously large profits of the oil industry alone could come close to balancing the budget. The measure finally adopted by Congress and signed into law for the taxation of these profits is a far cry from what would be equity in a just society.

Inflation has devastated welfare families. Take the case of New York State, one of the more generous states in the amount of welfare allowances. The average family of four in 1980 received $2,544 per year less in real income from welfare than it did just six years ago.

In the rush to balance the budget such families not only will receive no adjustments, they are likely to get less. But how do they survive? They accumulate debts, they don't pay their rent, their utility bills, or their food bills. They thus jeopardize many small businesses and property owners and widen the circle of human suffering, business losses, and peripheral unemployment. Is it these 1.3 million poorest people in New York, the majority of them children, who should be playing a prominent role in helping us out of our recession-depression?

We have reason to be deeply concerned about the human values at stake in our present time of trouble. We seem to learn very little from the past. A major presidential candidate made a speech in Detroit in May, 1980, in which he urged the abandonment of federal and state roles in public welfare programs. These, he insisted, should be returned to the local communities so that they might take care of their own.

This reminded me of Herbert Hoover's block-care plan.

It may be recalled that President Hoover decried the need
for federal intervention in taking care of the poor and disadvantaged. Instead he launched a plan whereby people in
each neighborhood would take care of those in trouble who
lived on their own block. There was only one major flaw in
the program. The people in the ghettos of New York and
Detroit, Chicago and Cleveland were all suffering. He asked
those who had nothing to share it with their neighbors,
those in the affluent areas were to take care of the affluent
in their neighborhoods. It was the Hoover administration
that counted those who peddled apples on the street cor-
ners as employed, and which maintained that "many persons left their jobs for the more profitable one of selling
apples."

But that was a long time ago. In 1949, however, *Barron's*,
the financial weekly, editorialized that apparently "the only
way to get a day's work out of a man is to threaten his children with starvation." I fear this philosophy, couched in
1980 language, continues to have credibility with many who
would return to the ideas of the past for solutions to the
even more complex problems of the present and future.

An important index to assess the value a society places on
individuals and families is the social expenditures as a percentage of the gross national product (GNP). The United
States has a long way to go before it begins to approach
even the middle rank of industrialized countries in terms of
its demonstrated concern for social programs. The most recent figures were developed in the mid-1970s by the Organization for Economic Development when it analyzed expenditures of the countries of Western Europe, Japan,
Canada, and the United States. In that period we were
spending 15.7 percent of the GNP on health, education,
and income maintenance. That placed us fourteenth among
the eighteen countries studied. Only New Zealand, Australia, Greece, and Japan expended a smaller proportion of
their national wealth. We know that the Scandinavian countries do better, but should we really rank below Germany,

Ireland, Italy, Belgium, France, and Canada? We should give pause when we spend half as much for social programs as the Netherlands and one-third less than France and Finland.

The aged are a major segment of our society under direct attack in 1980. We hear from political platforms of the need to contain and reduce expenditures in behalf of this major segment of our society. Few say that they are lazy and incompetent. Most agree that after a lifetime of work they should be entitled to incomes which enable them to live in decency and dignity in their years of retirement. But this is not the case for too many retirees. From time to time the media carry stories of the elderly freezing in unheated apartments, victims of crime, and themselves criminals as they are caught stealing food or clothing. The more sympathetic can be heard to say that when the elderly steal they are evidencing character disorders that come with senility. But I suggest that these are societal disorders that result from an inhumane approach to human well-being.

Look for a moment at the economic position of the aged as economic units consisting of a single person or a married couple living together. In a 1976 survey of a cross section of the population over age sixty-five, the Social Security Administration found that fully 25 percent had total incomes, including earnings and income from assets and pensions, that were below the poverty line. Nearly two thirds of those surveyed relied exclusively on Social Security benefits for pension income, and of this group almost a third received total incomes below the poverty line. Without Social Security it is estimated that fully 60 percent of all aged families would live in total poverty.

Yet the question raised continuously by spokesmen for both major political parties is whether we are not spending too much on Social Security. Serious proposals have been advanced to "contain the costs." New formulas are being advanced to reduce the minimum benefit, to tax half of benefits received, to eliminate death benefits, reduce or eliminate allowances for older children, and tighten eligibility definitions so that more people can be kept off Social Security and transferred to supplemental Security Income (welfare). Is it not appropriate to ask who speaks for this generation that is enjoying what our society happily dubs their "golden years"? Is this what this country is all about? Should they be bearing their "fair share" of expenditure cuts to control inflation?

I work in the auto and agricultural implement industries where unemployment today is already higher than it was at the bottom point of the 1974–75 recession. And unemployment is not restricted to blue-collar workers. It affects every category.

Our current serious difficulties have more than economic consequences. Our industries have been proud ones. They have paid well and provided good benefits. And because of a strong union and essentially forward-looking employers a good job has been done in employing blacks and other ethnic minorities who continue to be excluded from many of the better jobs in our society. But when layoffs come they are based on seniority. We do not know of a better system which would eliminate favoritism and provide equity. So the most heavily hit are the 40 percent to 50 percent blacks and other minorities who constitute the auto and auto supplier work force in the city of Detroit, for example. All too suddenly they are moved from the class of well-paid worker to that of potential welfare recipient. All too suddenly they are deprived of the dignity, decency, and hope which America can offer and was providing for them. Unemployment insurance is limited. Other jobs are practically nonexistent. Many of the small employers are going out of business never to return or are moving to the nonunionized Sun Belt.

Tens of thousands of these workers have been moved permanently, or at least for a long time, out of the work force. The class of the alienated has been enlarged. Programs like those envisaged in the Humphrey-Hawkins full employment bill are paper promises. So we need to be concerned for the unemployed, for their families, and for the society. And we need to speak for programs that will protect the integrity of that society which is again under siege.

Finally, health care is of crucial importance in a humane society. All of us are the victims of a system in disarray. Its costs continue to escalate at an inordinate rate and to constitute an important factor in fueling the fires of inflation. This has been well-known for at least twenty years. Successive presidents of both political parties have recommended that corrections be made. Endless numbers of polls show that the American people want a system of national health insurance such as exists in every other country of the world except South Africa. But a fragmented Congress and uncertain presidents have continued the present chaos.

Two statistics will illustrate how bad the situation is. We are currently spending $70 billion annually in federal funds for health care programs. Unless there is major intervention in the system, by 1985 we will require for that one year an additional $62 billion in federal funds alone. Is this inflationary?

In 1975 thirty million Americans lost their health insurance coverage primarily because of unemployment. The number is likely to be in the same ball park in 1980. Add to this some eleven million Americans eligible for Medicaid and not receiving it, because they are unwilling or unable to apply, or kept out by restrictive state rules, and the dimensions of the problem become apparent.

It is trite to state that lack of availability of health care is a matter of survival for all of us. It is perhaps less apparent that becoming ill or disabled and not receiving good care results in increasing numbers of people who become permanently dependent, and increasing numbers of children who grow into adulthood incapable of participating fully in the society of which they are a part.

There is in Congress a carefully structured proposal, the Health Care for All Americans bill, which can make good care available for all and at the same time contain the wildly inflationary costs. There are, then, solutions. The problem is that the solutions have not had sufficient political support to bring them before the people.

Gar Alperovitz stressed the importance of our value system in dealing with economic priorities. No decision on economic policy is devoid of political content, of the exercise of political judgment and choice. Gar Alperovitz has outlined constructive alternatives to the present repressive solutions advanced by the national political leadership to deal with our economic problems.

I have referred to the searing effects on people and on families of cutbacks in social programs now under way. Every social worker can bear witness that the damage will not be repaired by restoration of these programs several years from now when the economy recovers. The damage will have been done to children, the out-of-work minorities, the mentally ill, the elderly. The costs of remedial action will be high and the results meager.

A cabinet officer with whom I discussed this said to me, "You're right, but at present we are so few and our voices are not heard."

My thesis is that we are not few. We are advocates who speak for many, and we need to recognize that it is through the political process that we will humanize our economy. We must be aware that in the political arena we are confronted with an administration uncertain about solutions, and a Congress in which public policy is made without the benefit of party responsibility which would make such policy more coherent and programmatic. Both of these phenomena call for a more active political role for advocates in the field of social welfare. I suggest a general outline for an action agenda:

1. We need to inform ourselves about the range of issues in social policy and the facts which surround each of them.

2. We need to take responsibility for action through the National Association of Social Workers and other professional channels.

3. We need to get the boards of social agencies into social action at a local level, working with Congressmen and state legislators.

4. We need to see to it that funds are available locally, through United Funds, city councils, federal and state governments, so that the poor and the ethnic minorities can get help in organizing themselves for social action.

5. We need to join with other groups in an effort to get the largely uninvolved ethnic minorities and the poor to register and vote in local, state, and federal elections.

6. We need to form new coalitions and focus our efforts on a single issue or a set of related issues, including CETA funds, more adequate support for public welfare programs, mental health services for dischargees from state mental health institutions, strengthening Social Security, and enacting national health insurance. Natural alliances among organized labor, the NAACP and the Urban League, the Progressive Alliance, church, civic, and fraternal groups can be most effective in pressing for constructive social change, just as the right-wing organizations have been so effective in concerted action on a limited number of issues.

7. We need to assume a larger role in electoral politics, working with candidates for public office and elected officials on a program of social change.

In these times of severe hardship for millions, we must recognize that political action for constructive social change is a moral imperative. A humanized economy requires a choice of alternative methods for dealing with its problems which take into account the problems and needs of the people. Our success in developing alternatives to the present state of affairs will be a test of social imagination and vision. And the choices we make as a nation will be the fundamental political decisions of our time.

Call it old-fashioned, call it liberal, call it social welfare— I call it American to put people before profits, to select those economic measures to restore our economy that will provide both short- and long-range protection to all groups in our society. I call it American to treat the poor, the el-

derly, the unemployed, the sick as though they were equal
partners in what is still the wealthiest country in the world.

Franklin D. Roosevelt understood this when he told us
forty-seven years ago: "The test of our progress is not
whether we add more to the abundance of those who have
much. It is whether we provide enough for those who have
little."

The Independent Sector and Voluntary Action

BRIAN O'CONNELL

For eighteen months during 1978 and 1979, the committee which created the organization INDEPENDENT SECTOR examined the role, impact, shortcomings, and future of the nonprofit nongovernmental side of our national life. The committee included many of the long-time leaders of the field, such as John Gardner, its chairman; Alan Pifer, Landrum Bolling, and Glen Watts, but it also included many of the sector's newer faces and causes, such as Carl Holman of the National Urban Coalition; Raul Yzaguirre of the National Council of La Raza; and Ruth Abram of Women's Action Alliance. That diversity made the job a good deal more difficult, but it also made it a good deal more relevant.

The committee began work with a piercing analysis of whether philanthropy, volunteering, and independent institutions really do make an important difference in society today. They went at the task with an almost chilling skepticism, stripping away the myths and shibboleths which so often produce only a romanticized interpretation of the sector's role and goodness. For example, at our very first meeting, brutally unattractive comparisons were made between what some government entities are doing about equal opportunity contrasted with what many voluntary organizations are not doing about equal opportunity. In subsequent sessions, we acknowledged that the government has been

BRIAN O'CONNELL is President, INDEPENDENT SECTOR, Washington, D.C.

brought to, and is held to, its current level of effort only through the tenacious and courageous work of some citizen groups. This was one example of the process we followed to sort out the relative weaknesses and strengths on the voluntary side. In the end, not one of the committee members dared to exaggerate the sector's merits.

Even when we viewed the sector in its naked state, there remained both evidence and conviction that individual freedom depends on, and flourishes in, this independent albeit imperfect sector. It provides individuals with allies, options, outlets, and power. Moreover, it provides society with innovation, experimentation, criticism, and reform. Even in an imperfect state, these are essential qualities for a society which cherishes individual freedom. The committee concluded that though it is foolish and terribly unattractive to exaggerate or romanticize the sector's contributions, it is more foolish and downright dangerous to fail to recognize and to preserve what this sector represents to our uniqueness as a country and to our chances to be unique as individuals.

AN OVERVIEW OF THE STATE OF HEALTH OF THE SECTOR

The organizing committee also examined the health of the sector itself. Here too, most of us were to undergo a marked reorientation. After starting to enumerate the problems facing the sector and the attacks upon it, supposedly sufficient to blow us out of the water altogether, we were brought up short by a far more impressive review of the current strengths and contributions of the sector. One of the most important findings in the organizing committee's report is that the sector is alive and well. In just the past decade, the sector has given rise to an amazing array of new efforts on behalf of many significant causes including women's rights, the aged, voter registration, refugees, preservation, conservation, consumerism, native Americans, population control, experimental theater, mental health, international understanding, neighborhood empowerment and on and on.

Americans are organizing to influence every conceivable aspect of the human condition. Increasingly, we are willing to stand up and be counted on almost any public issue. We organize to fight zoning changes, approve bond issues, oppose or propose abortion, improve garbage collection, expose overpricing, enforce equal rights, and protest wars.

Volunteer: National Center for Citizen Participation, says that 45 to 55 million Americans volunteer. The last Department of Labor study on this subject indicated that in 1974, 24 percent of the United States population volunteered. This was an increase of 8 percent over a similar survey in 1967. One of the most encouraging trends is that citizen participation now includes every economic group. What had been the province of the upper and middle classes has spread to every part of our society. Participation has finally truly begun to come of age. Another and related encouraging trend is the groundswell of neighborhood activity and organization. People have come to realize that if they depend on some grand design from above to produce relief and direction, they will wait forever.

The Gallup Poll organization recently completed two surveys which reveal that people overwhelmingly are willing to get involved in an unpaid way to improve their communities. Seventy percent of the adults surveyed in urban communities are "willing to serve on committees, to participate in neighborhood betterment activities, or to assist in the performance of social services."[1] From this and other experiences, George Gallup concludes: "For more than 40 years, we have been polling the people of the nation. And out of this experience I have come to the conclusion that our nation's greatest resource is the talent and brains of our citizens and a willingness to use them in the service of the nation."[2]

It is important to our national orientation and morale to know that people still care and still do have tremendous

---

[1] George Gallup, speech to National Leagues of Cities, November 27, 1978, St. Louis, p. 10.

[2] *Ibid.*, p. 1.

influence on their own lives, their communities, and their world. If the Organizing Committee's examination and report had ended right there and if that were the only message we could impart to the American people, our work would still have served an extremely valuable purpose.

In taking our examination an additional step, we found that despite the overwhelming good news, people have not just been seeing ghosts in discerning problems of considerable consequence. As the committee's report goes on to say, "Problems have been developing, however, which need the attention of everyone interested in preserving the place of the sector in American life." [3] The problems are these:

1. Volunteering in and for our traditional groups is down. These groups are the religious and human service organizations, museums, private libraries, private hospitals, privately supported secondary schools, and institutions of higher education and symphony orchestras.

Measured by numbers of people and hours in so-called traditional organizations, volunteering is down slightly, and when population growth is introduced, it is down significantly. This is certainly so for churches, long the mainstay for volunteering. Even the health agencies, which have been able to attract enormous numbers of volunteers, are now beginning to lose ground.

If one looks at this whole situation from the perspective of the current struggle of a church to hold its members and increase their involvement, or of a hospital to attract and hold service volunteers, the news may be viewed as bad. But if one looks at the balance from the perspective that more people are willing to be involved in their society, the news is very good.

The challenge for all of us is to find ways to tap the desire of people to be involved and to have some greater control of their own destinies.

[3] Organizing Committee report, December, 1979 (Washington, D.C.: INDEPENDENT SECTOR), p. 14.

2. There is skepticism and even cynicism about all our institutions, government, churches, foundations, "charities," and so forth.

3. Giving is steadily declining both as a percentage of the gross national product and as a percent of disposable personal income.

4. The sector clearly has its share of faults and frauds.

In a sector so given to experimentation and freedom, there is a temptation to hide behind an entirely *laissez-faire* doctrine. However, to the extent that the ineffectiveness of some institutions colors public perceptions of the sector as a whole and to the extent that the public is not well-served by such organizations, then all in the sector have a stake in achieving high standards of performance.

5. One of the major problems is that the sector is both everywhere and invisible. We are all involved with many of its organizations, but we do not really recognize its roles or even its existence as a distinct sector. People take for granted the freedoms it provides and sustains. One can complete a full and supposedly thorough formal education without ever hearing or reading about the major role of this sector in American life.

6. There is a rapidly growing pattern of government regulation which, in its complexity and patchwork, threatens to inhibit the freedoms of speech, assembly, and petition.

7. There are decidedly negative impacts on the sector as a result of changes in tax policy.

In the name of tax simplification, an increasing number of Treasury officials would abolish altogether the income tax deduction for charitable contributions. Others argue that because the government loses revenue when people deduct gifts from their taxable income, this money is really a tax expenditure and therefore government should have control over where that money is channeled and how it is spent. The genius of the original proposition that people should be free to support the causes of their choice and that government should do everything possible to encourage this aspect of pluralism is being subordinated to simplicity and to crisp lines of authority.

8. There is greater dependence on government grants, contracts, and other government funds by traditionally independent organizations.

We really do need to sort out where this is leading the individual organizations and the sector as a whole. We also need to work with government to develop more uniform and realistic accountability mechanisms so that initiative is not stiffled.

These problems make clear that the sector is not as effective as it should be and, more important, that it is in some danger of serious decline, particularly in the very quality that is its most significant characteristic, independence.

RELATIONSHIP BETWEEN THE GOVERNMENTAL AND
INDEPENDENT SECTORS

The future of the independent sector is very much dependent on its relationship to government. This involves government regulation of the sector, tax policies, and use of government funds by independent organizations. It also involves society's expectations and the needs of the two sectors.

Before one can realistically analyze the future roles of the two sectors, it is necessary to get the relationship into perspective. To begin with, it has become entirely too easy to adopt a simplistic antigovernment stance. It is essential to start with an awareness of *public* responsibility. It is true that government has far outdistanced the voluntary organizations' dollar investment in human services and that government has assumed many of the obligations previously borne by independent institutions. Significantly, this is the result of our awareness that democratic government is the basic representative of the people when problems are so large as to call for the ultimate expression of organized neighborliness.

It is essential to a clear view of what is transpiring to acknowledge that much of the growth of government has been induced by segments of the voluntary sector advocating greater expenditures for health, research, education, the arts, social welfare, and so many other necessary investments in our future. It has also been induced by many of us advocating far greater oversight of equal opportunity, environmental impact, consumer involvement, and so many other examples of glaring neglect in our past. Now these institutions are caught in a contradiction between their traditionally independent posture and their accountability to government.

The only way to sort out honestly the future roles of the two sectors is to analyze how our society can best provide services to people. The principal alternatives are:

1. *A totally government-operated effort.* Such an arrangement would certainly clarify accountability and would not muddy up organization charts; but it lacks alternatives, experimentation, and maximum citizen influence.

2. *An all-voluntary effort.* Despite the fantasies of some pipe dreamers who remember some good old days that never really existed, we obviously are not going to go in this direction.

3. *A combination of the two.* It would be cumbersome and more difficult to hold accountable, but it would provide the flexibility, alternatives, and citizen influence which reflect the hard lessons of the past.

I suspect that most social welfare professionals favor the combination and assume that is the way we will go. The assumption is so widespread that much of the talk today is of the vendor role of the sector, and most of the debate is whether the channel of support should be vouchers, fees, or contracts. For assurance and rationale, we point to the Wolfenden Report on the future of the voluntary sector in Britain, to the American Enterprise Institute's studies on mediating structures, to the scores of other such "evidences" of the value of pluralism, and to the lessons each of us has learned on the worth of *community* participation, *citi-*

zen involvement, and *community* control. We note almost with relief that people of all political and philosophical persuasions are beginning to point out the practical limitations of big government and the value of providing for dispersion of power and for alternatives.

Even in the face of all this evidence and conviction and assumption, I am not really sure that the combination of sectors is, in fact, the way it will work out. I have eight serious doubts:

1. In the current budget cutbacks at all levels of government, I hear from many professionals that the earliest and heaviest slices are taken from the programs of voluntary agencies.

2. As we acknowledge the interrelationship of human problems and needs and the breakdown of total systems to serve the whole person or the whole family, it is very easy to imagine more and more policy-makers concluding that we must have a simple integrated system which in its simplicity might not accommodate such complications as contracts and vouchers.

3. Legislators are tightening the screws of accountability, and the people they hold accountable are not very comfortable or credible when, in those moments of hot lights and frigid cross-examination, they try to explain a breakdown in terms of decentralization or the limitations on their control.

4. Accountability mechanisms are becoming so controlling, for example in the health field, that the very arguments for voluntary organizations—flexibility, responsiveness, citizen control, experimentation, and the like—are no longer really germane.

5. Planning, in my experience, flows naturally in the direction of those who have the money to implement the plans. It is also my experience that those who have the money tend to think first about what *they* want to do with it.

6. In our growing preoccupation with the vendor role and the rationalizations why government should do more of its public business through voluntary organizations, we in-

creasingly sound more self-serving than public-serving.
Without the characterizations of objectivity, dedicated volunteering, and contributed support, we may have lost our
ace (and maybe even our face cards too).

7. Even the contributed dollars are beginning to follow
government's lead. Foundations and corporations in Cleveland, for example, have significantly revised their priorities
to respond to a massive, one-for-three, challenge grant
from the National Endowment for the Arts. Several United
Way's in Ohio are buying a small piece of the public mental
health system at the expense of building the citizens' mental
health movement, and foundations nationwide are responding to do their share to implement a vast array of government studies and plans to save libraries, create summer
jobs, improve international understanding, and on and on.

8. In the growing governmental efforts to exercise
greater public control, or at least oversight, of the independent sector, all in the name of protection of the people, the
independent voice of the sector is being muffled.

With these doubts and concerns very much in mind, I
submit that we have two major jobs to do in the 1980s if
there is to be a viable voluntary sector around in the 2000s.
The first job is to gain a better grasp of how the public will,
in fact, be best served, with what model or models or by
what principles or according to what values, and then to
develop the power—intellectual, creative and political—to
make it happen.

The second job is to recognize that in the current debate
about the government-independent sector roles, and in the
current stampede for government funding, we are losing
track of the far larger issue, the maintenance of a society
conducive to *independent* voluntary action.

On the first—the right model or principles or values—the
only advice I would presume to offer has to do with citizen
control and participation, including and indeed emphasizing consumer involvement in articulating needs, planning
services, operating programs, and evaluating results. The

more I work with people and communities the more faith I have in the capacity of human beings to respond to responsibility with common sense and practicality.

My own guess is that whether one starts the examination with a prejudice for a public model, a private model sustained by government dollars, or a combination of the two, a sensible final product is likely to look pretty much the same: a healthy balance between (*a*) *responsibility* of democratic government; (*b development* of institutions and programs which are encouraged by every conceivable device to be creative, responsive; and caring, and (*c*) citizen participation and influence.

If in our heart of hearts we believe that the best way to serve people requires a partnership of government and voluntary organizations, then we cannot just assume that the common sense of it will prevail. I hope that at least some of my eight doubts help convince the social welfare profession that is not the way we are headed.

As important as a balance or alternatives might be, even that is decidedly secondary to clearing the way for new and independent groups and causes and experiments to emerge in the future.

The significant negative of putting substantial government money into voluntary agencies is the automatic compromise of the independence of those organizations. As valuable as their direct services are, they are still decidedly secondary to the role of the voluntary sector to act as independent advocate and critic. Many groups which accept substantial government funds will, of course, continue to perform in advocacy-critic roles, but when the real crunch develops, their reliability for independence just cannot be assured.

Today's voluntary agency personnel are wonderfully principled and fiercely independent, but will their successor executives and boards be so alert to compromise? Will they *really* be willing to lop off essential programs which deal with pressing human needs if that is the price for calling for the replacement of an inadequate public official? How many sensitive executives will *really* be ready to terminate able providers if there is a need to demonstrate that independent advocacy is even more important than our service function? How many boards that are proud of their services and unused to raising the private dollars to pay for them will *really* opt for quarreling with the source of support? And how credible will be such a board's efforts to influence appropriations if it can be tagged with even a particle of self-interest? Additionally, it is my experience that the large provider of service which is substantially dependent on government funds tends to use up much of its social action clout dealing with the legislation, appropriations, and administrative red tape associated with the agency's own program.

These tests become particularly pointed when one realizes that the most likely source of government funds is usually the government agency which covers the same area of human need and which, therefore, the voluntary organization should be monitoring. Some agonizingly important priorities could have been advanced if my former agency, the Mental Health Association, had been willing to accept support from the National Institute of Mental Health. But accepting such support would lead to loss of a real measure of independence, both to criticize the institute and to go before Congress and the administration to advocate for it.

Although the debate on the use of government funds by voluntary organizations is still raging, the reality is that this new funding pattern is already established and most voluntary agencies are quickly following it. Even if one opposes such support, the forces pushing the other way are prevailing, and all the voluntary agencies can do is to understand what is happening well enough to capitalize on the positives and try to compensate for the negatives.

The solution to encouraging the independent voice of the voluntary sector while at the same time expanding its service function must start with a conscious determination or reaffirmation that though there are multiple roles that the voluntary sector performs, it is its independent voice in public matters that is the quintessential value. Anything that compromises the sector's capacity to be independent diminishes the function for which society depends on it.

Attention to services is important, but to the extent that it obscures or takes us away from enhancing the independent role of the voluntary sector, society is not best served. The higher value is to provide the means by which tomorrow's reformers might get at us all.

THE NEW ORGANIZATION: INDEPENDENT SECTOR

After completing its analysis of the place of the sector in our lives and detailing the contributions and weaknesses of the sector, the Organizing Committee concluded that the sector is not as effective as it should be and, more important, that it is in some danger of serious decline. For that reason, the committee concluded that it is essential to find ways to deal with the problems and weaknesses. Not surprisingly, it was concluded that the best way to mobilize a positive and massive effort is to involve the thousands of organizations which already relate to the millions of individuals who already have a conviction about volunteering and giving and pluralism.

The committee therefore proposed that the new organization should be seen as a meeting ground where the diverse interests of the sector can comfortably come together to determine how to pursue their individual and collective interests in strengthening the capacity of the private sector to be of public service.

The interpretation of what this curious new organization, INDEPENDENT SECTOR, is all about is possibly best contained in our roster of 230 strikingly varied organizations. They are remarkably different. They are sometimes quarrelsome, often competitive, and always fiercely independent. But in the composite they represent that special tradition of giving, volunteering, and not-for-profit initiative that has made

America unique. The common denominator is their shared determination that people will have an opportunity to influence their own lives and the kind of society in which they live.

The roster includes groups as different as the American Theatre Association, United Negro College Fund, Sloan Foundation, Overseas Development Council, Audubon Society, U.S. Steel Foundation, Opera America, and National Council of Churches. These and indeed all of the 230 have vastly different purposes, but common to all is a commitment to alternatives, options, innovation, pluralism, and individual freedom.

The basic job of INDEPENDENT SECTOR will be to create a favorable nationwide climate for philanthropy, voluntary action, and independent organizations. It will pursue that job through five program areas:

Relationship with Government to deal with the infinite interconnections between the two sectors, but particularly to ensure the healthy independence and continued viability of non-governmental organizations.
Public Education to improve understanding of the sector's role and function in giving people alternatives, greater opportunities for participation and for creating a more caring and effective society.
Research to provide a body of knowledge about the independent sector and about how to make it more useful to society.
Communications within the sector so that shared problems and opportunities may be identified and pursued.
Encouragement of Effective Operation and Management of Philanthropic and Voluntary Organizations to maximize their capacity to serve individuals and society.[4]

The Organizing Committee and the 230 organizations which have already joined share a belief that giving, volunteering, and not-for-profit initiative are what have made America unique and they share a conviction that it is the mission of INDEPENDENT SECTOR, to help keep it that way.

The upheavals of the 1960s and 1970s have brought all of us to an appreciation of how essential it is for people to

[4]*Ibid.*, pp. 21, 22.

have some control of their own destinies. Whether it is expressed as "doing one's own thing," or empowerment, or making our institutions responsive and responsible to the people they were designed to serve, we are all now rigidly alert to the value and joy of having options and alternatives and having the power of citizens to experiment, influence, and reform. These quintessential characteristics of individual freedom are served and fostered by America's independent sector. The sector's role in our society is the giving, volunteering, and not-for-profit initiative which has made America so wonderfully unique. It is the mission of INDEPENDENT SECTOR to help keep it that way.

—

Community Empowerment

THE CRITICAL ROLE OF NEIGHBORHOODS

ARTHUR J. NAPARSTEK

I BECAME INTERESTED in small communities and neighborhoods a number of years ago when I took my son back to my own community, on the lower East Side of New York. I remembered that neighborhood as one that was multiracial, multiethnic. It was a neighborhood or community—and I use the two words interchangeably—that had organizational and cultural support systems. In many ways, it was a community that had a dual accountability system. When we were kids, the worst thing we could do was play stick ball on the streets (that's with a little pink ball, "Spaldeen," and a broomstick) or break a window. If the police mistreated us, they were held accountable because they were a part of those support systems. If the kids on the block mistreated the police, we were held accountable because our fathers were shamed and they heard about it informally.

Much of the authority in that community came from within; it was not imposed from outside. When I took my son back there, I found a city neighborhood once alive with a sense of belonging, tradition, and roots replaced by architecturally grim, monolithic public housing projects: a new type of slum, one with little hope of culture and community, one in which gangs and violence abounded. I was sick over that. That did not have to happen. That is a tragedy.

ARTHUR J. NAPARSTEK is Director, Washington Public Affairs Center, University of Southern California, Washington, D.C.

It resulted, I believe, from the myopia of urban planners and policy-makers in New York City as well as the state and federal levels.

With my son, I visited a second neighborhood of my youth where my father had a little dry cleaning business. He came to this country in the 1930s, and opened up a store in the South Bronx. I remember the South Bronx as a neighborhood or series of neighborhoods made up of black, Puerto Rican, Irish, Jewish, and Italian families. Today it is a wasteland. In 1979 it was estimated that there were sixty fires a night in the South Bronx. Housing abandonment abounds. The area is truly a tragedy, and there are South Bronxes throughout the country.

Why did that happen? As a result of unrented housing and discrimination, decisions to disinvest from that community were made by lenders and public officials in a variety of ways. I saw it at a very personal level. The building inspectors, the fire inspectors, the health inspector would come by my father's store seeking graft because they knew there was a breakdown in accountability in that community. The garbagemen either would not take that extra step to pick up the garbage or, if they did, they banged the hell out of the cans because they did not care about the neighborhood. In 1961 my father sought a $5,000 loan to fix up the façade of the store, and the banker said that one didn't want to put money into that store because the neighborhood was deteriorating. Everybody turned their back on him.

Real estate interests, in collusion with city officials, practiced racial steering. As a consequence, one million Puerto Rican individuals and families were steered into two areas of the city—Spanish East Harlem and South Bronx. Neither community had the support systems and the socioeconomic infrastructure needed to support individual and family life for those newcomers to New York.

A third area of my youth was where my extended family lived, and that was Brooklyn Heights. I remember Brooklyn

Heights as a beautiful little community five to ten minutes from downtown New York by subway. Working-class and poor people lived there, elderly people lived there—it had support systems. Today you could not buy a brownstone in Brooklyn Heights for $250,000.

Fast-buck operators, speculators, the externalities of the marketplace took over. People in that community lost control. We now call it gentrification, a British term; in other words, the gentry moved in. More significantly, the process displaced people. This type of community exists in Washington, D.C., in San Francisco, in Los Angeles, in Chicago, in cities throughout the country. Several lessons can be drawn from this: either don't live next door to me, or something is terribly wrong with our policies. Our policies, in the words of former Governor Michael Dukakis of Massachusetts, created wastelands in the cities, slums in the suburbs, and suburbs in the rural areas.

THE ABSENCE OF A NATIONAL POLICY TO PRESERVE
NEIGHBORHOODS

The past decades have witnessed enormous suburban expansion within regions, movement toward the Sun Belt, growth in social programs and, of course, in population and the gross national product. It is my thesis that government policies have stimulated this growth at the expense of existing communities which have been undermined, both by government policies and the popularity of the Sun Belt.

We do not have a national growth policy which provides guidance to state and local officials on how best to serve the mutual self-interest of a region and substate regions, cities, small communities, and neighborhoods. Generally, reform efforts designed to improve governmental accountability get bogged down by the centralization/decentralization debate. For example, there are those who believe that government effectiveness can only be brought about through the reaggregation of political and administrative power at the metropolitan level. The other position is the opposite: that greater governmental responsiveness can be achieved through a process of disaggregating power to cities and their neighborhoods.

I am now convinced that the key choices of urban policies must be made at the metropolitan area, city, small community, and neighborhood levels, not at the national level or the more limited state levels. One of our fundamental mistakes is that policies have not focused on people. And people in most metropolitan urban areas (and I believe also rural areas) live in neighborhoods or small communities, and not cities. If the neighborhood dies, the city begins to die. Generally, people's emotional and economic investments are in their small community neighborhoods. Yet our public policies have not supported the small community neighborhood as the locus for service delivery. We have completely overlooked it. We have completely destroyed those organizational and cultural networks, those support systems, those mediating structures (or whatever we want to call them) that provide support for individual family life.

Policy-makers in Washington and in state capitals throughout the country often treat all small community neighborhoods the same. Our programs are based on assumptions of monoculturalism. Yet we know that different neighborhoods have different needs; that different people deal with crises in different ways; that Italians in Federal Hill, Providence, meet their needs differently from Polish people in South Milwaukee, or from Jews in Philadelphia; that Hispanics meet their needs differently from blacks in Detroit, who meet their needs differently from blacks in Birmingham or Green County, Alabama; and so on and so forth.

One of the most impressive attributes of American cities and neighborhoods as a whole is their diversity. They vary enormously in total population, area, density, climate, age, reliance upon public transportation, relationship to outlying suburbs, racial composition, growth rates, economic vitality, age distribution of the population, form of government, amount of housing vacancies and abandonment, crime rates, and fiscal health and stability. Because of this diversity, no single set of policies can possibly be effective in all, or even most, of the nation's large cities and neighborhoods. Yet all our policies and programs are packaged on the assumption that all people are going to deal with their problems and needs in the same kinds of ways. We have never legitimized pluralism and diversity in this country. As a result, we do not have a policy which provides us with the programmatic strength and the conceptual handle to deal with the issues of ethnicity, class, race, and geography. This is one of the reasons we have service delivery systems that in many ways are characterized by urban apartheid—service delivery for one group of people and a different and inferior system for another group of people.

In policy terms, a neighborhood is not seen in the total context but as an isolated entity. We have not made the linkage between where people live in the neighborhood or small community, the city, the state, the federal government, and the world. We know more about national and regional economies than we do about neighborhood economies.

When the flow of funds is disrupted, we can end up with disinvestment and decline. Let me be more specific. I worked in Gary, Indiana, in the late 1960s. I learned how important these linkages are between the neighborhood, the city, the state, the country, and the world. Let me be precise. I was working for the mayor I consider to be one of the best mayors in the country: Richard Hatcher. We went ahead and in 1969 obtained many millions of federal dollars; however, we did not realize how powerless we really were.

When I started working in Gary, there were 38,000 people employed at U.S. Steel; by the time I left Gary, almost 20,000 people were laid off. Decisions made in Pittsburgh and New York on the basis of what was happening in the Ruhr Valley and Japan wiped out half the work force in the

city. We started a Model Cities program, we built two neighborhood facilities, and so on. We had concentrated code enforcement, we had employment programs, and so on and
so forth. What we were doing was building those programs
in areas of the city's neighborhoods that were being red-
lined. ("Redlining" means that banks and savings and loans
do not provide credit for inner-city people.)

There was no way for those human service or economic
development programs to work. No way at all. There was
no way those employment programs could have worked.
The deals we made with the U.S. Steel workers and the rest
could not work, all because 20,000 people were laid off
from U.S. Steel. We did not make the connection. We did
not think in those terms. We did not think in terms of what
constitutes the proper preconditions for success. We did not
identify the disincentives that were structured into the system and created negative preconditions and made it impossible for anything to work.

Several years later, I worked in Toledo trying to help revitalize a small commercial strip of sixty or seventy stores in
the black and Hungarian neighborhoods of the Birmingham district of Toledo. We were able to talk the city council,
which was also the zoning board, into using $500,000 of
Community Development Block Grant Funds to create a
high-risk revolving loan fund for those stores. The council
was not making the connections between the stores, the
schools, the housing, and human services. The city council
approved the half-million dollar loan fund. We were followed by developers who asked permission to build a shopping center a mile and a half away from that commercial
strip. The city council approved it, thus bleeding the mag-
net stores off the commercial strip and into the shopping
center. I went to the city manager, the mayor, and the president of the city council immediately after that decision and
said: "Why in the world did you do that? You may have just
risked $500,000 of public money." They never made the
connection.

Later I worked in Newark, New Jersey, which also has a fine mayor: Ken Gibson. There are good community groups there, and 30 percent to 40 percent of the city is dependent upon public services. Yet, the financial arrangements between the city of Newark, the county of Essex, the state of New Jersey, and the federal government are antiquated and anachronistic, filled with disincentives that create negative preconditions. More money leaves Newark, with this dependent population, than stays in the city. As a result, property is assessed at a higher and higher level each year. Five years ago, a $60,000 house in Newark would pay a property tax of $5,000 to $6,000 per year. In Richfield, New Jersey (an all-white, no-crime, good schools neighborhood), a $60,000 house would pay only $1,500 a year in property tax. This is a distincentive that creates negative preconditions and makes it impossible for anything to work, and Ken Gibson is up against it. We were faced with it when we started to deal with the housing abandonment probem there.

In policy terms, we need to understand those government incentives which also stimulate the exodus of light industry from the cities. We have laws arising out of the tax reform act that provide incentives for light industry to move out. After they moved out, we have tried to create compensatory programs to get people back to work—after the job opportunities are lost. We need to look at that situation.

Another problem is the constant parachuting of programs into communities and neighborhoods with the "made in the statehouse" or the "made in Washington" labels. On the way to the eighth floor, while at the Department of Housing and Urban Development several months ago, there were two bureaucrats in the elevator with me. They were saying that "if you take a 202 program and tie it to 312 and you link to to Section 8, you are going to have a dynamite neighborhood revitalization program." Not once did they talk about people. Not once. Not once did they talk about the proper preconditions for melding federal subsidy

and incentive programs with local conditions. Not once did
they realize that a Section 312 housing program in the
south end of Boston, for example, will lead to gentrification
and displacement, which is what happened; or that Section
8 public housing subsidies in another part of a city could
lead to abandonment of business. We have to begin thinking in those terms.

Our policies support the parachute notion but also lead
to fragmentation, and that leads to inaccessibility and limited accountability. Rules and regulations, Title XX, community development block grants, urban development action grants, Economic Development Agency grants, and so
forth, have legal, administrative, and fiscal obstacles built
into them that make it impossible for people to gain some
control over the programs that they need.

I worked with a group of welfare mothers in Cochran
Gardens, a public housing project in St. Louis, which is con-
tiguous to the old Pruitt Igo site, that public housing project
which was blown up several years ago. These folks wanted
to get a day care center and they wanted to utilize Title XX
money because they wanted to become vendors, and they
did not want dependency. They were unable to do it because of the mess of administrative rules and regulations
they had to deal with on the state and federal levels. One
almost has to carry a lawyer around on one's back in order
to cut through that kind of red tape and legal obstacles.

We are all so very vulnerable because the funding cycles
and the evaluation cycles are so different from each of the
funding sources on the city level, the state level, and the
federal level. The amount of money that community groups
and governments spend on overhead just to keep their
books clean is unbelievable, and it takes a lot of courage on
the part of their leadership to be able to do that. We have
looked for ways in which the federal government can provide leadership, and I believe that process will not start in
Washington, it will start locally. Only then can a Title XX
program be integrated with a Section 202 housing project

(housing for the elderly). We have to look at ways in which churches and synagogues can accept Section 202 funds for housing developments. We know that, in most instances, the best Section 202 programs are those run by neighborhood-based institutions; they have the greatest degree of accountability.

How do we build partnerships? It is necessary to have a three-sector approach: the community, the public sector, and the private sector. When meeting with community groups and working in different communities around the country, I hear a lot of talk about people wanting power, people wanting this, people wanting that. I do not see that at all. People feel things are out of control; they want to get some degree of control over their lives. I hear people really saying three things. People want equity (fairness), which they determine in different ways. Objectively, they determine equity in terms of: "Is there a return on my investment?"; "I pay property taxes, am I getting services?" Or: "Is there a return on my involvement? I'm involved in the process, am I getting any kind of return?" Or: "Is my neighborhood being treated fairly compared with others that are considered to be similar to my neighborhood?" That is how people determine equity.

People want security. They want economic security, social security, and physical security. People do not want their kids to come home beaten up. They do not want to be mugged on the street. They do not want their welfare or Social Security checks stolen from their mailboxes. People want a sense of sufficiency, access to those locality-relevant neighborhood-based institutions that are supposed to be serving them. When people have a sense of equity, security, and sufficiency, they often feel somewhat empowered to deal with the problems confronting them; and that is an important kind of process. When they feel they are living under conditions of inequity, insecurity, and insufficiency, people feel alienated and will leave that neighborhood if they have the resources. If they do not leave, or cannot leave, because they do not have the resources, then they will opt out in other ways.

I also hear people saying that they want to develop partnerships with the public sector and the private sector, but they want the community sector to be part of that. It must be a partnership with parity, not a situation where one sector is power-up and the other sector is power-down. I often go to meetings where the private sector (consisting of big corporations or small businessmen) defines the problem based on data generated from market surveys, chamber of commerce reports, or consulting reports. The public sector generally defines the problem based on data from planning departments. And the community sector comes in with feelings. These meetings just blow up, and people do not talk to one another.

We have to look for a process which can lead to the devolution of authority in the public sector. By "devolution" I mean where authority comes from a higher order to a lower order, where the people closest to those citizens who receive the services have the power to make decisions and are held accountable.

Devolution of authority must occur where citizens become more involved in the decision-making processes concerned with how resources are to be spent. It is political and administrative decentralization. Simultaneously, we have to begin looking at the empowerment process from the community side. Devolution from the public sector and empowerment from the community take place simultaneously. There will be tension; but that is what democracy is all about. It is the way to bring about parity and also partnership with parity. The same is true with business. With the devolution of big corporations and the empowerment of small business we get those checks and balances.

We must stop providing grants that just create dependency. We have to think instead of catalyzing activities so that local communities can deal with their problems as they see

The Art of Humanizing a Welfare Department

THOMAS H. WALZ

Robert Pirsig, in his bestseller *Zen and the Art of Motorcycle Maintenance,*[1] contrasted two attitudes toward the upkeep of motorcycles: classicist and romantic. Classicists are people familiar with the mechanical structure and rational organization of the machine, who derive as much satisfaction from maintaining the machine as from using it. Romantics, on the other hand, feel threatened by the complexity of maintaining the machine, and see the value of motorcycles in their capacity to provide thrills and affordable transportation.

The modern welfare department, like the motorcycle, can be seen as a complex machine—based on principles of rational organization—which requires considerable maintenance for its continued functioning. The "classicists" in welfare departments are generally found among relative newcomers to the field: professional managers, planners, and systems analysts. The "romantics" are administrators with a social work orientation and humanistic outlook. Some degree of tension between these two views exists within nearly all social welfare organizations, although the advocates of "modern management" seem to have the upper hand at present.

Translating these two schools of thought into administra-

THOMAS H. WALZ is Director, Iowa Gerontology Project, University of Iowa, Iowa City.
[1] Robert Pirsig, *Zen and the Art of Motorcycle Maintenance* (New York: William Morrow & Co., 1974).

tive approaches, one may start from the proposition that the alternatives cannot be integrated, but only placed in balance. Given this assumption, one may propose that scientific management is a necessary—but not sufficient—condition for improving welfare administration.

As current trends seem to favor the classicists, it might prove fruitful to begin with a review of the principles of bureaucratic organization:[2]

1. Organizational goals are measured predominantly in terms of productivity and efficiency.

2. Organizations grow to a size that optimizes economies of scale.

3. Hierarchies of authority, with clear lines of responsibility and accountability, govern the structure of organizations.

4. Organizations depend upon authority of position; allegiance and cooperation are due to whoever holds the position.

5. Organizations are divided into specialized functional subgroups, with specialists working only within designated areas.

6. Control and decision-making are highly centralized, with specialists making rational decisions based on factual information.

7. Responsibilities are defined by job and role prescriptions, and are carried out with total objectivity.

8. Uniform policies and procedures are adopted to assure equitable and predictable application.

9. Physical environments are designed to maximize efficient production.

10. Communication is written, formal, and follows clear lines of authority.

11. Information flows upward to facilitate top-level decision-making, and downward, in the form of directives, further to rationalize bureaucratic behavior.

---

[2] For a brief summary of classical and modern organizational theory see Bengt Abrahamsson, *Bureaucracy or Participation* (Beverly Hills, Calif.: Sage Publications, 1977), pp. 85–89.

Ironically, classical organizational theory seems to be designed to cure the problem—the model—it creates. Merely choosing bureaucracy as an organizational model produces a range of costs which management is expected to minimize. In a recent article Elgin and Bushnell[3] cited sixteen problems common to large, complex organizations:

1. Diminished capacity for individuals to comprehend the entire system

2. Diminished public participation in decisions

3. Declining public access to decision-makers

4. Growing participation of experts in decisions

5. Disproportionate growth in costs of coordination and control

6. Dehumanization of interactions between people and the system

7. Increasing levels of alienation

8. Increasing challenges to basic value premises

9. Unexpected and counterintuitive consequences of policy actions

10. Increasing system rigidity

11. Increasing number and uncertainty of disturbing events

12. Narrowing span of diversity of innovation

13. Declining legitimacy of leadership

14. Increasing system vulnerability

15. Declining over-all performance of the system

16. Growing deterioration of the over-all system unlikely to be perceived by most participants in that system.

Given these problems, could we not design an organizational model to mitigate or even eliminate these costs? The organizational model that I propose is based on a theory of "inverted bureaucracy." Just as the bureaucratic model is rational and scientific, the alternative model would be humanistic and intuitive. Because human cooperation and participation are ultimately the critical values in achieving productivity, organizational theory needs to recognize the

[3] Duane S. Elgin and Robert A. Bushnell, "The Limits to Complexity: Are Bureaucracies Becoming Unmanageable?" *The Futurist*, XI (1977), 337–51.

importance of human development as a legitimate organizational goal.

What follows is an explanation of the theory of inverted bureaucracy through an exposition of the alternative principles upon which it is based. These principles are derivative of, but in direct contrast to, the bureaucratic principles.

THE PRINCIPLE OF A PRIORI HUMAN SOCIAL PURPOSES OF SOCIAL ORGANIZATION

People gather together to confirm their social nature, and this act of social interaction distinguishes the human animal. Human development through social interaction is of equal importance to any economic or material reasons for human grouping, in both formal and informal organizations.

Welfare departments, therefore, are organized for several purposes. Clearly, the production of vital items needed by society—social services and/or income-transfer payments—should be done efficiently and effectively. However, the style of administration, the attitudes and considerations made to the people who make up the system, is important to the co-product of the organization: human development. This suggests that administrative policies and procedures should optimize the quality of human experience for workers and clients while retaining reasonable concern for costs.

THE PRINCIPLE OF HUMAN SCALE

We cited sixteen problems associated with organizational size, yet the trend in welfare has been toward larger, more centralized organizational arrangements. In some instances, this may take place in order to circumvent the sometimes oppressive local administration of welfare. But more likely, larger organizations are chosen to achieve the economies of scale that motivate industrial organizations to grow and consolidate. Such factors as economic advantage or exercise of control tend to dominate the decision.

However, to facilitate human development, organizational scale must be limited.[4] Although no fixed number of people can be specified, organizations appear to become impersonal and bureaucratic when individuals do not know or cannot relate to others in the organization beyond their job role. To afford human development, considerable interaction on a personal as well as a professional level should be possible.

Accordingly, this principle suggests the descaling of welfare administration back to local and neighborhood administration, although aggregating the local experience would be necessary for some macro-planning and policy development purposes. Unfortunately, little research has been done on this question. We do know, however, that alienation and dehumanization become larger problems as the scale of welfare organizations continues to increase.

THE PRINCIPLE OF HUMAN NEED SATISFACTION

Although the importance of human development within the welfare setting can be easily acknowledged, implementing this objective organizationally is more difficult. Most administrators wish to deal humanely with their workers and clients, but few have found the secret of how this can be done within a bureaucratic context.

Ego psychologists tell us that people typically need a clear definition of personal identity, respect for their individuality, a positive self-concept, adequate love and support, some reasonable control over their own destiny, opportunity for challenge, and a sense of security.[5] The challenge for the administrator is to establish work environments and administrative processes that respond to the basic human needs of worker and client alike.

Of course, in any effort to meet basic human needs, one cannot neglect considerations of economy and efficiency. The problem is one of balance. Generally speaking, admin-

[4] E. F. Shumacher, *Small Is Beautiful* (New York: Harper & Row, 1973).
[5] Reference is made to such ego psychologists as Erich Fromm, Theodore Maslow, and Gordon Allport.

70 *Humanizing a Welfare Department*

istrative practices that acknowledge needs for individualization, positive self-concept, affection, challenge, and security need not add to administrative cost. In producing a context in which human needs may be satisfied as the work gets done, the important factors include attitudes, milieu, feelings of trust, and a solid dose of leadership.

THE PRINCIPLE OF PARTICIPATION[6]

Bureaucratic centralization produces apparent efficiencies in the decision-making process: uniform decisions, based upon complex data, may be implemented throughout the system. However, the costs of centralization may well outweigh the benefits. Centralization insures that only a small number of staff are directly involved in making decisions; to the majority fall the tasks of supplying data and enforcing decisions made from above. For most people, the creativity and responsibility of policy development are lost.

To correct this, a healthy administrative model requires broad participation in decision-making. At a minimum, those affected by a decision should have some influence upon the decision itself. The time and effort involved in this "participatory management" process should be offset by the reduction in effort necessary for "selling" the decision or enforcing the directive. Broad participation makes for responsible and accountable behavior by those who have a part in the decision-making, since such involvement reinforces a sense of identification with the institution.

The concept that all decisions can be derived from empirical data is simply not adequate. If workers and clients were authentically listened to and their opinions regularly solicited, decisions would be enriched by a depth of experience and by qualitative impressions that mere facts cannot convey. Such efforts to date, however, have been little more than window dressing.

Daniel Bell, in his seminal work on postindustrial society,

[6] See Abrahamsson, *op. cit.*, pp. 199–221 for a discussion of participatory administration.

warns that the trend toward top-down management will come into direct conflict with the growing tendency of all persons to demand participation as a right.[7] Obviously, this issue goes beyond the administration of welfare. Given the increasing complexity of American society, participation of individuals in decisions which affect their lives may become the critical issue of our age.

THE PRINCIPLE OF FUNCTIONAL GENERALIZATION AND
VERTICAL INTEGRATION

Although the bureaucratic model argues that specialization is the key to productivity and efficiency, the problems with specialization are severalfold. Persons who are given restricted work-role definitions often have limited vision concerning the relationship between their own function and the over-all purpose of the agency. Moreover, repeated performance of a particular function can increase boredom and thereby reduce efficiency.

Life itself is a matter of rhythm and change, with a core of stability and sameness, and work life is no different. Generalization means to build an understanding of a broader range of information and skills leading to comprehension of the work system as a whole.

Vertical integration means to structure organizational life so that people at various levels in the organization take some responsibility for work efforts at other levels. While a primary assignment is necessary to provide stability, the opportunity to cross over within the work hierarchy is extremely useful in building agency cohesion.

It is particularly sad in welfare administration to witness the hardening of the arteries of the personnel system, reinforced by merit system regulations and collective bargaining contracts. A caseworker dare not type a letter, even if his secretary is severely overworked, for fear of breaching a la-

[7] Daniel Bell, *The Coming of Post-industrial Society* (New York: Basic Books, 1973), pp. 162–64.

bor contract. A supervisor dare not assist on a case for similar reasons.

Simplified structures and procedures and a reduced range of programs would greatly reduce the need for much of today's specialization. We rarely reflect upon the educational costs in time associated with developing our welfare specialists—time which must be spent before the efficiencies of using specialized people pay off. And, given the high staff turnover in welfare, we can rarely collect on the desired efficiencies of the skilled specialist.

THE PRINCIPLES OF THE AUTHORITY OF MERIT AND
LEADERSHIP TURNOVER

In most bureaucracies, workers are usually evaluated by their supervisors. Yet most persons in authority have power over others only in so far as those they command choose to obey. Given this reality, it would seem proper to evaluate a person largely by the perceptions of those they purport to manage. Evaluations in this respect would become more like votes of confidence or entitlements to continue in some level of authority.

Too frequently within bureaucracies, persons arrive at positions of authority through seniority, default, or other reasons not necessarily related to merit. Once there, an incompetent person is almost impossible to dislodge. It does not seem too radical to argue that leadership should be earned both through performance and the support of those below. Both upward and downward mobility in organizational life should not only be permitted, but encouraged. Moreover, in human service organizations, it would seem imperative that supervisors and administrators be rotated to direct-service assignments as an occasional reminder of agency and client reality at the line level.

Obviously, upward mobility will be cherished as long as rewards continue to be concentrated at the top. Certainly, special rewards are necessary for those who assume the heavy responsibility of supervision and administration.

However, these responsibilities are rarely any greater in service terms than the burdens upon persons working protective services or otherwise caring for the welfare of needy people. I frankly believe we overestimate the value of the administrative level and accord it far too much power and recognition.

THE PRINCIPLE OF PRIMARY COMMUNICATION

Bureaucracies are built of paper and characterized by memo cultures. It is in the very design of a bureaucracy that communication becomes difficult. In large-scale organizations, opportunities for face-to-face communication are reduced, levels of trust drop, and memoranda become quasi-legal documents. However, the immensity of paper flow soon leads to information overkill. In self-defense, even important memos and directives are diverted into the round file.

It would seem that the whole concept of public welfare as a mutual aid system—an expression of personal concern on the part of the state for its citizens—should be characterized by primary communication. This personal level of relationship should characterize not only worker-client relationships, but also intrastaff and worker-administrator dealings as well.

In communicating we need all the information we can get. Writing simply does not convey the texture of the spoken word, which depends upon voice inflection, lip formation, and eye contact to deliver the full impact of meaning. This principle simply argues for a return to the communications basics.

THE PRINCIPLE OF DESIGN PSYCHOLOGY

Physical environments are the ego extensions of organizations. When the computer is given better quarters than the waiting areas for clients, we are being told where the department's priorities really lie.

The physical arrangements of most bureaucracies are

geared toward encouraging efficient production at minimum cost. This economy-of-scale principle is reflected in standardized furnishings with low-cost and low-maintenance requirements, frequently reflecting a single color design. The result is a flat, sterile environment which all too often reflects the dehumanizing management processes of bureaucracy.

To counter this principle would be, of course, to design the work environment to accommodate both productivity and human development. Comfortable, attractive, and personal space would not hinder production, and by reducing the stresses engendered by the sterility of the bureaucratic landscape, might actually enhance work efficiency (the so-called "Hawthorne effect").

Public budgets, of course, limit the luxury of public work environments, but low-cost or no-cost efforts may be made to humanize, personalize, and enrich our agency settings. In most cases management needs only allow what comes naturally; people are usually willing to decorate and personalize their own spaces. Personal touches on busses in Mexico and taxis in Colombia not only reflect the personalities of the chauffeurs, they also give public transit an exciting and important human face.

THE PRINCIPLE OF SUBJECTIVITY AND ITS COROLLARIES

Man is a subject, not an object. Unfettered objectivity in the administration of welfare can produce severe consequences, including procedural rigidity and a "by-the-book" approach to management.

Objectivity as a goal of bureaucratic organization was introduced as a method of curbing the government patronage system that had grown during the last half of the nineteenth century. The impersonal delivery of government services, it was felt, would help to improve equal access to those services. The development of uniform benefits and procedures has unarguably led to a reduction of controversy and human error.

Unfortunately, pure objectivity does not provide government with the flexibility to respond to unique human needs, or to develop creative solutions to novel problems. Man is objective only when he acts like a machine. Organizations based on a machine metaphor must enforce the principle of objectivity; likewise organizations based on a human metaphor require at least a degree of subjectivity.

Again we are not in an either/or situation. While some routinization of policy and procedure is essential, so is freedom to invent, expand, and individualize those policies and procedures. A manual simply cannot replace human judgment. Standard procedures should ideally be guidelines for organizational behavior, with enough flexibility to allow creative input at all levels of the organization.

THE PRINCIPLE OF THE CONVIVIAL TOOL

The final principle that belongs to the theory of inverted bureaucracy is borrowed from Ivan Illich,[8] the premier organizational analyst of our time. A convivial tool is a policy or procedure simple enough for most people to understand and use without the aid of an expert.

Although bureaucratic organizations do not intentionally seek complexity, large and highly specialized organizations cannot help but depend upon esoteric practices and language. Bureaucratic language is a vocabulary to which only the specially trained are privy. To the extent that this language is used to exclude the uninitiated from decision-making, obfuscation becomes power.

To humanize organizational life requires a fundamental simplification—a reduction in the volume of policies to a manageable number, a demystification of procedures, and a resistance to technologies controlled by an elite corps of specialists.

Welfare is a human service. Organizational models for the administration of welfare should reflect consistency be-

[8] Ivan Illich, *Tools for Conviviality* (New York: Harper & Row, 1973).

tween ends and means. To regard welfare as simply another "industry" suitable for profit-oriented management models is to defeat the unique social function of human services.

I firmly believe we have gone too far in rationalist approaches to large organizational management. The rational model works only when kept in balance with the ten principles of inverted bureaucracy I have presented.

It is only when a system is in balance that harmony can exist. With harmony, the whole may become greater than the sum of its parts.

Black Americans and Neoconservatism

THE WHITNEY M. YOUNG, JR., MEMORIAL LECTURE

ROBERT C. WEAVER

Two RECENT developments typify what is happening to black Americans. The gains that were made in the 1960s and early 1970s have been decelerated and are threatened, while the relative deprivation of the disadvantaged increases. Furthermore, a poll of registered voters in mid-February of 1980 found that only a fifth favored more government attention to blacks.[1] Benign neglect has become an attitudinal reality.

CURRENT STATUS OF BLACK AMERICANS

Since even before emancipation the progress of blacks has been measured in terms of changes over time. Obviously, this approach has some validity, but in a multiethnic and multiracial democracy, a more significant index is the relative position of groups in that society. Most black Americans accept this point of view, as do those who take seriously the announced goals of American democracy.

In discussing the status of black Americans, there is a tendency toward excessive generalization. Citing median in-

ROBERT C. WEAVER is Distinguished Professor Emeritus of Urban Affairs, Hunter College, City University of New York.
[1] These data are taken from a summary of the New York *Times*/CBS News poll as reported in the New York *Times*, February 20, 1980.

comes and unemployment rates, some affirm that blacks have made but limited economic progress and their relative status has retrogressed. Others see significant progress in the expansion of the middle class and blacks' recent access to professional and managerial jobs.

So far as incomes and unemployment are concerned, two somewhat inconsistent phenomena persist simultaneously. There has been both an absolute and a relative increase in the economic status of well-trained blacks with a decline in the status of the unskilled, poorly trained, and inexperienced, as well as of others who remain outside the mainstream. Median figures for the total black population fail to reveal this dichotomy. Moreover, although they understate somewhat the progress of the upwardly mobile, they minimize the deprivation of the masses of blacks.

For example, the number and proportion of blacks in relatively high-income managerial employment have increased significantly since the mid 1960s. But those involved and the rest of the black middle class are still a relatively small proportion. In 1977 only 9 percent of all black families had incomes above the Bureau of Labor Statistics level of $25,-200 for a "higher" standard of living, and 24 percent had incomes above $17,106, the BLS "intermediate" level. While this represented a significant historical quantitative gain, 24 percent of whites enjoyed the "higher" and 49 percent the "intermediate" standard. Moreover, the proportion of black families at the "higher" standard had declined since 1972.[2]

None of these data reveal qualitative changes. More important than the achieved positions in upper management and a few corporate directorates, a growing number of blacks serve in junior management where they are favorably positioned for upgrading. This fact is also a fundamental

[2] Robert B. Hill, "The Economic Status of Black Families," in *The State of Black America 1979* (New York: National Urban League, Inc., 1979), pp. 31–32; Sheila Rule, "Black Middle Class Called Vulnerable: Conference Says Recent Gains Are Periled by Economic Decline and Hostility of Majority," New York *Times*, March 30, 1980.

element in motivating more black youths to pursue training in business administration and related fields.

In white-collar and industrial employment, the equal opportunity executive orders and civil rights laws of the 1960s accelerated departures from the color caste patterns of employment. Those now in moderate- and lower-middle-income brackets have been the chief beneficiaries. For them, however, the impact of recession and inflation seems to be more severe than for their white prototypes.

The economic status of less affluent blacks has deteriorated even more rapidly. Between 1976 and 1977 the number of black families below the official poverty level increased by 20,000; the number of similar white families decreased by 20,000.[3]

During recent decades, the rate of joblessness among all youth has been higher than that for all other major elements in the labor market. Beginning in 1958, an increasing differential between white and black youth developed, and by 1977 official figures reported 37 percent unemployment for blacks and 14 percent for whites.[4] Many economists have long asserted that when the discouraged who have withdrawn from the labor market are included, a significantly larger proportion of black youth are jobless.

By 1970 the racial differential in unemployment among teen-agers was at least twice as large for blacks as for whites in eight large central cities. Six years later, unemployment for all teen-agers had grown appreciably. For black youths the increase was dramatic, ranging from 42 percent to 58 percent in seven of these cities. White unemployment in these cities ranged from 12 percent to 25 percent.[5]

High unemployment among youth is attributed primarily to structural changes in our economy and insufficient de-

---

[3] Hill, *op. cit.*, p. 32.

[4] *Economic Report of the President*, 1978 (Washington, D.C.: U.S. Government Printing Office, 1978), Table B-30, p. 292.

[5] *Some Facts Related to a Profile of Unemployment in New York City* (New York: U.S. Department of Labor, Bureau of Labor Statistics, 1978; mimeographed), p. 13.

mand for labor. The first involves less need for unskilled workers and a shift from blue-collar to white-collar labor. The impact of the second change is seen in the significant rise of unemployment among young men aged 16 to 19 when there is only a slight increase in unemployment among male workers aged 35 to 44. Black victims of racial discrimination are especially affected by a lessened demand for labor.[6]

As awesome as these developments are, a recent, unpublished Labor Department study found that earlier figures understated the situation. Even this alarming development was characterized as "only the most visible dimension of relative deprivation."[7] Black and Hispanic youths are consigned to lower-wage and lower-skilled jobs than whites. They must travel longer than white youths to reach the unskilled and blue-collar jobs, which are increasingly concentrated in suburbia, reflecting the relationship between residential segregation and employment opportunities. In contrast to conventional wisdom, the survey states that "the evidence suggests that the majority of these young people are not unsuccessful because of inflated expectations."[8]

THE PHILOSOPHY OF THE NEOCONSERVATIVES

In light of the true status of black Americans, how can one account for the retreat from support of government action to alleviate the deprivation of disadvantaged blacks and to accelerate the upward mobility of all blacks?

It is obvious that the nation is in a conservative mood. This attitude, while in part responsive to institutional, political, economic, and social developments, is not self-generating. The rationale for conservatism has long been articulated in this country. Its champions have not hesitated to proclaim their philosophy, refusing to compromise intellec-

[6] Leonard Silk, "Unemployment Among the Young," New York *Times,* November 28, 1980.

[7] Philip Shabecoff, "U.S. Study Finds Big Jobless Rate in Youth Ranks," New York *Times,* February 29, 1980.

[8] *Ibid.*

tually with what they consider the errors and dangers of radicalism or the misdirected sentimentality of liberalism. In recent decades, a new political and economic outlook has emerged, voiced by intellectuals, many of whom were formerly liberals and/or socialists. They speak and write from the prestigious universities, their work appears in magazines read by intellectuals and opinion-makers, and they are among the editorial writers of the better daily newspapers. Increasingly, they influence public officials. Their philosophy is appealing in a generally affluent society harassed by inflation. Their sophisticated prose attracts many who might be repelled by the conventional conservative appeal.[9]

We are inundated by assertions about the inefficiency and ineffectualness of public action, used to justify greater, if not almost complete reliance upon the market to allocate resources. And the argument seems in part credible, because of the forensic skills and literary capabilities of its new set of proponents. Seldom do they crassly reject concern for the disadvantaged; rather they delineate the limitations of reform, the alleged inherent defects of governmental efforts, and the asserted rapidly declining deprivation in American society. Nowhere is this more apparent than in their treatment of poverty:

Many people who in writing about poverty want to prove that it is limited and requires no further Federal action have confused the number of the poor and how they live. Their incomplete analyses have added to public misunderstanding and inhibited development of sound legislation and public policy.[10]

In reality, cash-transfer programs, such as Social Security and Supplementary Security Income, have reduced the growth of poverty, thereby achieving their intended purpose of allowing millions of persons to maintain decent living standards. The impact of these programs, however, has been offset by a paucity of job opportunities which provide

[9] Peter Steinfels, *The Neoconservatives: the Men Who Are Changing American Politics* (New York: Simon and Schuster, 1979), p. 74.
[10] Woodrow Ginsburg, "Still Poor," New York *Times*, January 14, 1980.

adequate income. At the same time, food stamps and other in-kind benefits are not adequate substitutes for sufficient cash income to afford the freedom of choice which the champions of the market never cease to stress. Finally, the poverty index, like the index of unemployment, has many serious deficiencies. Recent research has established that both underestimate the incidence of the phenomenon they are designed to measure.

Similarly, public approaches designed to reduce unequal treatment of minorities and women are criticized as going too far, and the prevalence of discrimination is minimized. Indeed, it is asserted that by the close of the 1960s discrimination was no longer a major barrier to employment and that blacks were making significant gains before affirmative action programs were launched. Observing that both race and class are involved in determining the status of blacks, some of the neoconservatives accentuate the impact of class, while ignoring that lack of upward mobility is primarily a racial phenomenon. In this context there is an attack upon affirmative action. Open admission in higher education, regardless of how it is accomplished, is identified as reverse discrimination and unnecessary.

It is repeatedly affirmed that the Great Society was a failure and its programs flawed. This, of course, was the position of the Nixon administration and found support among some former liberals, many of whom had established reputations in the social sciences and were to join the ranks of the neoconservatives. The combination of the new administration's repudiation and some social scientists' collaboration rendered this position conventional wisdom in a growing segment of society. Even as this occurred, equally qualified researchers challenged the evaluations of the neoconservatives. In one appraisal of the Great Society, appearing in a journal edited by Irving Kristol and Nathan Glazer, high priests of the neoconservatives, Eli Ginsberg and Robert Solow concluded in 1974:

There is nothing in the history of the 1960's to suggest that it is a law of nature that social legislation cannot deal effectively with social problems, or that state and local governments or private enterprise will always do a better job than the "Feds." We can find no support for such sweeping generalizations.[11]

More recently, others, notably Sar A. Levitan and Robert Taggart, have reviewed a series of Great Society programs and challenged the opinions that they were failures. They assert that this erroneous conclusion "continues to hold sway over decision makers and the public, generating a timidity and negativism which has retarded needed and possible progress."[12] Defenders of the Great Society recognized its weaknesses, and many accepted the adverse impact of its inflated rhetoric. But many who repudiated the effort resorted to inflated rhetoric when they spoke of throwing money at problems while also proposing to throw federal money to state and local governments and thereby avoid difficult domestic issues.

The weaknesses in conservatives' and neoconservatives' broadside attack upon public action to achieve social goals are well demonstrated in the area of subsidized housing. The Housing Act of 1968, Section 236, authorized a program designed to expand greatly lower-income rental housing. In January, 1973, the Nixon administration declared a moratorium on all subsidized housing, with special reference to Section 236. The administration was soon joined by the detractors of the Great Society in asserting that the programs were ill-designed and ineffective.

In October, 1973, Henry J. Aaron, writer of an authoritative study of housing subsidies who earlier pointed out some of the defects in Section 236, said this before the Housing Subcommittee of the House of Representatives:

[11] Eli Ginsberg and Robert M. Solow, "Some Lessons of the 1960's," *Public Interest,* Winter, 1974, p. 212.

[12] Sar A. Levitan and Robert Taggart, *The Promise of Greatness* (Cambridge, Mass.: Harvard University Press, 1976), p. viii.

It is important for the critics to acknowledge that existing programs [of housing subsidies] have provided high quality of housing for more than two million low and moderate income families who would otherwise have paid far more for worse housing, that they have mobilized a most extraordinary coalition in behalf of the poorly housed, ranging from the National Association of Homebuilders through organized labor to the National Welfare organizations, and that they are capable of bringing benefits of life in new communities to many who would be too poor or too dark otherwise to gain access. Whatever the flaws of these programs, their authors can take pride in their positive accomplishments.[13]

And these accomplishments were noteworthy in light of the Nixon administration's operation of the programs. The agency administering them, the Federal Housing Administration (FHA), was decimated as the Department of Housing and Urban Development (HUD) was reorganized annually from 1969 through 1972. According to the Civil Service Commission, there were many violations of the merit system in HUD's appointments, often involving replacement of qualified personnel by incompetent and inexperienced officials to handle complicated programs.[14] Despite these impediments, the document HUD issued nine months after the moratorium in an attempt to justify it stated that minority families were served by the programs to a considerably greater degree as a percentage of the total number of eligibles than other low- and moderate-income families. Anthony Downs suggested that this planned achievement became a basis for stopping the effort.[15]

A most impressive evaluation of Section 236, both because of its access to extensive official data and the time of execution (almost a decade after the program's enactment), is that made by the General Accounting Office (GAO), dated January, 1978. This analysis, like others, found administrative weaknesses in the program. However, it char-

---

[13] Henry J. Aaron, *Hearing of the Subcommittee on Housing of the Committee on Banking and Currency of the House of Representatives*, 90th Cong., 2d Sess., 1968, p. 789.

[14] *Housing and Development Reporter*, March 20, 1974, p. B-1.

[15] Anthony Downs, "The Successes and Failures of Federal Housing Policy," *Public Interest*, Winter, 1974, p. 138.

acterized Section 236 as "the foremost example of Government assistance for privately developed rental housing," adding that it "was intended primarily to serve moderate income tenants, and it does. . . . The program provides good quality multifamily housing."[16] The report noted that defaults and mortgage failures were cited by HUD as the major reason for suspension of Section 236. At the time of the moratorium, its failure rate was no greater than that of the nonsubsidized middle- and upper-income FHA rental program, which was excluded from the moratorium. In addition, the GAO reported that between 1970 and late 1974 Section 236 produced nearly a quarter of a million lower-cost rental units—more than half the new rental units produced in this price range. When combined with public housing and rent supplements, it produced 82 percent of the low- and moderate-income rental units during the same period. Failures in the program were attributed principally to problems during construction, inexperienced and underfinanced nonprofit sponsors, underestimated operating and utility costs, inadequate rent schedules, and inadequate monitoring by HUD.[17]

Involving innovative approaches, it was inevitable that the Great Society could not fulfill all its lavish promises. But many of its components, despite some defects, demonstrated that public action was effective in dealing with social problems. Model Cities, despite Congressional conversion from a demonstration to an operative program with woefully inadequate funding, showed how a federal program could successfully target assistance to poor and minority groups in central cities. It provided performance standards

[16] General Accounting Office, *Section 236 Rental Housing—an Evaluation with Lessons for the Future* (Washington, D.C.: General Accounting Office, 1978), pp. 1, 4, 5. More recent evaluations of Section 236 fail to recognize that it was designed as a moderate-income housing program rather than one targeted at reaching the severely disadvantaged or hard-to-house population. "Are Housing Allowances Effective?" *Research Report from MIT-Harvard Joint Center for Urban Studies*, No. 21 (1980), p. 5.

[17] *Section 236 Rental Housing—an Evaluation with Lessons for the Future*, pp. 7, 13 *et seq.*

for citizen participation without destroying the role of the mayors.

The war on poverty was somewhat of a misnomer from the start. It was never adequately funded and it could not compete for funds with a war in Asia. But, like Model Cities, it did much to energize ghetto residents for political action. Head Start was characterized as a "bust." Yet current studies at Cornell University are finding that teen-agers who participated in the program had much less need of remedial work, were less likely to drop out of school, and encountered fewer problems with the law than those of similar backgrounds who had not attended Head Start.[18]

A more accurate appraisal of recent actions to ameliorate social problems would permit society to profit from past experiences and upgrade present and future activities. Most important, it would repudiate the neoconservatives' assertion of the helplessness of public programs to deal with social issues.

Such an approach is a virtual "cop-out," and a dangerous one at that since it has great appeal in our society, where it is fiscally attractive and assuages the consciences of those who otherwise might be troubled by deprivation amid widespread well-being. It is so appealing, so escapist, and so opportunistic that it may well encourage glorification of the "good old days" when government paid little attention to the nation's poor and the victims of discrimination.

OVERRELIANCE UPON THE MARKET TO ALLOCATE RESOURCES

Another consequence of the denial of the effectiveness of public action is an unrealistic reliance upon the market, particularly as the instrument for allocation of resources. This is perhaps the most crucial issue raised by the neoconser-

[18] Saul Kapel, "It Really Was a Head Start for Poverty Kids of the '60's," New York *Daily News*, January 31, 1980.

vatives. It is an appealing economic rationale for the notion that the least government is the best government.

Proponents of complete or almost complete reliance upon the market stress the consumer's access to information and his breadth of choice. Much that is said about this has substance, if a bit exaggerated. Surely, however, the consumer often is not well-informed; witness the need to recall faulty automobiles and the barring of widely sold drugs proved to be dangerous. In our society, where the commercialized sector is ever expanding, individual preferences are often either unavailable or priced beyond one's reach.

Democracy is said to be a system in which those who decide, decide for others. As pointed out, this also occurs in the private sector. Those who pay for community goods are said to be ignorant of their burdens; but, as Proposition 13 in California demonstrates, they are learning even if, in part, they are misdirected in terms of ultimate economic and social impact.[19] They also are becoming increasingly conscious of the magnitude of transfer payments and rightfully concerned with the efficacy of public spending.

The neoconservatives, like the conservatives, create the impression that we have an almost flawless market and public bureaucrats incapable of serving national interests. This I challenge, while agreeing that there is need for restraint and selectivity in, as well as constant analysis of, public intervention in the allocation of resources.

Neoconservatives make repeated references to the excesses and dangers of unrestrained political action, especially in public allocation of resources. This appears to be one of the consequences of the absence of a social norm of behavior which leads to informal social controls and restraint. John Rawls holds the "intuitively" acceptable view

[19] Wallace Turner, "San Francisco Feels Impact of Tax Cuts: Like Other Communities in State, City Is in Financial Bind as a Result of Proposition 13," New York *Times,* March 9, 1980; see also John Herbers, "Experts Expect Budget Cuts to Hit Prosperous as Well as Poorer Cities," New York *Times,* March 30, 1980.

that individuals can be expected to restrain the exercise of their individual powers in the interest of protecting the fabric of their society if, but only if, they believe the society as a whole to be just.[20]

Another weakness of the neoconservatives and conservatives is their cavalier treatment of equity. The practical consequences of this neglect are all too apparent. Mass unemployment is socially less depleting than class unemployment. The continuing poverty among minorities and especially among black youth in a generally affluent society is an explosive situation, threatening our economic, social, and political system. Youths are inclined to be turbulent, and they and many others who share their poverty, joblessness, and lack of legitimate opportunities are prone to enter the street life of crime. Alienated from society, both have little or no vested interest in it or its economic and political institutions.

A cardinal and pervasive issue in a mixed economy is how much reliance should be placed upon the market to achieve economic as well as social objectives. Once public services and welfare become a significantly increasing part of consumption, there is a corresponding tendency to minimize the differences between the functions of the private and public sectors. Over a decade ago Norton E. Long wrote:

Consumership becomes the synonym for citizenship and all problems are solved by the workings of the political analogue of the market. This reduction of politics to economics has an escapist attraction. But it won't work. Even the democracy of the buck requires political action to insure the freedom of the market from noneconomic discrimination.[21]

For example, to assume a free and competitive market in a situation of *de facto* widespread residential segregation is to assure such market-approved discrimination.

[20] John Rawls, *A Theory of Justice* (Cambridge, Mass.: Harvard University Press, 1971). The term "intuitively" is appropriated, as other parts of my analysis, from Fred Hirsch, *Social Limits to Growth* (Cambridge, Mass.: Harvard University Press, 1976).

[21] Norton E. Long, "Local Government and Renewal Policy," in James Q. Wilson, ed., *Urban Renewal: the Record and the Controversy* (Cambridge, Mass.: M.I.T. Press, 1966), p. 433.

There are, obviously, many problems and potential dangers related to public allocation of resources, although much neoconservative literature exaggerates them. One of the most pronounced fallacies is that of viewing political and bureaucratic activity as the same as market activity and considering both as means to private ends. In such a context, political and bureaucratic activity tends to be inherently inefficient. The proponents of this approach then conclude that political action should be minimized. But in our society dedication to efficiency at the cost of crass inequality, injustice, and social turmoil raises the question of the desirability of sacrificing a certain amount of efficiency for greater equality. One can have a dedication to efficiency, deplore waste, and also recognize that a concern for efficiency alone is an inadequate and, at times, a dangerous criterion for economic and social action.

Existing limitations of the market do not dictate neglect or abandonment of it as a major instrument of resource allocation to meet the needs of the individual. There is, however, a tyranny of small decisions involved. And the market has its bias: to cater to those particular demands that are amenable to commercialization. This, in turn, limits what is made available to those goods and services that the market is technically suited to provide.[22] If what people want is not in this category, it does not become available, thereby often retarding rather than advancing social objectives and suggesting the need for public intervention. In deciding where such intervention should be targeted and how it should be designed, efficiency, obviously, is an important criterion.

Neoclassical economics is an unreliable base upon which to determine public policy. Leonard Silk, an economic columnist of the New York *Times,* has told us why:

Conventional economists, through most of the past century, have concentrated too narrowly on increasing the efficiency and growth of production, while paying too little attention to the distribution of wealth and income, or to the still wider issue of social

[22] Hirsch, *op. cit.*

justice. They have assumed that efficiency was the obvious (or implicit) objective of their discipline, but that the study of social and economic justice was beyond the reach of "economic science." The economists, with rare exceptions, treated equality and inequality, justice and injustice, as matters for . . . [others], but not for themselves qua economists.[23]

Economic freedom can be defined as the right of individuals or businesses to act autonomously, generally free of governmental constraints and direction. Most economists devoted to *laissez-faire* as well as libertarians as a whole consider economic freedom as a necessary condition for all freedom. Silk, however, aptly affirms that economic freedom and social justice are really quite different values.[24]

There is a role for the market and for public action in the allocation of resources. With competition and fairly equal bargaining power, the market performs well. Indeed, far more efficiently than public actions.

On the other hand, many public goods and services are not provided by the market. But in contemporary society many of these have great human and social significance, although not all can be made available. It is specious, however, to assert rather arbitrarily that all or almost all types of goods and services can be supplied by the market, to apply its standards of performance to goods and services it was never designed to produce, and then decide that what can be provided with a reasonable degree of efficiency should not be made available. This not only flies in the face of political reality but retreats from a concern for greater equality and justice, thereby weakening the fabric of society.

The artful advocacy of the neoconservatives has done much to popularize exaggeration of the progress that blacks have made, acceptance of the concept that public action to deal with social and economic issues is futile, and unrealistic reliance upon the market. These concepts are the major ra-

---

[23] Leonard Silk, *The Economists* (New York: Basic Books, 1976), p. 253.
[24] *Ibid.*, p. 264.

tionale for the rise of what Vernon Jordan describes in these words:

In the 1960's there was a general consensus shared by whites and blacks alike, that an activist government should achieve full employment, reverse the effects of discrimination, and revitalize the cities. Today that consensus has been shattered. In its place we see the formation of a New Negativism in America that calls for a weak, passive government; indifference to the plight of the poor; abandonment of affirmative action, and letting the cities twist slowly, slowly in the wind.

. . . Race is central to the rising support of the New Negativism. People are not merely saying "No" to high taxes and inflation, they are saying "No" to inclusion of Black and Brown people into the mainstream.[25]

The late Arthur Okun struggled in the last years of his life to reconcile the liberal tradition with the harsh realities inflicted by inflation. He refused to accept recession as the cure. Rather, Okun asserted that there needs to be a balance between equality and efficiency. "He knew there was no remedy in reckless inequality to improve efficiency or in massive inefficiency to enhance equality."[26]

The economic future of black Americans will be determined largely in the context of the controversy over the issue of the balance between equality and efficiency. Because of this, those who influence the attitudes and policies relevant to the balance and related issues have a profound impact upon blacks.

[25] Vernon E. Jordan, Jr., address at the Annual Meeting of the National Conference of Catholic Charities, Kansas City, Mo., 1979, p. 3.

[26] "Arthur Okun's Challenge," New York *Times,* March 25, 1980, p. 18; see also Richard F. Janssen, "Art Okun: the Economist as Philosopher," *Wall Street Journal,* March 26, 1980, p. 22.

Social Work, Caring, and Human Resource Development

BURTON GUMMER

T HE BEGINNING of a decade is an ideal time for taking stock. It sets the mood for looking over what one has been able (or unable) to accomplish in the preceding ten years, what one's current situation is, and what the prospects for the future look like. As with people, no less with a profession such as social work, the beginning of a decade is a propitious time for looking backward, inward, and forward. Aside from its symbolic appeal, there are pressing practical concerns which necessitate this kind of assessment at this time. The profession is beset by a variety of pressures and strains which, if not dealt with effectively, can undermine our capacity to maintain any role (let alone a significant one) in the conduct of America's social welfare institutions.

The most striking development in social welfare since 1950 is the tremendous growth in its size and scope. In 1950 a total of $12.7 billion was spent by all governments, federal, state, and local, for social welfare (excluding health and education); by 1975 this figure had risen to $177.4 billion, an increase of nearly 1300 percent.[1] In 1950 there were 75,500 people employed in social welfare; by 1970 this figure had risen to 217,000, and the current number is nearly half a million.[2] In 1950 there were about 12,000 peo-

BURTON GUMMER is Associate Professor, School of Social Welfare, State University of New York at Albany.

[1] Alfred M. Skolnick and Sophie R. Dales, "Social Welfare Expenditures, 1950–1975," *Social Security Bulletin*, XXXIX, No. 1 (1976), Table 10, p. 9.

[2] Sheldon Siegel, *Social Service Manpower Needs: an Overview to 1980* (New York: Council on Social Work Education, 1975), pp. 5, 12–16.

ple with an MSW degree working in the social services; current estimates put that figure at around 100,000. While it is increasingly clear that this rate of growth will not continue into the 1980s, even with serious cutbacks in current and projected spending, the welfare system will still be enormous compared to twenty-five years ago, and concerns with its proper management and operation will continue to mount. There appear to be long-term trends in social welfare which can be expected to persist even if current expenditure levels stabilize or continue to grow.

FEDERALIZATION

Since the 1930s the role of the federal government in social welfare has steadily expanded, with 1966 being the watershed year when, for the first time, the federal share of public social welfare expenditures exceeded that of state and local governments. By 1975 the federal government was providing 58 percent of the total public expenditures for all social welfare (excluding health and education). It is safe to say that the federal government is in the welfare field to stay. Our welfare state may be a "reluctant" one in terms of the political rhetoric surrounding it, but it is nonetheless real, accounting for over half of the expenditures in the federal budget.[3]

The federal role in welfare has, until recently, been primarily a fiscal one, with the actual operation of social welfare services left to the states, the localities, and the voluntary sector.[4] While this is still generally the case, there is a definite trend toward more and more federal involvement in the operation of social welfare programs at the local level. This is occurring in two ways: a tightening of federal guidelines for, and monitoring of, grants to the states (in the social services this occurs primarily through Title XX of

[3] Skolnick and Dales, *op. cit.*, p. 4.
[4] Bruce L. R. Smith, "Accountability and Independence in the Contract State," in Bruce L. R. Smith and D. C. Hague, eds., *The Dilemma of Accountability in Modern Government: Independence versus Control* (London: Macmillan, 1971), pp. 3–69.

the Social Security Act); and the assumption of direct administrative responsibility for the cash-benefit programs in public assistance. While Title XX still reflects the delicate balancing act that traditionally takes place between the federal and state governments in regard to the amount of fiscal and program control to be delegated to the states, the trend over the past decades has been decidedly in the direction of greater federal control.[5]

With the introduction of Supplemental Security Income in 1974, a process was begun of transferring administrative responsibility for the public assistance program to the Social Security Administration, culminating in 1977 with the elimination of the Social and Rehabilitative Services (the federal "welfare agency") when the last and largest of the public assistance programs, Aid to Families with Dependent Children (AFDC), was transferred to Social Security. We can expect to see increased administrative consolidation of the social insurance and social assistance programs in the future, with important implications for human resource development and deployment in these areas.

One probable consequence of this transfer of administrative responsibility will be, as Terrence Smith argues, the ascendance of the program and administrative philosophy of the Social Security Administration (SSA) and the continued diminution of the influence of professional social workers in the operation of the cash-assistance programs. He argues that because of its size, power, and influence, the Social Security Administration will be able to "exert pressure on Federal and State AFDC staff to conform to its own tradition, values, and mode of operation."[6] The approach of the SSA,

[5] Martha Derthick, *The Influence of Federal Grants: Public Assistance in Massachusetts* (Cambridge, Mass.: Harvard University Press, 1970); Martha Derthick, *Uncontrollable Spending for Social Services Grants* (Washington, D.C.: Brookings Institution, 1975).

[6] Terrence P. Smith, "Planning for Public Welfare Manpower: Shifts/Effects on People and Practice" (paper presented at the Northeast Regional Conference of the American Public Welfare Association, Newport, R.I., 1978), p. 9; see also Thomas H. Walz and Harry J. Macy, "The MSW and the MPA: Confrontation of Two Professions in Public Welfare," *Journal of Sociology and Social Welfare*, V, No. 1 (1978), 100–17.

moreover, is predicated on the Weberian model of a rational bureaucratic structure, with emphasis on standardized, routine procedures, impersonal treatment of clients, reduction or elimination of discretionary decision-making at lower administrative levels, and loyalty to one's office and department. This will result, Smith contends, in the creation of an organizational climate in cash-assistance programs that is inimical to the traditional social work orientation which stresses a humanitarian and empathetic concern for the client, emphasis on professional judgment, discretion at the service level, advocacy on behalf of the client, and an inherent strain between the worker and the organization.[7]

The experience of the past few years in the staffing of public welfare programs, both cash and services, has, in fact, been one of reductions in social work educational requirements for line positions. Even at supervisory levels, long the domain of the professional social worker in public welfare, there is evidence of an increased demand for management skills. In a recent study of the hiring preferences of county welfare directors, Rino Patti and Ronald Rauch presented the directors with three profiles of the "ideal" type of job applicants: "locals" with extensive agency experience but without formal training in social work; "professional practitioners" with extensive experience and training in direct-service technologies; and "administrative specialists" whose major qualification was formal and specialized training in administration.[8] When asked who would be their first choice for a line supervisory position, almost as many directors indicated the administrative specialist as their first choice (29.7 percent) as did those directors who preferred locals (35.5 percent) or professional practitioners (34.8 percent).[9] Further support for the increased emphasis on man-

---

[7] Smith, *op. cit.*, pp. 11–14; see also Michael Sosin, "Social Welfare and Organizational Society," *Social Service Review*, LIII (1979), 392–405.

[8] Rino Patti and Ronald Rauch, "Social Work Administration Graduates in the Job Market: an Analysis of Managers' Hiring Preferences," *Social Service Review*, LII (1978), 569–70.

[9] *Ibid.*, Table 2, p. 572.

agerial skills in social welfare practice is found in a survey of the job experiences of one school's MSW graduates during 1971–76 conducted by David Sherwood and Michael Daley. They found that "first jobs typically involved a fair amount of direct service or administrative support. . . . There soon developed a clear pattern involving a shift into administrative support and administration."[10]

While the role of the manager has continued to grow in the public welfare sector, particularly in the cash programs, the schools of social work have failed to keep up with this development. From 1968 to 1975 there was a 42 percent increase in the total number of graduate social work students, but the average number of students majoring in administration increased only 1.5 percent between 1968 and 1971 and only 3 percent between 1972 and 1975.[11] There are important technical and ideological dimensions to this problem, notably the relative lack of expertise in management subjects among social work faculties, and the opposition of many to what is perceived as the inherent social and political conservatism of managerial functions. However, another factor seems to go much deeper and, in the long run, may prove a real obstacle to social work's large-scale involvement in the preparation of administrators for social welfare. It may well be that the work and professional ethos surrounding administration may be essentially antithetical to the work and professional ethos that most people entering social work value.

The art and science of administration clearly have their roots in the efforts to rationalize the operations of big organizations, whether public or private, for profit or nonprofit. From the efficiency studies of Frederick Winslow Taylor to the decision theories of management's first Nobel

[10] David A. Sherwood and Michael R. Daley, "Curriculum Directions for an Upgraded MSW: Administration for Everyone?" *Journal of Education for Social Work*, XV, No. 2 (1979), 65–71.

[11] Bernard Neugeboren, "Barriers to Education in Social Work Administration" (paper presented at the Annual Program Meeting of the Council on Social Work Education, Phoenix, 1977), p. 3.

Laureate, Herbert Simon, the management professions have taken as their primary assignment the application of rational models of choice and structure to modern organizations. The kinds of personal characteristics most valued in this work, moreover, derive from what is needed to pursue rational behavior. Specifically, managers are expected to be instrumental and calculative in their interpersonal relationships, to emphasize cost factors in decision-making, to concentrate on goal attainment and outcomes, and to exhibit loyalty to the organizations for which they work.

The roots of professional social work, on the other hand, are found in the efforts of an industrial and commercial society to care for those harmed or victimized by the very processes of industrialization and commercialization. From the first professional prescriptions of Mary Richmond to the latest position papers of the National Association of Social Workers, the social work profession has taken as its primary assignment the provision of care to the dependent, deprived, debilitated, and demoralized citizens of American society. As such, the personal characteristics most valued in this work are those of authenticity and empathy in interpersonal relationships, concern with the qualitative aspects of decisions about human needs and services for meeting them, emphasis on process and treatment, and the willingness to advocate on behalf of one's client, even with one's employing organization.[12] The strains that Smith sees developing between the SSA and the professional social worker may be the prototype of a growing conflict between the profession and public welfare in general.

The federalization of a large segment of the social welfare system presents a major challenge to the social work profession in terms of its ability to adapt its training and educational capabilities to respond to a rapidly shifting en-

---

[12] For a thoughtful discussion of the differences between clinical and managerial orientations to social services, see Rino Patti and Michael Austin, "Socializing the Direct Service Practitioner in the Ways of Supervisory Management," *Administration in Social Work*, I (1977), 267–80.

vironment. There are some indicators of imaginative and creative responses from the profession, particularly in the burgeoning area of continuing education. The work of Patti and his colleagues, for example, on what is involved in enabling clinically trained social workers to make the transition to supervisory and administrative positions is an example of one such attempt to develop ways for the profession to respond to changes in the welfare system.[13] If preparation for managerial careers in social welfare by social work is to move beyond its present token status, the policy recommendations coming out of this and similar studies will have to find their way into the accrediting and credentialing criteria of the professional associations of social work. The next decade will be a critical one in this respect. Without aggressive action on the part of the profession, its influence in a major segment of social welfare will continue to wane.

INCREASING RESIDUALISM OF PUBLIC SOCIAL SERVICES

Richard Titmuss once observed that "separate state systems for the poor, operating in the context of powerful private welfare markets, tend to become poor standard systems."[14] In short, services for the poor become poor services. The American public welfare system is almost exclusively a system for the poor, or a residual system. There are some who argue that there are signs of a move toward a more universal system of services since some publicly financed services are now available to individuals in middle-income brackets.[15] The evidence, however, lends support to the opposite prediction for future developments. That is, the public social services, and those services provided through vol-

[13]Rino Patti et al., "From Direct Service to Administration: a Study of Social Workers' Transitions from Clinical to Management Roles—Analysis and Recommendations," *Administration in Social Work*, III (1979), 131–51, 265–75.

[14]Richard Titmuss, "Choice and the Welfare State," *Commitment to Welfare* (New York: Pantheon Books, 1968), p. 143.

[15]Neil Gilbert, "The Transformation of Social Services," *Social Service Review*, LI (1977), 624–41.

untary agencies but publicly funded in most part, are becoming more, not less, residual as their clienteles become, relative to the rest of the population, poorer, more chronically ill, more deviant, and, in general, more marginal to mainstream developments in the society.

There is now a fairly substantial body of research and analysis supporting the argument that there are two welfare systems in the United States, divided along economic, ethnic, and racial lines, with the public sector assuming major, if not exclusive, responsibility for the poor and nonwhite.[16] Moreover, not only are clients of public agencies poor, they are beset with more social, health, economic, and psychological problems, their problems are more intractable and chronic, and their over-all life chances considerably less sanguine than those of the nonpoor. The implications for the kinds of services that public agencies need to provide, and who will provide them, are critical for the social work profession.

Specifically, we can expect increased pressures for services that are directly related to meeting the immediate consumption needs of the dispossessed. While this is readily apparent in programs such as public assistance where there has been, at least since the mid-1960s, a marked skepticism about "talking cures" in general, these pressures are now making themselves felt in other areas. Community mental health centers, for instance, are experiencing a marked change in clientele as they have to deal with the growing number of deinstitutionalized patients. The service needs of this group, moreover, lend themselves more to community organization and case management skills than they do to the traditional therapeutic training of most professionals in mental health. The problem of worker "burnout," long considered an occupational hazard unique to public assistance

[16] A recent review of the major studies in this area, along with new data on the extent to which the poor and nonwhite are overrepresented in all kinds of institutional facilities, is presented in Murray Gruber, "Inequality in the Social Services," *Social Service Review*, LIV (1980), 59–75.

and child protection, is now being discussed in the well-appointed offices of some of our better clinics.

Not only are agencies experiencing demographic shifts in the nature of their clientele, the nature of the relationship between social agency and client has altered significantly in the past fifteen years as a result of what Mayer Zald terms "the politics of rights":

The politics of rights is made possible or facilitated by the growth of organizations and groups devoted to the advocacy of the rights of the dispossessed. . . . Sometimes drawing upon people closely linked to the group at risk . . . at other times drawing upon individuals and organizations with less clear "interests" . . . these organizations take as their mandate the use of the courts, the media, and the legislature to raise the quality and quantity of goods and services allocated to their client population.[17]

The organization of clients into politically and administratively effective advocacy groups may have an impact on professional social work more important than federalization since this gets at the heart of professionalism itself. That is, these groups present a challenge to the ultimate authority of the professional to have the final word concerning the definition of the problem confronting the client and what should be done about it.

If the trends toward more advocacy on behalf of, and by, clients continue, we can expect marked changes in the relationship between service providers and consumers. These changes, moreover, will probably move in directions that range from the muting of some of the more authoritarian aspects of professional-client interactions to the aggressive deprofessionalization of entire sectors of service.[18] What form the changes will take in a particular field will depend

[17] Mayer N. Zald, "Trends in Policy Making and Implementation in the Welfare State: a Preliminary Statement" (rev. version of a paper presented at Conference on Human Service Organizations and Organizational Theory, Center for Advanced Study in the Behavioral Sciences, Palo Alto, Calif., 1979), p. 13.

[18] See Donald Feldstein, "Do We Need Professions in Our Society? Professionalization versus Consumerism," *Social Work*, XVI, No. 4 (1971), 5–11; Willard Gaylin et al., *Doing Good: the Limits of Benevolence* (New York: Pantheon Books, 1978).

on the organizational and political strength of a professional group and their ability to resist challenges to their prerogatives and perquisites. Given the importance that professionalization has had for the development of social work since the turn of this century, threats to its professional status will not be taken lightly. There is already evidence indicating that professional social workers, given the choice, prefer to practice with clients and in organizations that enhance rather than detract from their status as professionals. In a recent survey of the employment characteristics of professional social workers, David Hardcastle and Arthur Katz found that only 2 percent of those in their sample reported working in the area of "poverty and its elimination."[19] They also found that "private practice and practice in the profit sector appear to be proportionately on the rise."[20]

IMPLICATIONS FOR SOCIAL WORK

Émile Durkheim once remarked that "the categorical imperative of the moral conscience is assuming the following form: *Make yourself fulfill a determinate function.*"[21] This is sound advice for both individuals and professions, and the present challenge to social work is to identify clearly the functions it can usefully fulfill. When one surveys the current status of social work practice, it seems as if we are a long way from heeding this advice. Carol Meyer describes the state of that practice as

a mélange of practice approaches, theories, and models. . . . Schools of social work educate students in accordance with the idiosyncratic interests of their faculties; students learn one model of practice and not others; professional communities often prefer

---

[19] David Hardcastle and Arthur Katz, *Employment and Unemployment in Social Work: a Study of NASW Members* (Washington, D.C.: National Association of Social Workers, Inc., 1979), p. 43; see also Elizabeth Howe, "Public Professions and the Private Model of Professionalism," *Social Work*, XXV (1980), 179–91.

[20] Hardcastle and Katz, *op. cit.*, pp. 44–45.

[21] Émile Durkheim, *The Division of Labor in Society*, tr. George Simpson (New York: Macmillan, 1933), p. 43, emphasis in original.

to train students for particular agency practices; and MSW graduates cannot distinguish themselves from BSWs in regard to what
they actually do. Public and voluntary agencies are out of step
with each other, to say nothing of their relationship to private
practice. Clinical practice is being defined variously as psycho-
therapy, mental health work, private practice, psychoanalytically
based practice, work in clinics, MSW as opposed to BSW practice,
or practice as opposed to policy analysis. This is social work practice in 1979.[22]

This "organized anarchy," if allowed to continue, will seriously undermine social work's ability to represent itself as
a profession that can successfully fulfill a needed and defined function. Major efforts will have to be taken to develop agreement within the profession about priorities.
However, as much as organized anarchy threatens our effectiveness, so does the siren call of a profession unified
around a universally held set of goals and purposes. Professions in general are not tightly knit systems in which all
members agree about their mission; rather, they are more
accurately seen as loosely-coupled confederations of a variety of interests and positions, "pursuing different objectives
in different manners and more or less delicately held together under a common name at a particular period in history."[23] This is particularly true for social work because of
the turbulence of the political, economic, and social environments within which it exists. Because of that turbulence,
moreover, loose coupling can be functional since it permits
segments of the profession to develop adaptive strategies
for dealing with pressures they are facing but which others
are not.

There is a fine line, however, separating a loosely coupled
profession from an anarchic one, which is the situation with
which we are currently struggling. Calls for professional unity and a common base for social work practice become

[22] Carol Meyer, "What Directions for Social Work Practice?" *Social Work*, XXIV
(1979), 267-72.
[23] Rue Bucher and Anselm Strauss, "Professions in Process," *American Journal of
Sociology*, LXVI (1960), 325-34.

merely rhetorical when one considers the divergences within the field and the matrix of conflicting pressures and expectations coming from without. A major characteristic of a turbulent environment is the gross increase in the amount of uncertainty that units operating in such environments face. The strategy usually recommended for dealing with uncertainty is the development of a centralized planning capability so that relevant information from all parts of the environment can be brought to bear at a single decision point. This need for increased centralization tends to be true whether one is considering organizations, professions, communities, or entire societies. The challenge facing social work is in many ways a microcosm of the challenge confronting the society as a whole where the political, economic, and cultural pressures of a world community are producing increased demands for central control of our politics, our economy, and now our welfare systems. The ability of social work to maintain an integral role in the social welfare institutions of this society will depend in great part on its ability to develop the organizational mechanisms, either through the existing national professional associations, or new ones created for that purpose, that will enable the profession to coordinate the diverse activities that go on under its name and guide these into coherent and socially useful and needed directions.

A National Family Policy for the Chronically Ill Elderly

JULIANNE S. OKTAY and *HOWARD A. PALLEY*

AN INCREASING number of policy analysts have been urging that the United States adopt public policies aimed at achieving family well-being. Daniel P. Moynihan cautions:

A nation without a conscious family policy leaves to chance and mischance an area of social reality of the utmost importance, which in consequence will be exposed to the untrammeled and frequently thoroughly undesirable impact of policies arising out of other areas.[1]

Although much of the literature on family policy is oriented to the care of children, recently this area has become an issue of concern to those interested in both the well-being of the functionally impaired elderly and their caring relatives.[2]

In modern industrial society, many of the economic, protective, educative, and recreational roles of the family have

JULIANNE S. OKTAY is Assistant Professor, School of Social Work and Community Planning, University of Maryland at Baltimore.

HOWARD A. PALLEY is Professor, School of Social Work and Community Planning, University of Maryland at Baltimore.

[1] Daniel P. Moynihan, "Foreword to the Paperback Edition," in Alva Myrdal, *Nation and Family* (Cambridge, Mass.: M.I.T. Press, 1968), p. x; emphasis in original.

[2] Elizabeth S. Johnson and Barbara J. Bursk, "Relationship between the Elderly and Their Adult Children," *The Gerontologist*, XVII (1977), 90–96; Stanley J. Brody, S. Walter Poulshock, and Carla F. Masciocchi, "The Family Caring Unit: a Major Consideration in the Long-Term Support System," *The Gerontologist*, XVIII (1978), 556–61; Abraham Monk, "Family Supports in Old Age," *Social Work*, XXIV (1979), 533–38.

declined in favor of, or in comparison with, the utilization of other societal institutions. We believe that national policies can utilize the family to provide important protective, educative, and affectional roles for the chronically limited elderly.

It is appropriate that national family policy be directed toward the elderly, for the large majority of them are in close contact with family. Shanas[3] in the late 1950s found that 90 percent of the elderly in the United States had children, and that while only 36 percent lived in the same household as their children, 24 percent lived within walking distance and 25 percent lived a short ride away. Even across great distances, family ties still often remain close.[4] In times of illness, older people overwhelmingly turn to family members. The probability of an elderly person living with adult children is negatively related to his or her level of health. Sussman[5] has shown that there is widespread acceptance of familial responsibility for the elderly, and that 81 percent of families indicate they would agree to take in an older relative under some circumstances.

In spite of this acceptance of responsibility by the family, there are indications that the family will not be able to continue the current high degree of care of the elderly without financial and service supports. Treas[6] reviews demographic data to show that reduced fertility means that there will be fewer children to share the burden of elderly parents in the future. While in 1910 there were three 35–44-year-old women for each widow over 55, in 1973 there were only 1.2. Also, high rates of marriage have eliminated the "maiden aunts" who may have been most available for care

[3] Ethel Shanas, "Family Responsibility and the Health of Older People," *Journal of Gerontology*, XV (1960), 408–11.

[4] Rose Dobrof and Eugene Litwak, *Maintenance of Family Ties of Long-Term Care Patients: Theory and Guide to Practice* (Washington, D.C.: U.S. Government Printing Office, 1977).

[5] Marvin B. Sussman, *Social and Economic Supports and Family Environments for the Elderly*, final report (Washington, D.C.: U.S. Administration on Aging, 1979).

[6] Judith Treas, "Family Support Systems for the Aged: Some Social and Demographic Considerations," *The Gerontologist*, XVII (1977), 486–91.

of the elderly in the past. Finally, inflation and women's liberation mean that the remaining daughter frequently is not only married but in the work force as well. Thus the family of the future will have fewer resources available for the care of the elderly ill. Also, there is some literature to suggest that caring for elderly sick relatives is stressful for families and may even result in the physical and/or mental breakdown of caregivers.[7]

Current national social policy provides little support for family members caring for aged relatives. However, several demonstration projects are underway in this area. (Most of these provide reimbursement under Medicaid or Medicare for services provided to the patient by family members.)

Reporting on a program in New York designed to support families caring for elderly relatives, Gross-Andrew and Zimmer[8] note that the most frequently needed services were housekeeping and personal care. A surprisingly high number of respondents were interested in counseling services. Families caring for relatives with mental confusion needed companions or escorts. A small number of families needed transportation and money to modify their homes.

Current thinking about services to support families caring for elderly relatives has been influenced by Litwak's work on relationships between formal organizations and primary groups. This work is built on the assumption that primary groups such as families are best able to perform some functions (nonuniform, nontechnical, unpredictable) and that bureaucracies best perform other tasks (uniform, technical, predictable). Thus in devising programs to support families,

---

[7] J.R.A. Sanford, "Tolerance of Debility in Elderly Dependents by Supporters at Home: Its Significance for Hospital Practice," *British Medical Journal*, XXIII (1975), 471–73; Sandra Newman, *Housing Adjustments of Older People* (Ann Arbor, Mich.: Institute for Social Research, University of Michigan, 1976); Gerald Eggert et al., "Caring for the Patient with Long-Term Disability," *Journal of the American Geriatric Society*, XXXII (1977), 102–14. Brigita Krumpholz et al., *Caregivers Coping Ability Project* (Baltimore: University of Maryland School of Medicine; in progress).

[8] Susannah Gross-Andrew and Anna H. Zimmer, "Incentives to Families Caring for Disabled Elderly: Research and Demonstration Project to Strengthen the Natural Supports System," *Journal of Gerontological Social Work*, I (1978), 119–33.

formal organizations have to find a balance which does not replace or discourage the family. The need is for programs which are flexible, and which build on the strengths which families provide.

In sum, programs for the chronically ill aged need to be developed with an understanding of the family unit. Programs need not replace families, as an institutional emphasis does. Rather they need to be designed carefully to complement the family's strength, and to provide substitute services where families are not available. Families need support in order to fulfill whatever responsibility they want to accept concerning dependent elderly members. Current programs such as tax-credit programs, Social Security, Supplemental Security Income, health benefit programs, and social service programs should be examined from the point of view of utilizing the family unit. The goal should be to encourage, not to punish or ignore, the families who choose to care for elderly relatives in need of long-term care.

ACUTE VS. CHRONIC CARE

Patterns of reduced fertility and advances in medical science, such as antibiotics, have resulted in an aged population which is growing both numerically and proportionately. Those over 65 now make up 11 percent of the population, and the oldest category (75 plus) is growing at the fastest rate. As medical science has been able to control most of the acute illnesses which were prime causes of morbidity at the turn of the century, chronic diseases are now the major diagnosis of persons over 65 years of age. Chronic illness is characterized by gradual onset and progressive degeneration. It is often difficult or impossible to treat and is of lifelong duration. Chronic conditions include heart disease, arthritis, diabetes, cancer, and visual or hearing defects.

Over 22 million Americans are over 65 years of age. According to estimates of the National Center for Health Statistics, 81 percent of these persons have at least one chronic condition, and many suffer from several chronic problems. Forty-five and a half percent of the chronically ill elderly have activity limitations caused by these chronic illnesses, and 34.9 percent have major activity limitations.

Chronic conditions result in different patterns of health care utilization. In short-term acute hospitals, the average length of stay is seven days; in chronic-disease hospitals it is 141 days, and in nursing homes 2.8 years.[9]

As Brody observes:

The nature of chronic impairment implies a deficit over a period of time. An episodic response is ineffective and inappropriate to the need for rehabilitation. Instead continuity of care is necessary, a spectrum of services provided by a variety of disciplines and professions . . . whose collective goal is the maintenance and improvement of the individual's level of functioning.[10]

Thus, the acute illness medical model is not adequate to deal with the needs of the chronically ill. These needs are social, psychological, and economic as well as medical. A chronic condition resulting in limited functioning affects an individual's sense of self-esteem and well-being. The chronically ill person may be less able to earn a living and to engage in social activities. Such a person may be unable to meet basic needs, such as shopping, housekeeping, cooking, eating, bathing, and dressing. Excessive medical expenses combined with inflation and decreased earnings lead to impoverishment. Thus what is needed is a broad range of services to meet a complex set of interrelated needs. These services range far beyond the medical to include homemaker, personal care, transportation, social and recreational, and social services. Such services must be adequate, accessible, and well-coordinated.

Unfortunately, the community-based services now available to the chronically ill elderly in the United States fall far

[9] Judith LaVor, *Long-Term Care: a Challenge to Service Systems* (rev. ed.; Washington, D.C.: U.S. Department of Health, Education, and Welfare, Office of Planning and Evaluation, 1977).

[10] Stanley J. Brody, "The Thirty-to-One Paradox: Health Needs of the Aged and Medical Solutions," *National Journal*, XI (1979), 1870.

short of this goal. Certainly such services are not uniformly available on a national basis. Health services which are available are skewed toward needs of acute rather than chronic illness. The main health programs used by the elderly are Medicare, specifically designed primarily for those over 65, and Medicaid or Medical Assistance, designed to serve the needs of the medically indigent.

MEDICARE

Community-based services under Medicare involve home health and supportive services as ordered by a physician. Medicare, as part of health insurance benefits, covers up to 100 home visits for home health care per illness under its hospital insurance provision (Part A) and 100 visits per illness under its supplementary medical insurance provision (Part B). Service coverage includes some social services, intermittent nursing care, physical therapy, speech therapy, home health aide and housekeeping services (Part A only), and medical equipment and supplies as ordered by a physician. Any state-certified home health agency is eligible to receive reimbursement for services provided to patients eligible under the Medicare titles.

By 1975, about 500,000 persons received Medicare reimbursable home health services, a rate of 20.2 persons per 1,000 enrollees. Total charges amounted to $227 million, an average of $454 per individual served. Ninety-four percent of those served were aged. By 1978 the amount spent for home health services had risen to $563 million, which for the first time exceeded the amount spent on nursing home care.[11]

In spite of this increased emphasis on home care, a significant problem with home health care services provided under Medicare remains the tendency to emphasize the skilled medical component of home health care services. Thus while Medicare provides for home health care ser-

[11] U.S. General Accounting Office, *Home Health—the Need for a National Policy to Better Provide for the Elderly* (Washington, D.C., 1977).

vices, these services tend to be oriented to acute, quickly receding conditions amenable to "cure" through skilled nursing care rather than to the supportive and long-term rehabilitative care needed by many chronically ill elderly.[12]

In 1975, under Medicare, approximately 62 percent of all home health visits were for nursing care, and 26 percent were for home health aide visits.[13] Home health aides, who could conceivably provide a broad range of supportive services in the home, are in fact limited by Department of Health and Human Services regulations which define home health aide services as "essentially those which would be performed by a nurse's aide in an institution." Such regulations largely restrict such aides to bedside care services. While they can assist clients in bathing, personal grooming, exercising, and training in self-help skills, and in taking medication, there is little else these aides can do. They can perform services aimed toward "keeping the room of a bedridden patient a safe environment, prepare food and wash dishes."[14] Other housekeeping duties such as doing the laundry and grocery shopping are permitted only on a short-term basis under Part A.

While social services are covered for those patients who meet the Medicare requirements for home health services, the large majority of home health agencies simply do not provide such services. A 1974 study of home health care services under Medicare noted that of the 2,329 home health agencies certified by Medicare at the time, only 607 provided social services. The same study noted that 75 percent of hospital-based home health programs provided social services, but only 15 percent of state and local health

---

[12] Julianne S. Oktay and Francine Sheppard, "Home Health Care for the Elderly," *Health and Social Work*, III (1978), 36–47; Katherine Ricker-Smith and Brahna Trager, "In-Home Health Services in California: Some Lessons for National Health Insurance," *Medical Care*, XVI (1978), 173–89.

[13] Wayne Callahan, "Medicare: Utilization of Home Health Services, 1975," *Research and Statistics Note No. 2* (Washington, D.C.: U.S. Department of Health, Education, and Welfare, Health Care Financing Administration, 1978), pp. 1–5.

[14] U.S. Department of Health, Education, and Welfare, Social Security Administration, *Medicare Home Health Agency Revision No. 4*, Section 205.4, 1967, p. 15.

departments did so. Even in agencies offering social services, the social worker may be involved only in initial assessment. In some cases one worker is expected to serve an entire caseload involving hundreds of patients.

In sum, home health services under Medicare continue to be skewed to those most medically related. The focus of Medicare home health services on post-acute care of short-term health crises ignores some important health needs. Thus, failure to assist an aged arthritic person on a regular basis in tasks such as bathing, dressing, and simple household chores, forces such persons into institutionalized care. Given the widespread prevalence of limiting chronic conditions in the aged population, the services which are reimbursable under Medicare are not those which are needed by the majority of the population over 65. Badly needed supportive services such as household help and personal care are covered only if skilled care is needed as well. Thus large numbers of persons in need are not able to receive home services through Medicare.

MEDICAID AND TITLE XX

Medicaid, a joint federal-state program for the needy, is another source of funding for home health care for the elderly. In 1975, $113 million from federal and state sources went for Medicaid home health care benefits. By 1978 this amount had reached $197 million.

Statutorily, the Medicaid program is less restrictive than Medicare since there is no federal requirement for prior hospitalization nor is there a limit on the number of visits. Also, personal care given by a nonfamily member is reimbursable, as are nonmedical services such as household duties and assistance with activities of daily living. In practice, however, the Medicaid home health services are severely restricted by the states. Many states have adopted the Medicare regulations covering home health services. Only a few states, including Oklahoma and Connecticut, currently make use of provisions allowing for personal care and nontechnical services.[15] There is a wide variation among states in home services allowed under Medicaid. New York, which has the most complete package, in the 1977 fiscal year consumed 81.2 percent of total Medicaid expenditures for home health care.[16] Obviously, the level of home service care received by needy individuals in other states was quite circumscribed.

Thus while the Medicaid program has the potential to provide comprehensive home health service for the chronically ill elderly who are impoverished, the ability of the states to set limitations has meant that such programs rarely are offered. Instead, when available, services for the most part are oriented to the acute, limited needs of a small segment of the needy population.

Existing home health care services in the United States under Medicaid (and Medicare) are only partially developed with respect to the provision of assistance to the elderly with chronic impairments. The goal of home health services in the United States as a matter of systematic national family policy for the chronically limited elderly should be to increase the effectiveness of health care, to reduce inappropriate costs, to improve the functioning of such elderly persons, and to reduce social strain on caring relatives. A national family policy emphasizing broadly defined and widely available home health care services would be most appropriate in terms of meeting the needs of the chronically ill elderly who face a high risk of long-term institutionalization. Evidence exists that such expanded home health services use also would reduce inappropriate inpatient services.[17]

Furthermore, in spite of some successes, Title XX (the

[15] Denise Humm-Delgado and Robert Morris, "Family Policy and the Disabled: Examples of Family Payments for Long-Term Disability" (Waltham, Mass.: Florence Heller Graduate School of Advanced Studies in Social Welfare, Brandeis University, 1976; mimeographed), pp. 9–12.
[16] U.S. Department of Health, Education, and Welfare, Health Care Financing Administration, *Data on the Medicaid Program: Eligibility, Services, Expenditures* (Baltimore, 1979), p. 51.
[17] John Hammond, "Home Health Care Cost Effectiveness: an Overview of the Literature," *Public Health Reports*, XCIV (1979), 306.

social service provisions of the Social Security Act) has not been an adequate vehicle for the development of a truly national social service delivery system with a clear focus regarding the meeting of social service delivery needs of the chronically ill elderly. Within the Title XX block grant method of financing, studies by Schram[18] conclude that, relative to their numbers and needs, the aged receive a less than equitable share of social service funds in spite of some successful state service programs in Michigan, Alabama, and California. This is so because of the demands of existing social service programs, competition for service commitments between client groups, and state statutory mandates regarding the maintenance of present levels of funding for state social service programs combined with the federal funding limits of Title XX.[19] The U.S. Commission on Civil Rights 1979 report concerning age discrimination in programs receiving federal financial assistance concludes that the states in their responses to the competing demands for Title XX funds tend to discriminate against the elderly.[20]

Often utilization of service under Title XX has been skewed toward children. As an official of the Denver Department of Social Services observed regarding Title XX resources:

What has happened is the workload we have been given in terms of child abuse and neglect and the areas [*sic*] of families . . . has taken almost all our resources, and what we basically said is that we will pay as much attention as we can to the protection of the aged in terms of exploitation or abuse. We have tried to give emphasis to nursing home placement . . . and that's about the extent of it. The rest of the staff we have had has been pretty well delegated to the protection of children.[21]

Furthermore, the U.S. Commission on Civil Rights 1979 report noted that in public hearings Title XX program ad-

---

[18] Sanford F. Schram, "Elderly Policy Particularism and the New Social Services," *Social Service Review*, LIII (1979), 89–90; Sanford F. Schram and Richard Hurley, "Title XX and the Elderly," *Social Work*, XXII (1977), 101.

[19] U.S. Commission on Civil Rights, *The Age Discrimination Study, Part II* (Washington, D.C.: Government Printing Office, 1979), pp. 14–51.

[20] *Ibid.*   [21] *Ibid.*, p. 27.

ministrators testified that they depend on programs which were authorized by the Older Americans Act to serve older persons "and as a result limited resources are available for serving older persons" under Title XX.

THE OLDER AMERICANS ACT

Another dimension of the failure to establish a systematic family policy toward the chronically ill elderly is the nature of the Older Americans Act. Title III, the most expensive program under the act, devotes the major share of funds to advocacy of a larger share of funds for the elderly in other programs such as Title XX. In 1976 an estimated 7,086,210 elderly persons received services under approved Title III projects. Title III funding for the administration of Area Agencies on Aging and peripherally for social services amounted to $93 million in fiscal 1976. Such fundings were primarily to pay part of the cost of administration of Area Agencies on Aging, *"and the funding of social services by the State Agency where there is no Area Agency."* [22] The limited amount of social services actually received by elderly individuals *utilizing Title III funds only* in fiscal 1978 was as follows:

SERVICES PROVIDED UNDER TITLE III FUNDS
IN FISCAL YEAR 1978

Type of Service	Units of Service
Transportation	2,546,138
Home services	759,070
Legal and other counseling	266,157
Home repair and renovation	95,000
Information and referral	2,861,770
Escort	377,000
Outreach	1,604,000
All other services	4,200,000
Total	12,709,135

Source: U.S. Department of Health, Education, and Welfare Office of Human Development Services, *Administration on Aging Annual Report, Fiscal Year 1978* (Washington, D.C., 1979), p. 7.

[22] U.S. Department of Health, Education, and Welfare, Office of Human Development Services, *Administration on Aging Annual Report, Fiscal Year 1976* (Washington, D.C., 1977), p. 9, Emphasis added.

As of December 31, 1979, state obligation of federal funds for in-home services, a category which includes homemaker and home health aides, visiting and telephone reassurance, as well as chore maintenance, amounted to only $25,751,255. The fiscal 1980 federal budget continues to fund social services under Title III at a low level ($246.97 million). This funding is provided in order to maintain social services at present levels as well as to provide transportation services, assist senior center operation, and maintain other activities supportive to the nutritional program.[23] For fiscal year 1980, the Title VII Nutritional Program was funded at an authorized level of over $277.5 million. This program was expected to provide over 580,000 meals per day. *Only 15 percent of such meals would be provided for the homebound.*[24]

A major problem of programming under the Older Americans Act is the low appropriation level which does not permit development of national programming at a level which meets the needs of the elderly with chronic conditions of a physical or psychological nature. Moreover, the Administration on Aging is not geared to the establishment of systematic norms for meeting the nonmedical needs of the chronically ill elderly or caring relatives or of developing a national infrastructure of services to meet such needs systematically. That is, it is not a truly national social service delivery system with a clear focus on developing a national family policy for the chronically ill elderly.

INSTITUTIONAL CARE VS. FAMILY-CENTERED CARE

We have argued, in part, that the federal community-based health programs for the elderly are oriented to acute rather than chronic illness. We have also contended that present social service programs do not provide an adequate supply of high-quality social service supports needed by the chronically ill elderly. This is so in spite of the fact that the large

[23]"News of Federal Agencies," *Aging*, XLVI (1979), 229–300.
[24]U.S. Office of the President, *The Budget of the United States, Fiscal Year 1980—Appendix* (Washington, D.C.: Government Printing Office, 1979), p. 482.

proportion of functionally limited elderly suffer from chronic rather than acute problems. The result is that a great number of chronically ill elderly are not receiving aid from any federal program. The majority of these are meeting their needs for long-term care through family and friends. The Congressional Budget Office in a 1977 report estimated that of the 5.5 to 9.9 million functionally disabled, only 1.9 to 2.7 million receive help from any government programs; 3 to 6.7 million receive help from families, and 8 to 11.4 million receive no long-term care at all.[25] It is clear that the role of the family is enormous in this area. Indeed, even those who receive care from government programs are often also receiving care from family members.[26] Despite the extensive role of the family in the provision of long-term care for the chronically ill elderly, in their emphasis government programs are designed to serve individual patients in a manner which all but ignores the role of the family. For example, in the Medicaid program emphasis on care for frail elderly persons is placed on long-term institutional placement, despite the fact that the physical, social, and psychological needs of functionally impaired elderly persons are often not best served by such institutional arrangements.

Data regarding the Medicaid program validate the fact that the focus of this particular program is heavily weighted toward institutional arrangements. In fiscal 1978, Medicaid benefits totaled $18.4 billion. The federal share of such personal health expenditures was 56 percent.[27] Medicaid payments were heavily institutional—39 percent of Medicaid payments went to nursing homes (over $7.2 billion) and 37 percent went to hospitals (over $6.8 billion). Eleven percent

[25] U.S. Congressional Budget Office, *Long-Term Care for the Elderly and the Disabled* (Washington, D.C.: Government Printing Office, 1977). Although these figures are not limited to the elderly, the elderly compose the most substantial part thereof.

[26] U.S. General Accounting Office, *op. cit.*

[27] Robert M. Gibson, "National Health Care Expenditures, 1978," *Health Care Financing Review,* I (1979), 29.

of payments were made for physicians' services ($2 billion), and medically related home health service was only one service included under the general rubric of "other health services." Expenditures in this latter category were $246 million, or slightly more than one percent of Medicaid expenditures.[28] Medically related home health expenditures under Medicaid, regardless of some recent increases, have been negligible.

Institutionalization is also encouraged by the lack of adequate community-based alternatives. The discharge unit in the hospital generally finds it much easier to place a patient in a nursing home than to locate and activate the complex network of community-based services which would be needed. Often, considerable effort must be expended, and then if just one needed service cannot be managed, transportation, for example, the whole plan collapses.

This emphasis on institutional care is unfortunate in that most older persons are loath to choose this option. They wish to remain independent as long as possible and turn to family, friends, or community-based options such as boarding homes if they become functionally limited.[29] In fact, it appears that this is what usually happens. Comparison of the institutionalized and noninstitutionalized elderly show that those in nursing homes are generally people who have limited family resources and/or are in the most severely disabled group. A recent study by Pfeiffer determined that while 7 percent of the elderly in the community are extremely impaired, 76 percent of those in institutions are so impaired.[30] It has been agreed that 15 percent to 25 percent of those in institutions could be maintained in the community if adequate support were available. This seems most feasible for people with mild levels of disability, since recent

[28]*Ibid.*

[29]Shanas, *op. cit.*; Philip Brickner et al., "The Homebound Aged: a Medically Unreached Group," *Annals of Internal Medicine*, LXXXII (1975), 1–6.

[30]Eric Pfeiffer, ed., *Multidimensional Functional Assessment: the OARS Methodology—a Manual* (Durham, N.C.: Duke University Center for the Study of Aging and Human Development, 1976).

studies indicate that community-based care for a severely disabled individual with no family support would be very costly.[31]

There has been increasing interest in community-based alternatives to institutional care largely because federal health programs have become so costly. Also, several studies have suggested that home care services can prevent institutionalization.[32] However, more recent findings are not conclusive regarding cost savings or decreased rates of institutionalization where community-based alternatives are available. In a large study of day care and homemaker service programs authorized by Section 222 of the Social Security Amendments of 1972,[33] the National Center for Health Services Research found that reduction in cost due to decreased rates of institutionalization among the study populations were more than made up in program costs. In the homemakers group, rates of institutionalization were no lower than among the controls, but rates of hospital use were higher. Both community-based programs, however, seemed to result in lower death rates and higher contentment, improved functioning, and more social activity. Skellie, Coan, and Jourdan[34] also reported reduced death rates in populations receiving community-based services (alternative living services, day care, and home services) and no significant difference in rates of institutionalization.

Two studies indicate that home care is less expensive than

[31] Richard M. Burton et al., *Nursing Home Cost and Care: an Investigation of Alternatives* (Durham, N.C.: Duke University Center for the Study of Aging and Human Development, 1974); U.S. General Accounting Office, *op. cit.*

[32] Margaret Nielson, Margaret Blenkner, and Martin Bloom, "Older Persons after Hospitalization: a Controlled Study of Home Aide Service," *American Journal of Public Health*, LXII (1972), 1094–1101; Brickner et al., *op. cit.;* Burton Dunlop, *Determinants of Long-Term Care Facility Utilization by the Elderly* (Washington, D.C.: Urban Institute, 1976).

[33] William G. Weissert, Thomas H. Wan, and Barbara B. Livieratos, *Effects and Costs of Day Care and Homemaker Services for the Chronically Ill: a Randomized Experiment* (Washington, D.C.: National Center for Health Services Research, 1980).

[34] F. Albert Skellie, Ruth E. Coan, and Louis F. Jourdan, "Community-based Long-Term Care and Mortality: Impact One Year after Enrollment" (paper presented at American Public Health Association Annual Meeting, New York, 1979).

institutional care at levels of mild and moderate disability, if there is family support.[35] However, in cases where disability is severe, nursing home cost is lower if costs to the family are considered.

It would be unfortunate if these studies were to lead to a continued emphasis on institutional care, since looking at cost alone overlooks the very important issues of quality of care and quality of life. In fact, there is widespread agreement in studies on community-based programs that these programs are more effective than institutions in improving or maintaining health, mental functioning, life satisfaction, and social activities.[36]

To summarize, current policies of emphasis on acute illness in home health programs, and on institutional rather than community-based settings, have resulted in an enormous gap in coverage of the need for long-term community-based care for the chronically ill elderly. This gap is currently being filled by families. Because of the important role of the family in caring for the dependent elderly, policies need to be aimed at the family-based setting.

In view of the acute medical care service orientation of home care service under Medicare and often under Medicaid, as well as the inability of current social service provision under the Older Americans Act and Title XX to meet the needs of the elderly with chronic conditions who need service supports to function in their communities, a national family policy is essential with respect to the chronically ill elderly and caring relatives. Such a family policy should provide on a systematic national basis for a variety of community health and social services. The development on a national basis of systematic social service supports and ancillary health-functioning services should enable elderly in-

[35] Jay Greenberg, *Cost of In-Home Services* (Minneapolis: Governor's Council on Aging, 1974); U.S. General Accounting Office, *op. cit.*

[36] Neville Doherty, Joan Segal, and Barbara Hicks, "Alternatives to Institutionalization for the Aged: Viabiliity and Cost Effectiveness," *Aged Care and Services Review*, I (1978), 1–8; Gross-Andrew and Zimmer, *op. cit.;* Weissert, Wan, and Livieratos, *op. cit.*

dividuals with chronic limitations to continue to function in the community and should assist concerned relatives who wish to maintain relationships with such elderly persons outside a custodial institutional setting wherever possible. Such a national family policy should de-emphasize the curative medical model for assisting the elderly in those situations in which it is an inappropriate model.

Among the community health and social services which should be available to the chronically ill elderly as a matter of national family policy are physical rehabilitation aid in the community, nutritional assistance, as well as nonmedically oriented long-term personal care, homemaker and chore services. Social services which would include social work family service assistance (including counseling), should also be available to the chronically ill and concerned relatives. Finally, as child day care assists working parents, systematically available senior day care centers and respite care would help the aged and assist concerned and involved children and other relatives. Also, a system of cash allowances or payment for services rendered would help families to provide home or community care for their elderly relatives. Other cash incentives could be made available to allow families to make structural alterations in existing homes in order to accommodate chronically ill elderly relatives.

Whatever the specific services or economic incentives provided, as a matter of national policy it is important that they be designed in a highly feasible manner that will serve to build on the strengths of families rather than replace them.

International and Domestic Policies Regarding Refugees

THE FIELD of refugees worldwide is extremely broad, and the past year has seen an explosion of refugee problems in the world. I will address primarily the current Cuban situation.

At this moment the United States is deeply involved with the international community in helping people to survive under desperate circumstances in Cambodia, in Pakistan, in Somalia—literally millions of people, most of them women and children, without medical assistance, without hope, except for what this country and other nations can provide.

So the 1980 Annual Forum would have been a timely opportunity to review our refugee policies and programs even without the sudden influx of more than 60,000 Cubans that began on April 21. Now it is essential to do so because so many Americans feel confused and threatened by the boat arrivals at Key West, the disorder in some of the camps, and the press reports about undesirable elements among the Cubans. These events are causing troubled Americans to ask basic questions:

How many can we absorb?

Isn't the Statue of Liberty obsolete?

Why are we letting Fidel Castro do this to us?

VICTOR H. PALMIERI is Ambassador-at-large and U.S. Coordinator for Refugee Affairs, Washington, D.C.
Editor's Note: As of October 20, 1980, 125,000 Cubans have entered the U.S., and 92 percent of them have been resettled.

From the beginning, our policy has centered on three points:

1. The humanitarian effort of saving lives and caring for people
2. Enforcing our laws
3. Gaining the support of the Miami and Cuban-American community to cut off the boat flow.

That policy has worked; through the Coast Guard's efforts only a few lives were lost out of the more than 60,000 Cubans who made the dangerous voyage. The law has been enforced, first by fines against boat owners and then by boat seizures and arrests. Finally, we are winning the support of the Miami Cuban-American community, and the boat flow from Key West to Cuba has been cut off since the President's declaration of last week. The response to the Cuban emergency has been impressive by any standard.

Since April 21, 1980, we have received and cared for over 60,000 human beings, transporting them by bus and airlift to processing centers in Miami, Eglin Air Force Base (Fla.), Fort Chaffee, Arkansas, and the just-opened center at Indiantown Gap, Pennsylvania—instant cities where health screening, security checks, and sponsorship assurances for resettlement are being carried out. About 35,000 individuals have been released to families or resettlement sponsors. Of these, about 1,000 a day are currently being released to sponsors and families. This has been a cooperative effort involving 12 federal agencies, over 1,500 federal employees in Miami alone, state, county, and city officials, all the major national voluntary organizations, and local community groups of all kinds.

Why are there such severe problems at the camps?

Consider what these people have been through: stripped of everything they own; kept for long periods in camps at the port of Mariel in Cuba; often forcibly separated from friends and family; enduring the hardships and dangers of the voyage to Key West; and then more weeks of processing and waiting before they can be reunited with relatives or friends. Nevertheless, we are not going to permit short cuts on health screening or security checks.

We are going ahead with exclusion proceedings for all those who have committed serious crimes in Cuba or here. So far we have more than five hundred individuals in detention.

Where are we headed in regard to status and benefits for the Cubans who will be resettled here?

First of all, Congress is deeply involved in the issue of funding and status. We have been briefing the key committee members on an intensive basis. In the current Congressional budget deliberations, seeking quick decisions on new budget requests is not recommended. The issues are extraordinarily difficult. We need to minimize the fiscal burden imposed on states and localities, particularly south Florida. We need to provide assistance to avoid the costs of long-term dependence. But we also need to avoid creating incentives for increased flows from the Caribbean and Latin America.

Basically, these are federal government problems, and the administration is approaching them on that basis. There will be educational aid funds for both children and adults in areas with large numbers of Cubans. There will be expanded services for health screening and community health centers provided by the Department of Health and Human Services. There will be resettlement grants to aid voluntary organizations. The availability of other major assistance programs such as Medicaid, remains to be resolved.

Now to those persistent questions.

First, "How many can we absorb?" The answer is not all, but many. Second, the Statue of Liberty will never be obsolete because America's role as a beacon of freedom is a central part of our tradition and our strength as a free people. But we do have to have controls to protect against sudden massive inflows, and we have to have policies that are equitable for different racial groups, such as, for instance, the Cubans and Haitians in south Florida.

The other persistent question is: "Why are we letting Fidel Castro do this to us?" There are two answers to this. One is that a nation with a strong humanitarian tradition is vulnerable if an adversary chooses to send people here in a way that risks lives. We will always try to save lives and care for people. None of us would do otherwise.

The other answer is that we can deal with our problems, the confusion and the cost and the inconvenience, if we stay calm and work together. But Castro mày not be able to deal with his problems, and we should keep in mind what the whole world knows: the boat flotilla has been an eloquent witness to the failure of his system and the success of ours.

Social workers are the social service leaders of our nation. We can continue our tradition as a symbol of hope and refuge to persecuted peoples only with their support.

Despite all the problems they are coping with in our cities and towns today, we should recall that the record of history is clear: whenever we have helped others to come here and build a new life, whether it was the Irish in Boston long ago, or the Italians in New York City, or the Chinese in San Francisco, or the Cubans in Miami, there have been problems at the start but afterward we have always been able to say, "by helping these people, we have helped ourselves."

Poverty in Female-headed Households

NANCY S. BARRETT and *ROBERT L. CROSSLIN*

THE EXTENT of poverty among female-headed households in the United States is alarming. One out of three have incomes below the official poverty level—and one out of two with children below the age of 18 are in poverty. This compares with only one out of fifteen families in America generally (including those headed by females) and one in twelve of all families with children under 18.[1] During the 1960s, the United States made tremendous strides in reducing both the absolute and the relative incidence of poverty: the proportion of all Americans living in poverty dropped from 22.4 percent to 12.1 percent. However, there was very little progress against poverty during the 1970s. By 1978 the incidence of poverty had fallen only slightly, to 11.4 percent of the population. During this period the number of persons in male-headed households living in poverty *declined* by 2.1 million to 11.6 million. On the other hand, those in female-headed families *rose* by 1.7 million to 12.9 million.[2] The failure to reduce the incidence of

NANCY S. BARRETT is Deputy Assistant Secretary of Labor for Policy, Evaluation, and Research, Washington, D.C.
ROBERT L. CROSSLIN is Acting Director, Office of Wages and Labor Relations, Office of the Assistant Secretary for Policy, Evaluation, and Research, U.S. Department of Labor, Washington, D.C.

The opinions expressed herein are solely those of the authors, and do not necessarily represent the official views or policies of the U.S. Department of Labor.

[1] U.S. Department of Commerce, Bureau of the Census, Current Population Reports, *Consumer Income*, p. 60, No. 119, March 1979.
[2] *Ibid.*

poverty in United States during the last decade was due entirely to the rising number of female-headed households with inadequate, poverty-level incomes.

The nature of the problem is made clearer by considering the sources of income of female- and male-headed families in the United States. In 1977, 40 percent of all female-headed families supported themselves with earned and unearned income only (no transfer payments). In contrast, the similar figure for male-headed families was 71.2 percent. Thirty-one percent of female-headed households below the poverty level had public assistance as their sole source of support. Still, 31.7 percent of female-headed households in poverty had some amount of earned income, although it was not enough to provide a decent standard of living for their families. These figures indicate that transfer payments are a source of income for the majority of female-headed households, and even among working-mother household heads, a large percentage do not 'earn enough to keep them out of poverty.[3]

Distressing as these facts are, the situation is likely to become even worse in the years ahead as the number and percentage of female-headed households continue to grow. The consequences are tragic in terms of social, psychological, and economic effects on females and their families. Poverty is now a women's issue. We must understand the main causes of poverty among female-headed households, and work diligently toward effective solutions on all fronts.

CAUSES OF POVERTY IN FEMALE-HEADED HOUSEHOLDS

CHANGES IN FAMILY STRUCTURE

Changes in life style during the 1970s have produced a significant increase—32 percent—in the proportion of female-

[3]*Ibid.* Poverty is defined here as an annual family income at or below the official poverty income level established by the Bureau of Labor Statistics for given-sized

headed families from 10.9 percent of all families in 1970 to 14.4 percent in 1978.[4] The age and marital status distributions of this group changed dramatically also. Whereas only 16.9 percent of the women who headed such families were aged 25 to 34 in 1970, by 1978 that age group accounted for one fourth of the total. Also the proportions who were never married, or were divorced, rose from 10.9 percent to 15.6 percent, and from 22.5 percent to 33.8 percent, respectively. Concomitantly, the proportion who were widowed dropped from 42.8 percent to 28.9 percent.

These trends show no signs of reversing. One out of every two marriages today is likely to end in divorce. While most eventually remarry, disproportionately many divorced women face the prospect of below-poverty incomes for some period of time.

CONTINUED LOW EARNINGS OF WOMEN

In general, the gap between male and female earnings has not been narrowing. In fact, the ratio of female/male median earnings has been virtually constant at 60 percent since 1967.[5] Although the Equal Pay Act was passed in 1963, and has contributed greatly to lessening earnings differentials *within* occupations, the basic problem continues to be the occupational distribution of women workers, both within and between occupations.

There has been a sizable increase in the proportion of working women, especially those heading families and holding professional and managerial jobs, and proportionately fewer working as operatives and private household workers. But the fact is that the overwhelming majority of women family heads remain in traditionally low-paid female occupations. In 1978 over three fourths of employed women

families. In 1977 the poverty level for a female-headed family of four was $6,162. This compares with $5,512 (1977) for forty hours of full-time work per week at the minimum wage of only $2.65 per hour.

[4] *1979 Employment and Training Report of the President* (Washington, D.C.: U.S. Government Printing Office, 1980).

[5] U.S. Department of Commerce, Bureau of the Census, *Current Population Reports*, Series P. 60, various issues.

TABLE 1

MAJOR OCCUPATION GROUP OF EMPLOYED WOMEN HEADING FAMILIES AND MARRIED WOMEN, HUSBAND PRESENT, MARCH OF 1970 AND 1978

Numbers in thousands; percent distribution

Occupation Group	1970 Total	Women Heading Families 1978					Married Women, Husband Present	
		Total	Never Married	Married Husband Absent	Divorced	Widowed	1970	1978
White-collar	51.5	57.5	58.8	50.1	63.6	49.7	60.8	65.8
Professional-technical	10.8	13.0	14.1	12.3	14.5	9.3	15.4	17.0
Managers, administrators, except farm	5.4	6.7	6.0	4.8	7.5	7.1	4.7	6.9
Sales	5.0	4.6	2.9	3.9	4.9	5.9	7.1	7.0
Clerical	30.3	33.2	35.8	29.1	36.7	27.4	33.6	34.9
Blue-collar	19.7	18.4	19.4	21.4	17.0	17.9	18.0	15.2
Crafts	0.9	2.3	2.3	2.1	2.5	2.3	1.3	1.8
Operatives, except transport	} 18.0	14.7	16.4	18.4	12.7	14.1	} 16.3	11.7
Transport equipment operatives		0.3			0.4	0.6		0.9
Nonfarm laborers	0.8	1.1	0.7	0.9	1.4	0.9	0.4	0.8
Service	27.8	23.6	21.8	27.4	19.3	31.0	19.5	17.6
Private household	6.9	3.4	4.1	5.9	.9	6.2	3.5	1.9
All other services	20.9	20.2	17.7	21.5	18.4	24.8	16.0	15.7
Farm	1.0	0.5	0.1	1.0	0.2	1.3	1.9	1.3
Total employed: Number	2,785	4,414	607	912	2,018	877	17,497	21,614
Percent	100.0	100.0	100.0	100.0	100.0	100.0	100.0	100.0

SOURCE: U.S. Department of Labor, Bureau of Labor Statistics.

heading families were in sales, clerical, operative, and service occupations.[6]

Attitudes about job options for women appear to be changing very slowly. It is hoped that attitudes and, especially, the number of opportunities for women to move into other occupations will change more rapidly in the future.

In addition to occupational segregation, another factor holding down women's wages is the failure of women to move upward in the career-ladder hierarchy. The pattern over the life cycle is for male earnings to rise sharply in the mid-twenties and thirties, so that males in the 35-to-44 age bracket are earning twice the median income of the 18- to 24-year age group. Women, on the other hand, gain very little over the life cycle. Although the median income of full-time, year-round female workers aged 35 to 44 is more than the median for 18- to 24-year-olds, the difference is less than $2,000. For males, the difference is around $8,000 (1975 dollars).

It is often thought that women are concentrated at the bottom of the job hierarchy because they lack the work experience of men of the same age. Although it is true that many women interrupt their working life at some point when they are raising children, the trend is for women to remain at work longer than used to be customary. The growth that has occurred in the female labor force since the mid-1960s has been primarily due to a drop in the exit rate of women rather than to an increase in the entry rate. This trend is quite clear. Since 1968 entry probabilities for both full-time and part-time female workers have increased only slightly, while exit probabilities have declined dramatically for both groups (see Table 2). Since the growth in the female labor force has resulted from an increased labor force attachment of women rather than a relative increase in the number of inexperienced workers, the average female

[6] Janet L. Norwood and Elizabeth Waldman, "Women in the Labor Force: Some New Data Series, U.S. Department of Labor, Bureau of Labor Statistics, 1979, Report No. 575; and unpublished B.L.S. statistics.

TABLE 2

PROBABILITY OF LABOR FORCE ENTRY AND EXIT FOR FEMALES AGES 16+
1968–79 ANNUAL AVERAGES

Probability of	1968	1969	1970	1971	1972	1973	1974	1975	1976	1977	1978	1979
Entry into full-time labor force[a]	2.3	2.4	2.5	2.6	2.6	2.6	2.7	2.8	2.9	2.9	2.9	2.9
Exit from full-time employment	4.2	4.1	3.6	3.4	3.6	3.7	3.5	3.0	3.2	3.0	3.0	3.0
Exit from seeking full-time work	30.5	32.1	33.4	31.4	26.7	25.4	28.9	33.1	22.0	23.0	20.7	22.0
Entry into part-time labor force[b]	2.7	2.8	2.9	2.9	2.9	3.0	3.0	2.9	3.0	3.0	3.1	3.2
Exit from part-time employment	17.9	16.4	14.8	13.6	13.8	13.7	12.7	11.9	12.1	11.5	11.6	11.2
Exit from seeking part-time work	58.0	61.1	63.8	60.4	46.5	50.1	51.0	54.0	42.1	44.1	40.9	42.9

[a]Full-time labor force includes persons working full time and persons seeking full-time work.

[b]Part-time labor force includes persons working part time voluntarily and unemployed persons looking for part-time work.

Note: Probability of entry into, or exit from, the labor force is equal to the number of persons who entered (or left) the labor force in period t (where t is an average month in the year under study) divided by the number of persons in the labor force in period $t - 1$.

SOURCE: Carol Leon and Robert W. Bednarzik, "A Profile of Women on Part-Time Schedules," *Monthly Labor Review*, October, 1978, and unpublished B.L.S. statistics.

worker is gaining work experience. If there were not resistance to moving women up in the job hierarchy, the increased labor force attachment of women would be resulting in their increased representation in higher-ranking jobs.

However, just as the sociology of the labor market resists equal pay for women, it also resists moving women into positions of authority, particularly those with supervisory responsibility over men. Hence, the rationalization that women are not interested in jobs with upward mobility continues to dominate thinking about women's promotional opportunities.

LACK OF SUPPORT SERVICES

Another myth is that public policy has responded to women's changing roles and aspirations. In fact, one of the most astonishing aspects of the massive movement of women into the labor force is that it has occurred in the absence of accommodating public policies and the availability of support services that would take over some of the tasks women performed when they were full-time homemakers.

Six million preschool children have mothers who work, and the vast majority of these children are in makeshift care. By 1985, there will be around 12 million preschool children with working mothers, yet no serious consideration is being given to child care policy. When most preschool children were being cared for at home by their mothers, the idea of government involvement did seem to conflict with what was regarded as a private family responsibility. Today, most working mothers desperately need a place outside their home where their children can receive reliable, loving care. It is difficult to overestimate the psychic and emotional costs incurred by the many working women who are unable to find decent care for their children.

WORK DISINCENTIVES IN THE WELFARE SYSTEM

The present welfare system discourages women from working by its provision that able-bodied women who happen to be mothers should not be expected to work. (The United States is the only country that pays welfare benefits just for being a mother.) While this aspect of the welfare system has the same strong emotional appeal as the idea of full-time motherhood, the fact is that nearly half of all women with preschool children do work. The current welfare support model for mothers is antithetical to the basic philosophy of the women's movement.

The provisions of the government's Work Incentive Program (WIN), which exempt women with children under the age of six from job search and work requirements, automatically exclude almost three fourths of the welfare population from participation in the labor force. Discouraging the participation of these women does them a long-run disservice, reducing their likelihood of successfully moving out of poverty when their children reach school age, due to a lack of skills and work experience. Continuing welfare dependency therefore results because the job and earnings opportunities do not offer a better alternative.

This is not to suggest that income support for poor women should be discontinued. Lack of access to decent jobs, lack of skills and employment experience, all add up to a need for income supplements, specially designed training and counseling programs, and solutions to child care problems. The Carter Administration's welfare reform proposals for jobs and cash supplements would reduce by over two million the number of people, in families with children, who have below poverty-level incomes. If enacted, this legislation will certainly be an important step in combating poverty in female-headed households.

UNDERREPRESENTATION OF WOMEN IN PUBLIC JOBS,
TRAINING PROGRAMS, AND APPRENTICESHIPS

Although women appear to be fairly represented in Comprehensive Employment and Training Act (CETA) programs, the jobs for which they are being trained are primarily traditional female occupations. The CETA system is currently attempting to upgrade the training and job placements of poor women. Demonstration projects aimed at ending the sex stereotyping of jobs, and the development of nontraditional employment opportunities for women, are now being carried out.

The separately funded WIN program also provides training, placement, and other employability services for welfare recipients. However, under this program too the starting wages of women are substantially lower than those for men. In 1978, the beginning wages of males averaged $4.01 per hour as opposed to $2.97 for women.[7]

Public, and private, apprenticeship programs, which are often critical for providing movement into the skilled trades, woefully underrepresent women. At the beginning .of 1978 women were only 2.2 percent of all registered apprentices.[8]

Given all these factors (changes in family structure; occupational crowding and segregation leading to low earnings; lack of support services; disincentives in the welfare system; underrepresentation in jobs, training, and apprenticeship programs), it is no wonder that poverty has become primarily a women's issue. We have created a welfare dependency, and yet poor females face occupational and sex discrimination if and when they enter the labor force.

---

[7] *1979 Employment and Training Report of the President*, p. 55.
[8] *Ibid.*, p. 57.

POLICY RECOMMENDATIONS

Significant reductions in the incidence of poverty will only come about through changes in attitudes, and by altering current public policies that hamper women's opportunities and incentives for earning decent wages.

We need more diligent enforcement of equal employment opportunity laws, especially innovations for successfully combating occupational segregation by public and private employers.

Women should be better represented in CETA, with an emphasis on providing women with training and jobs in nontraditional occupations. CETA training should be more flexible to accommodate the needs of poor mothers with preschool children. Day care could be provided, or training sessions could be held at night when women would find it easier to find care for young children. In addition, the U.S. Employment Service should provide specialized counseling and other services for women, some possibly at night.

We need policies, such as affirmative action approaches, to increase the proportion of women in apprenticeship programs.

The welfare system should be revamped to provide poor women with jobs and income supplements rather than income substitutes. In this vein the WIN program should be extended to all able-bodied welfare recipients; and the Carter administration's welfare reform proposals should be enacted.

The personal income tax should be computed on the basis of each individual's income, rather than on the basis of the combined income of husband and wife in order to increase the labor force participation and work experience of married women and thus reduce the likelihood that they may face poverty in the events of becoming a single head of household.

The Social Security system should be reevaluated in the

light of changing family structures so that every individual is guaranteed a minimal but adequate income. Divorce leaves many women without coverage, and elderly women lose their widow's benefits upon remarriage.

A comprehensive plan is needed to meet the child care needs of working mothers, and mothers in need of training, now.

While the war against poverty in the 1960s focused largely on minority males, the battle against poverty in the 1980s must focus on improving the economic situation of women.

Promoting Client and Worker Competence in Child Welfare

ANTHONY N. MALUCCIO

In the field of child welfare there is general agreement about the inadequacies and questionable effectiveness of the service delivery system. Study after study suggests that there is a wide gap between the promise of child welfare services and their performance.[1] For instance, while the goal of a permanent home for each child has become accepted at the philosophical level, it is still far from being realized in practice, for many children are drifting in temporary, inappropriate placements.

Various solutions to these problems are usually offered, including more staff, more and better training, improved practice technology, and social action or social reform. While all these remedies are important, none would deal adequately with a recurring problem, namely, the failure of the service delivery system to promote the competence of clients and social workers in carrying out their roles and coping with life challenges. Much could be accomplished if we reconceptualized and changed practice so that it might be more conducive to the effective functioning of clients as well as social workers.

Ways of achieving this objective are suggested by competence-oriented social work, an approach based on newer

ANTHONY N. MALUCCIO is Professor of Social Work, University of Connecticut, Greater Hartford Campus, West Hartford, Conn.

[1] David Fanshel and Eugene B. Shinn, *Children in Foster Care: a Longitudinal Investigation* (New York: Columbia University Press, 1978); Alan R. Gruber, *Children in Foster Care—Destitute, Neglected . . . Betrayed* (New York: Human Sciences Press, 1978).

bodies of knowledge from anthropology, biology, ecology, and psychology. In view of its emphasis on promoting the competence of clients and practitioners, this approach is especially suited to child welfare.

COMPETENCE-ORIENTED SOCIAL WORK[2]

Two decades ago Allport described the drive toward competence as a most significant force in human development and behavior: "We survive through competence, we grow through competence, we become 'self-actualizing' through competence."[3] Since then, competence has come to be regarded in various fields as an exciting and promising concept in understanding and working with human beings.

DEFINITION OF COMPETENCE

Although theorists and researchers from other disciplines have contributed much to the study of human competence, it is still a vague concept with multiple meanings. However, most writers agree with White,[4] who defines competence in biopsychological terms as the person's achieved capacity to interact effectively with the environment. White sees the key manifestations of competence as self-confidence, trusting one's own judgment, and the ability to make decisions.

The problem with this definition is that it places the burden on the human organism. In other words, competence is simplistically regarded as a property or trait of the per-

---

[2] This section is adapted from Anthony N. Maluccio, "Competence-Oriented Social Work Practice: an Ecological Approach," in Anthony N. Maluccio, ed., *Promoting Competence in Clients—a New/Old Approach to Social Work Intervention* (New York: Free Press, 1980), pp. 1–24.

[3] Gordon W. Allport, *Pattern and Growth in Personality* (New York: Holt, Rinehart & Winston, 1961).

[4] Robert W. White, "Motivation Reconsidered: the Concept of Competence," *Psychological Review*, LXVI (1959), 297–333; Robert W. White, "Strategies of Adaptation: an Attempt at Systematic Description," in George Coelho, David A. Hamburg, and John E. Adams, eds., *Coping and Adaptation* (New York: Basic Books, 1974), pp. 47–68.

son. It would be more accurate to view it as a transactional concept and define it as an attribute of the transaction between the person and the environment. Such a definition is emphasized in particular by Sundberg, Snowden, and Reynolds,[5] who propose the notion of ecological competence. These authors assert that an adequate consideration of competence should take into account all relevant personal dimensions, such as someone's skills, qualities, and expectations *and* their interaction with environmental stimuli and situational expectations.

COMPONENTS OF ECOLOGICAL COMPETENCE

Drawing from the formulation of Sundberg, Snowden, and Reynolds as well as related theoretical perspectives, I regard the major components of ecological competence as capacities and skills, motivational aspects, and environmental qualities. (This perspective on competence is similar to Ripple, Alexander, and Polemis's[6] "motivation, capacity, and opportunity" paradigm. However, it goes beyond it in such ways as emphasis on the dynamic interplay between people and their environments.)

Capacities and skills. This dimension includes capacities of the person in cognition, perception, intelligence, language, and physical health. It also encompasses a person's qualities in such areas as flexibility, tolerance for diversity, initiative or self-direction, reality testing, judgment, and tolerance for anxiety. In addition, it refers to specific proficiencies of an individual in areas such as athletics or interpersonal skills.

Motivational aspects. This category comprises the person's interests, hopes, aspirations—in short, the set of drives or energies variously described as competence motivation,[7] in-

---

[5] Norman D. Sundberg, Lonnie R. Snowden, and William M. Reynolds, "Toward Assessment of Personal Competence and Incompetence in Life Situations," *Annual Review of Psychology*, XXIX (1978), 179–211.

[6] Lillian Ripple, Ernestina Alexander, and Bernice W. Polemis, *Motivation, Capacity, and Opportunity* (Chicago: University of Chicago, School of Social Service Administration, 1964).

[7] White, "Motivation Reconsidered."

trinsic motivation,[8] or self-actualization.[9] These terms in essence refer to the human being's drive to deal with the environment, to seek stimulation, to cope with challenges, to accomplish, and to master.

Environmental qualities. The other major component of competence consists of significant environmental qualities impinging on a person's functioning at any given point. Examples include environmental resources and supports such as social networks, environmental demands, and institutional pressures and supports. Effective behavior requires a "goodness of fit" between personal abilities and environmental demands and supports. The complementarity or "goodness of fit" between people's needs and qualities and environmental demands and characteristics strongly influences adaptation and competence.

COMPETENCE-ORIENTED SOCIAL WORK

In conjunction with related formulations such as the life model of social work practice,[10] the concept of ecological competence leads to an approach that views the promotion of competence in human beings as a significant function of social work intervention. The approach reflects themes that are common to other perspectives on practice, but it is characterized by integrated emphasis on a number of features that have been discussed elsewhere [11] and are outlined here.

Humanistic perspective. Human beings are viewed as striving, active organisms capable of organizing their lives and developing their potentialities as long as they have appropriate environmental supports. The humanistic perspective leads to de-emphasis of pathology and recognition of each

---

[8] Edward L. Deci, *Intrinsic Motivation* (New York and London: Plenum Press, 1975).
[9] Abraham H. Maslow, *Motivation and Personality* (2d ed.; New York: Harper & Row, 1954).
[10] Carel B. Germain and Alex Gitterman, *The Life Model of Social Work Practice* (New York: Columbia University Press, 1980).
[11] Maluccio, *op. cit.*

person's multipotentialities, that is, actual as well as latent resources, strengths, and creativity.

Redefinition of human problems. Emphasis on coping and adaptation as transactional phenomena results in viewing human difficulties as "problems in living" or as manifestations of the poor fit or lack of mutuality between people and their environments. Problems are conceptualized in terms of the outcomes of transactional processes that create stress and place demands on the person's coping capacities.

Competence clarification. Assessment or diagnostic evaluation is reformulated as competence clarification, that is, as the process of identifying and understanding the person's competence in dealing with the environment at a particular time. Specific purposes are: (1) clarifying the unique capacities, skills, motivations, and potentialities of the client system; (2) clarifying the characteristics of the impinging environment that influence the client's coping and adaptive patterns; and (3) clarifying the "goodness of fit" between the client system and its impinging environment.

Redefinition of client and practitioner roles. Clients are viewed as partners in the helping process and as resources rather than carriers of pathology. Social workers are defined as enabling or change agents who play diverse roles and use varying approaches in order to provide the conditions necessary for clients to achieve their purposes, engage in their developmental processes, and carry out their tasks.[12]

Redefinition of client-worker relationship. To be effective in promoting competence, the relationship should be characterized by encouragement of client autonomy, reduction of the authority and power invested in the worker, and elimination of hidden agenda.[13] Workers should reduce social

[12] See Elliot Studt, "Social Work Theory and Implications for the Practice of Methods," *Social Work Education Reporter*, XVI (1968), 22–24, 42–46.

[13] Ann L. Hartman, "The Extended Family as a Resource for Change: an Ecological Approach to Family-centered Practice," in Carel B. Germain, ed., *Social Work Practice: People and Environments* (New York: Columbia University Press, 1979), pp. 239–66.

distance and nurture "a relationship that manifests openness, authenticity, honesty, and human caring."[14]

Focus on life processes and experiences. In intervention there is explicit use of the client's own life processes (such as life tasks and developmental crises) and life experiences (such as life events that unfold in the natural course of living). "Life itself is viewed as the arena of change: Life experiences, events, and processes can be exploited for their 'therapeutic value'. . . . Clients' own situations are used to generate opportunities for the productive use of coping, striving, and goal-directed action."[15]

Using the environment. Competence flourishes through a nutritive environment that is suited to the person's needs and qualities and that supports the natural life processes. Consequently, there is emphasis on understanding the environment with all its complexities and restructuring it in a purposive and systematic fashion.

Regular use of client feedback. The final feature is the use of client feedback, that is, having workers obtain, on a regular basis, the views of clients concerning their helping efforts. As discussed elsewhere,[16] client feedback can have a variety of positive consequences, such as providing opportunities for decision-making, reducing the social distance between client and practitioner, and increasing the client's sense of control over his or her life.

In short, competence-oriented social work practice essentially consists of changing the person-environment transaction so as to support and/or enhance the competence of individuals, families, and groups to deal effectively with the environment.

[14] Carel B. Germain, "Ecology and Social Work," in Germain, ed., *op. cit.*, pp. 1–22.

[15] Anthony N. Maluccio, "Promoting Competence through Life Experiences," in Germain, ed., *op. cit.*, p. 289.

[16] Anthony N. Maluccio, *Learning from Clients—Interpersonal Helping as Viewed by Clients and Social Workers* (New York: Free Press, 1979).

PROMOTING CLIENT COMPETENCE[17]

Child welfare is an ideal context in which to implement the competence-oriented perspective, since it is a field of practice in which social workers are clearly at the "crossroads of life"[18] and thus have opportunities to influence people-environment transactions.

EXPANDED DEFINITION OF THE "CASE"

To implement the competence-oriented perspective, we need to begin by defining a child welfare "case" more broadly than we do currently. Meyer suggests what might be involved in such an expanded definition:

. . . a boundary might be drawn around a certain number of city blocks, or, in rural areas, around a certain number of square miles. Within that area, all the components of child welfare transactions would be located—natural parents, child, foster parents, group home, crash pads—counseling center, administrative office, and so on.[19]

At present the comprehensive view of child welfare services proposed by Meyer is not widely reflected in practice. Consequently, as concluded in a nationwide survey of policies and programs for children in out-of-home care, the service delivery system is so fragmented and inadequate that it appears that families and children "don't count."[20] By redefining a child welfare "case" as Meyer indicates, we can provide services to children and families in the context of their natural life situations. We may thus have a better op-

[17]This section is in part adapted from Anthony N. Maluccio, "An Ecological Perspective on Practice with Parents of Children in Foster Care," in Anthony N. Maluccio and Paul A. Sinanoglu, eds., *The Challenge of Partnership: Working with Parents of Children in Foster Care* (New York: Child Welfare League of America; forthcoming).
[18]Bertha C. Reynolds, "Between Client and Community: a Study of Responsibility in Social Casework," *Smith College Studies in Social Work,* V (1934), 5–128.
[19]Carol H. Meyer, "What Directions Social Work Practice?" *Social Work,* XXIV (1979), 266–73.
[20]Children's Defense Fund, *Children without Homes* (Washington, D.C.: the Fund, 1978).

RESTRUCTURING THE ENVIRONMENT

The environment of most parents and children who come to the attention of child welfare workers is not sufficiently nutritive; that is, it does not support their coping and adaptive efforts. On the contrary, frequently the environment is so impoverished and depriving that it interferes with their strivings toward growth and competence.

A major function of social work intervention, therefore, is to help clients to restructure their environment, to modify or enrich it so that it is more suited to their needs and qualities and more conducive to their positive functioning. Children and parents need to have "an average expectable environment."[26]

Based on the particular needs of each family, restructuring of the environment can be accomplished in a variety of ways. In many cases, it involves helping parents to identify actual or potential resources in their social networks, such as neighbors, friends, members of the kinship system, or informal helpers. With certain ethnic groups, for example, the extended family may provide resources to help a parent care for a child so as to avert placement in an institution or foster home or to shorten the placement.

In other cases, enriching the environment may mean introducing a new person such as a homemaker or parent aide. Various interesting programs have been established involving paraprofessionals to educate and support parents.[27] The parents' environment is enriched so as to provide better opportunities for skills learning, need fulfillment, and competence development. For instance, the introduction of a supportive person such as a paraprofessional aide or an accepting grandparent figure can offer

[26] Heinz Hartmann, *Ego Psychology and the Problem of Adaptation* (New York: International Universities Press, 1958).

[27] Nancy A. Carroll and John W. Reich, "Issues in Implementation of the Parent Aide Concept," *Social Casework,* LIX (1978), 152–60; Lauren A. Spinelli and Karen S. Barton, "Home Management Services for Families with Disturbed Children," *Child Welfare,* LIX (1980), 43–52.

nourishment to the parents themselves, thus enhancing their capacity to give to their own children. As another example, enriching the parents' environment through participation in the activities of a residential treatment center can help to strengthen their parenting skills.[28]

In nearly all situations coming to the attention of child welfare agencies, parents need concrete services and institutional supports. In various demonstration projects it has been found that the number of children who return to their own homes increases significantly when parents are given intensive help along with adequate supports.[29]

EMPOWERING CLIENTS

Child welfare practice should also stress approaches that serve to empower clients—parents or children—that is, to help them to enhance their competence in dealing with environmental challenges. Various themes should be highlighted in this connection.

Knowledge from ego psychology, biology, ecology, and other fields can guide practitioners in finding ways to help clients develop their competence in dealing with life challenges. Above all, there should be de-emphasis of pathology, especially psychopathology, and greater emphasis on clients as active, striving human beings. In child placement, for example, there is a tendency to view the problems leading to foster care as reflecting primarily the psychopathology of the parents. There is inadequate attention to societal conditions that limit the power of parents and interfere with their coping efforts.

In the competence-oriented perspective, on the other hand, there is emphasis on the resources and supports needed by parents. "Human problems, needs, and conflicts need to be translated into adaptive tasks providing the

[28] Nadia E. Finkelstein, "Family-centered Group Care—the Children's Institution from a Living Center to a Center for Change," in Maluccio and Sinanoglu, eds., *op. cit.*

[29] Janet Lahti et al., *A Follow-up Study of the Oregon Project* (Portland, Oreg.: Regional Research Institute for Human Services, 1978).

client with opportunities for growth, mastery, and competence development."[30] For instance, a parent who is labeled abusing or neglectful can be helped to learn or relearn skills in child care. To accomplish this, the problem has to be redefined, not as one of child abuse or neglect but as a situation involving lack of knowledge or inadequate parenting skills. In short, the focus is on identifying and removing obstacles that interfere with the parents' coping capacities.

Empowering clients also means redefining them as resources. As they are given adequate opportunities, parents as well as children can mobilize their own potentialities and natural adaptive strivings. As demonstrated in recent years by the success of various self-help groups such as Parents Anonymous, parents can be recognized as resources who can help each other. It has been shown, too, that parents' organizations can lead to new roles for parents, new participation in rewarding activities, and ultimately a new sense of mastery as human beings and improved competence as parents.[31] Social work intervention should aim toward empowering clients to accomplish their purposes and meet their needs through individual and collective efforts.

PROMOTING WORKER COMPETENCE

The principles suggested by the competence perspective essentially apply to workers as well as clients. As human beings, workers also need an "average expectable environment"[32] in order to be able to carry out their roles and use and develop their potentialities.

Critics of child welfare services increasingly place on the workers the burden for various actual or supposed failures of the service delivery system. For instance, there is much

[30] Maluccio, "Promoting Competence in Clients," p. 290.
[31] Rosemarie Carbino, "Developing a Parent Organization: New Roles for Parents of Children in Foster Care," in Maluccio and Sinanoglu, eds., *op. cit.*
[32] Hartmann, *op. cit.*

talk about changing workers' attitudes and improving workers' skills through training. There is much concern about burnout, which is attributed largely to workers' personality factors or difficulty in dealing with job pressures. All of this may represent yet another effort to blame the victim.

Although there is no doubt that worker performance in child welfare needs to be strengthened, the solution to this problem lies not so much in the workers themselves as in their working environment. If one follows a competence-oriented perspective, there is much that is suggested in the way of changing the environment so as to promote the competence of workers.

RESTRUCTURING THE WORK ENVIRONMENT

There has been wide recognition of the strains and stresses that workers experience in child welfare practice, as they are confronted with complex demands and conflicting claims on their cognitive, emotional, and physical energies. In general, the problem has been attributed to the pressures of working with difficult, demanding cases. Increasingingly, we have also realized that various systemic factors put additional burdens on workers—factors such as limited resources, ambivalent societal opinions of their roles and the functions of child welfare agencies; the political context, with frequent investigations and exposés of public child welfare agencies by governmental and legislative bodies and the media; limited administrative support; insufficient recognition of their efforts; and so on and on. It is not an exaggeration to say that most child welfare workers function in an environment that is not conducive to their growth, their satisfaction, or development of their competence. It may be argued, indeed, that those who manage to cope effectively do so in spite of the system, in spite of the environment.

The environment of workers therefore must be restructured and enriched. Adequate opportunities must be provided to enable them to function productively. These include not only material resources and supports, but also opportunities for recognition, gratification, and positive feedback. They include opportunities to participate in policy-making and program-planning processes, to have an impact on the environment, and to exercise one's decision-making function. They include respect for workers on the part of administrators and the community in general. In short, the environment must provide conditions for competent functioning: opportunity, such as supports and resources; respect from others, which enhances self-respect; and power, which supports professional decision-making.[33]

These conditions hardly exist in practice today. For instance, while child welfare workers are required to make "life-and-death" decisions involving children, in most agencies they have to go through various channels to obtain access to a resource such as day care service for a client—if they can even do so.

REDEFINING THE ROLES OF WORKERS

The notion of changing the environment is abstract and global. Furthermore, the service delivery system is complex and difficult to restructure. One possible avenue for change lies in the area of workers' roles.

In most child welfare settings, workers often are overwhelmed by the complex and intense demands placed on them as they attempt to work with children and parents. A major problem is that the social worker is often required to be all things to all people: therapist for child and biological parents; consultant or supervisor with foster parents; case manager, advocate, and so on. Moreover, these multiple roles have to be carried out despite insufficient training, high caseloads, and limited resources.

Although the worker should play a central role in all child welfare cases, he or she cannot be expected to be omnipotent. His or her major role should be redefined as that

[33] M. Brewster Smith, "Competence and Socialization," in John A. Clausen, ed., *Socialization and Society* (Boston: Little, Brown & Co., 1968), pp. 270–320.

of a catalyst or enabling agent, someone who helps the client to identify or create and use necessary resources. The worker uses a variety of approaches and calls on a variety of resources in order to help provide the conditions necessary for clients to achieve their purposes, to meet life challenges, to engage in their natural life developmental processes, and to carry out their tasks.

The redefinition of workers' functions goes together with the redefined roles of foster parents and biological parents. In child placement, for instance, it has been shown that the goal of achieving permanent planning for each child is facilitated when foster parents are considered to be resources for biological parents.[34] Through role redefinition, parents, foster parents, and workers can unite to create new helping systems that are ultimately more effective and rewarding for everyone concerned.

This stance means that child welfare workers should de-emphasize insight-oriented, psychotherapeutic methods. It means that they should become expert in the use of community resources and natural helping networks as well as in the creation of new resources when there are service gaps in the community. It means that they should reallocate their own time and energies; for example, instead of putting excessive time into unproductive investigatory tasks such as home-finding, they could put more energy into working with parents. It means that they could adopt more educationally oriented roles aimed not at treating clients but at teaching them more effective ways of coping. It means that they would put more emphasis on home-based services[35] and reverse the historical trend of child welfare as a separation device.

[34] Cf. Patricia Ryan, Emily Jean McFadden, and Bruce L. Warren, "Foster Families: a Resource for Helping Biological Parents," in Maluccio and Sinanoglu, eds., *op. cit.*

[35] Sheila Maybanks and Marvin Bryce, eds., *Home-based Services for Children and Families—Policy, Practice, and Research* (Springfield, Ill.: Charles C. Thomas, 1979).

CHANGING THE THRUST OF EDUCATION AND TRAINING

Efforts to restructure the work environment and to redefine worker' roles should be complemented by a different thrust in education and training for child welfare practice. To begin with, we need to reexamine the pervasive emphasis on pathology—especially psychopathology—in our theories and our teaching. As shown in studies of client and worker perceptions of service,[36] the preoccupation with pathology manifests itself in numerous forms: in workers' determined quest for specific causes of their clients' difficulties; in their tendency to uncover intrapsychic conflicts; in their dissatisaction with the outcome of the service and their accomplishments or those of their clients; and in their persistent doubts about their clients' capacities to cope with future life challenges.

Practitioners, moreover, are effectively conditioned by the emphasis on pathology that permeates most theories of human behavior or personality development and most approaches to interpersonal helping. As with social work education in general, there is a need in child welfare to shift the focus from pathology to human strengths, resources, and potentialities. For instance, there should be more emphasis on the varieties of human coping strategies and creative ways through which human beings deal with life demands and expectations. In contrast to the typical normative stance, there should be full appreciation of the different capacities, styles, and qualities of people in different contexts. If this shift occurred, "practitioners would be more likely to view clients as proactive human beings who are capable of organizing their own lives to one degree or another."[37] They would then be better able to place emphasis "not on exploring pathology, but on finding, enhancing, and rewarding competence."[38]

[36] Maluccio, *Learning from Clients.*   [37] *Ibid.,* p. 198.
[38] Salvador Minuchin, "The Plight of the Poverty-stricken Family in the United States," *Child Welfare,* XLIX (1970), 124–30.

It is also urgent to teach students and workers ways of helping human beings to create or build on resources in their own ecological context and to develop their competence and power in transacting with the environment. For example, education should place more emphasis on such aspects as social networks, the role of natural helping systems, and linkages between informal helpers and the professional helping system.

Various approaches are emerging that should be useful: the ecological perspective on social work practice, with its focus on the mutuality and dynamic interaction between people and their environment;[39] task-oriented modalities, with their emphasis on formulation of client and/or worker tasks and stimulation of the clients' own cognitive powers and processes;[40] and educationally oriented practice models, such as "relationship enhancement,"[41] that highlight the teaching and learning of interpersonal skills and other coping strategies as means of preventing as well as treating problems.

Most of these approaches also involve resources and concrete services that are necessary to help clients make their environment more nurturing and more conducive to their growth and self-fulfillment. This suggests that educators need to stress a more active orientation toward the environment; they need to give more weight to nonclinical activities such as advocacy, situational intervention, and environmental manipulation—all of which have traditionally been neglected or have had limited prestige in the hierarchy of treatment modalities.

At the same time, there should be more emphasis on accountability to clients, not just to agencies or to funding bodies. This involves, among other aspects, training workers to act not only on the basis of their professional judg-

[39] Germain and Gitterman, *op. cit.*
[40] William J. Reid, *The Task-centered System* (New York: Columbia University Press, 1978).
[41] Bernard G. Guerney, Jr., *Relationship Enhancement* (San Francisco: Jossey-Bass, 1977).

ment and knowledge, but also in response to the client's definition of the "problem" and the client's ideas about what will be helpful. In essence, it involves teaching them to respond flexibly on the basis of their clients' needs, expectations, and life styles.

Finally, as a most important means of promoting competence, educational programs should stress preparation for autonomous practice. It is crucial to help develop workers' own capacities to think and to act professionally so that they may be ready for whatever tomorrow may bring.

CONCLUSION

In the face of diminishing resources, increased demands for service, and questions about the effectiveness of the service delivery system in child welfare, there is a danger of over-preoccupation with techniques and a narrowing of our vision. The competence-oriented perspective reminds us that, beyond concern with technology, we need to develop a grand design for service delivery that takes into account the many forces that help shape the functioning of clients and workers. It reminds us that, although the world's physical resources are limited, human resources are underutilized and can flourish in a nutritive environment.

Through an explicit focus on competence in education as well as in practice, child welfare in the 1980s could well become a major component of a revitalized social work profession.

Maternal Deprivation and Learned Helplessness in Child Neglect

JOAN M. JONES and R. L. McNEELY

THE CONCEPT of "learned helplessness" offers an intriguing explanation for the development and maintenance of patterns of passivity, apathy, avoidance, and depression which dominate and impair the psychological and interpersonal functioning of countless individuals. First discovered by chance, by Seligman and Maier,[1] in a laboratory experiment with restrained mongrel dogs, the variables associated with the occurrence of the phenomenon subsequently have been explored in experiments with various human subjects, including depressed patients[2] and nondepressed individuals.[3] In general, the findings have supported the premise that when human beings are exposed to one or more frustrating or aversive life events

JOAN M. JONES is Assistant Professor, School of Social Welfare, University of Wisconsin-Milwaukee.

R. L. MCNEELY is Associate Professor, School of Social Welfare, and Director, Center for Adult Development, University of Wisconsin-Milwaukee.

[1] Martin P. Seligman and S. F. Maier, "Failure to Escape Traumatic Shock," *Journal of Experimental Psychology*, LXXIV (1967), 1–9.

[2] W. R. Miller and Martin P. Seligman, "Depression and Learned Helplessness in Man," *Journal of Abnormal Psychology*, LXXXIV (1975), 228–38; W. R. Miller, Martin P. Seligman, and H. Kurlander, "Learned Helplessness, Depression and Anxiety," *Journal of Nervous and Mental Disease*, CLXI (1975), 347–57; D. C. Klein, E. Fencil-Morse and Martin P. Seligman, "Learned Helplessness, Depression and the Attribution of Failure," *Journal of Personality and Social Psychology*, XXXIII (1976), 508–16.

[3] D. C. Klein and Martin P. Seligman, "Reversal of Performance Deficits and Perceptual Deficits in Learned Helplessness and Depression, *Journal of Abnormal Psychology*, LXXXV (1976), 11–26.

which they have no control to terminate or alter, a state of learned helplessness may result. This state, specifically, the assumption of no control over the events of one's life, may produce behavioral changes such as undermining an individual's motivation to respond, retarding ability to learn that responding works, and/or causing other emotional disturbances, primarily depression and anxiety.[4]

The pragmatic applicability of the learned helplessness model as a viable framework which social workers and other mental health professionals can utilize in crisis counseling and in general clinical practice continues to be a topic of theoretical discussions,[5] scholarly critiques,[6] and clinical research with subjects with varied psychological and behavioral problems.[7] A review of these studies and of literature describing characteristics of prevalent types of neglectful mothers[8] prompted the authors to consider ways in which data they had collected in a comparative study of neglecting and nonneglecting mothers might be indicative of similarities in the patterns of behavior subsumed under the label "learned helplessness" and those exhibited by mothers of children evidencing maternal deprivation.[9] If such similari-

---

[4] Martin P. Seligman, *Helplessness: on Depression, Development and Death* (San Francisco: Freeman, 1975), p. 6.

[5] Carol E. Hooker, "Learned Helplessness," *Social Work* (1976), 194–98.

[6] Charles G. Costello, "A Critical Review of Seligman's Laboratory Experiments on Learned Helplessness and Depression in Humans," *Journal of Abnormal Psychology*, LXXXVII (1978), 21–31.

[7] Michael R. O'Leary et al., "Depression and Perception of Reinforcement: Lack of Difference in Expectancy Change among Alcoholics, *Journal of Abnormal Psychology*, LXXXVII (1978), 87, 110–12; William P. Sacco, and Jack E. Hockanson, "Expectations of Success and Anagram Performance of Depressives in a Public and Private Setting," *Journal of Abnormal Psychology*, LXXXVII (1978), 122–30; Robert C. Smolen, "Expectancies, Mood, and Performance of Depressed and Nondepressed Psychiatric Inpatients on Chance and Skill Tasks," *Journal of Abnormal Psychology*, LXXXVII (1978), 91–101.

[8] Norman A. Polansky, Christine De Saix and Shlomo A. Sharlin, *Child Neglect: Understanding and Reaching the Parent* (New York: Child Welfare League of America, Inc., 1977), pp. 21–53.

[9] The term "maternal deprivation" is used differently in the literature. Sometimes, it refers to children who have been reared entirely without a mother, for example in an institution (Seligman, *op. cit.*, pp. 143–44), and in other cases, it is used, as it will be here, to refer to mothers who neglect or deprive their children

ties were found to exist, a rationale would be provided for the utilization of assessment and intervention procedures with these mothers that have already proved effective with individuals manifesting learned helplessness.[10]

BEHAVIORAL SIMILARITIES IN LEARNED HELPLESSNESS AND MATERNAL DEPRIVATION

As conceptualized, the phenomenon of learned helplessness is predicated upon the assumption "that one's own actions have no influence on, or relationship to, the outcomes of events and experiences."[11] This assumption may result from a single intensely traumatic crisis, such as the unexpected death of a loved one; it may come from a change in life circumstances, such as loss of a job, that radically affects one's daily life patterns;[12] or it may result from the pervasive lack of control over basic life events, such as that experienced by individuals living in dire poverty.[13]

Whatever the etiology, once helplessness has been learned, and accepted as inevitable, individuals may generalize the expectation of noncontrol to other life situations. They may even begin to exhibit patterns of avoidance, passivity, and nonaction in those situations in which they do have control and can predict outcome.[14] Specific behaviors associated with learned helplessness include: isolation and withdrawal, as evidenced by an individual's preference to remain alone or to stay in bed much of the time; generally slow behavior; feelings of inability to act, manifested by nonaction or refusal to initiate new responses or to make decisions; and the general appearance of an "empty" person who has "given up."[15]

Many of the avoidance or passive behaviors exhibited by

of physical and emotional nurturance. See Robert Gray Patton and Lytt Gardner, *Growth Failure in Maternal Deprivation* (Springfield, Ill.: Charles C. Thomas, 1968).
[10] Seligman, *op. cit.*   [11] Hooker, *op. cit.*, p. 194.
[12] Seligman, *op. cit.*, pp. 1–6.   [13] *Ibid.*, pp. 159–65.
[14] D. S. Hiroto and Martin P. Seligman, "Generality of Learned Helplessness in Man," *Journal of Personality and Social Psychiatry*, XXXI (1974), 311–27.
[15] Seligman, *op. cit.*, p. 82.

mothers of severely physically neglected children whose conditions have been attributed to "maternal deprivation" are similar, if not identical, to those just described. Although Polansky, De Saix, and Sharlin identify five types of neglecting mothers—the apathetic-futile mother, the impulse-ridden mother, the mentally retarded mother, the mother in a reactive depression, and the psychotic mother[16]—it is mothers of the apathetic-futile type whose behaviors most consistently resemble those of learned helplessness. Apathetic-futile mothers have been described as "exhibiting a pervasive aura that nothing is really worth doing, seldom going after anything with a sense of energy or purpose, being unresponsive to attempts to mobilize them; and manifesting an emotional numbness which is not so alive as depression."[17] They also lack intense personal relationships beyond a kind of forlorn clinging, have low competence in most areas often associated with fear of failure and generally are unable to express important feelings.[18]

As noted, it was the striking parallels in the behaviors of victims of learned helplessness and the mothers of neglected children that led the authors to assess aspects of the lives of the neglecting mothers that might have influenced the development of feelings of noncontrol, and consequently resulted in their refusal to initiate basic nurturing responses or, in general, to retard any efforts to act on their own behalf in the best interests of their children.

THE STUDY

METHOD AND SELECTED FINDINGS

The study utilized social learning theory principles of behavioral development and maintenance as the framework

[16] Polansky, De Saix, and Sharlin, *op. cit.*, p. 21.
[17] *Ibid.*, p. 22.   [18] *Ibid.*

within which to identify and compare differentiating features in the daily lives of fifty-eight mothers, as well as differences in their nurturing knowledge and in the behavioral expectations they held for their children. Twenty-nine mothers of neglected children (*N* group) and twenty-nine mothers of nonneglected children (*N-N* group) were matched for maternal age, average intelligence, number of children, age and spacing of children, and Aid to Families of Dependent Children (AFDC) allotment levels.

Children whose mothers were selected for inclusion in the *N* group all manifested several of the criteria of retarded physical growth, inadequate medical care, and generally deficient nurturance which had been developed to substantiate severe physical neglect.[19] Children of *N-N* group mothers manifested none of these evidences of neglect. Subjects in both groups were surveyed regarding the number of daily life activities, events, and interactions in which they found enjoyment and the frequency with which they sampled them. The degree of their enjoyment of each item was indicated by their selection of one of four Likert-type responses, ranging from "not at all enjoyable" to "very, very enjoyable." They also responded to questions involving their nurturing knowledge, the behavioral expectations they held for their children, the frequency of their utilization of baby-sitters, and the number of household conveniences they possessed.

Initial analysis of the findings indicated that, in their daily lives, mothers of neglected children had fewer, and experienced significantly less frequently, "highly" satisfying life activities and interpersonal contacts and owned significantly fewer household conveniences than did their matched counterparts.[20] Similarly, there was a significant difference in the nurturing knowledge of the *N* and *N-N* group moth-

[19] Joan M. Jones and R. L. McNeely, "Mothers Who Neglect: Differentiating Features in Their Daily Lives and Implications for Practice." *Corrective and Social Psychiatry* XXVI (1980), 135–43.
[20] *Ibid.*

ers, with the *N-N* group scoring higher.[21] Although, clearly, a potentially important variable affecting the occurrence of child neglect, the extent to which mothers found various interactions with their children to be enjoyable was not determined in the initial data analysis.

As the authors began to explore similarities in the behavioral patterns of neglecting mothers and individuals manifesting behaviors indicative of learned helplessness, a subgroup of twelve items relating to mothers' interactions with their children was assessed to determine whether there was any difference between the degree of enjoyment or nonenjoyment that *N* and *N-N* group mothers derived from various activities with their children. For example, mothers were asked to indicate the extent to which they found from "no" enjoyment to "high" enjoyment in "teaching my child/children something" (colors, ABC's, and so forth) and in "reading/singing to my child/children."

Although no statistically significant difference was found in the degree to which mothers reported over-all activities with their children to be nonenjoyable or highly enjoyable, the mothers did differ significantly in the extent to which some of the individual items, examined separately, were reported to hold no enjoyment or to be enjoyable. For example, mothers differed significantly on the satisfaction/nonsatisfaction they reported they derived from "reading/singing to my child/children"; "breast feeding a baby;" "going out with my child/children to a fair, zoo, park"; and having a child of mine say he/she loves me." Mothers of neglected children found all of these to be less enjoyable than did mothers of nonneglected children.

As determined by weighted scores, *N* group mothers also differed significantly on the frequency with which they actually were able to experience activities with their children that they indicated would hold some degree of enjoyment. That is, mothers' reports of how much they would enjoy

[21] Joan M. Jones and R. L. McNeely, "Mothers Who Neglect and Those Who Don't: a Comparative Study," *Social Casework*, November, 1980.

specific activities with their children were weighted by how often they actually sampled these items. Points on the scale indicating the degree of enjoyment ranged from a score of o (I do *not* enjoy it at all) to 3 (I enjoy it *very, very much*). Similarly, the points indicating the frequency of sampling of each item in a given month ranged from o (I *never* experience this) to 3 (I *often* experience this). Scores of subjects were multiplied to produce a weighted measure which reflected both the enjoyment level and sampling frequency of an item.

It should be noted that this weighing technique does not completely differentiate among all combinations of life conditions. Specifically, scores of zero were possible for three different combinations of life conditions. Mothers might indicate no enjoyment for a number of activities with their children and yet be compelled to participate in them frequently. They might enjoy a number of activities in which they were never able to participate, or they might enjoy very few activities and participate in none.

In summary, not only did mothers of neglected children have fewer and sample less frequently highly satisfying daily life activities and interpersonal interactions, they also derived less satisfaction from certain activities with their children, and those activities they did find enjoyable, they experienced less frequently than than did mothers of nonneglected children. The potential for neglecting mothers to have the nonneglecting aspects of interactions with their children accentuated was further increased by their comparatively lower utilization of baby-sitters. Approximately 38 percent of *N* mothers stated that they never and/or rarely hired baby-sitters, in contrast to slightly less than 21 percent of *N-N* mothers. Almost 59 percent of *N* group mothers compared to about 38 percent of *N-N* group mothers never and/or rarely had friends baby-sit for them; 52 percent of the *N* group never and/or rarely had relatives baby-sit for them whereas only 21 percent of the *N-N* mothers never/and or rarely had such assistance.

ESTABLISHING BEHAVIORAL SIMILARITIES

Similarities in the behavioral patterns of neglecting mothers of the "apathetic-futile" type to those of individuals in states of learned helplessness become immediately apparent when general characteristics of the N group mothers' personal interpersonal behaviors are described. Mothers with histories of mental illness, mental retardation, or learning disabilities were not included in the N group, and the N group mothers who participated in the survey all exhibited behaviors previously described both as manifestations of apathy-futility and of learned helplessness. Specifically, many of the neglecting mothers interviewed, regardless of the time of day, from late morning to late afternoon, and regardless of the prearrangement of the interview time, were still in their bathrobes. Their children also were inadequately clothed, extremely dirty, and sometimes infested with lice. The conditions of all the N group houses reflected these mothers' total avoidance of any household or cleaning activities.

Although all N group mothers had agreed in advance to be interviewed, their verbal and facial expressions were flat of affect. Many of them sat, during at least the early part of the interview, staring blankly at television, responding to the survey items in dull monotones, and looking only occasionally at the interviewer. Similarly, requests or questions from their children or the crying of their infants prompted little or no response, and the severity of the diaper rash which most of the infants had, attested to the infrequency of changing and bathing. Although these descriptions are familiar to child-protective service workers, the life experiences and conditions contributing to the development and maintenance of neglecting mothers' feelings of hopelessness and, consequently, of helplessness frequently are not explored. Too, although their behaviors, or rather their non-behaviors, are suggestive of their having accepted a certain uncontrollability over their lives, the basis on which they have made this conclusion was not investigated.

The findings of this study suggest similarities between the ways in which behaviors of maternal deprivation and those of learned helplessness are developed and offer two possible explanations for neglecting mothers' apathy and inaction. First, because the number and frequency of highly enjoyed daily life activities, interpersonal contacts, and specific interactions with their children are significantly lower for mothers of neglected children, these mothers may have learned from consistent experience that they can exercise little or no control over the occurrence of pleasant events in their lives. Conversely, if daily life activities or interpersonal contacts with friends, relatives, and their own children are sufficiently unsatisfying and yet must be endured with some regularity, these same mothers may have developed feelings of helplessness predicated upon their inability to terminate unpleasant events.

Whatever the genesis of their feelings of uncontrollability, the fact that their daily lives are, indeed, marked by a dearth of positive events and interpersonal interactions or by the prevalence of nonenjoyable ones only serves to validate these feelings. Most important, helplessness, learned from living in chronically aversive life circumstances, may generalize, negatively affecting all aspects of an individual's adaptive behavioral repertoire and disrupting the ability to learn new behaviors.[22] This generalization of helplessness well may explain the development and maintenance of behaviors of avoidance and passivity manifested by mothers of neglected children.

GUIDELINES FOR ASSESSMENT AND INTERVENTION

As Seligman has shown, "forced exposure to the fact that responding produces reinforcement is the most effective way of breaking up learned helplessness."[23] Thus, a primary task with mothers of neglected children becomes the identification of conditions which are controlling and per-

---

[22] Seligman, *op. cit.*, pp. 36–37.   [23] *Ibid.*, p. 99.

petuating their perceptions of uncontrollability and the identification and creation of new sources of reinforcement.

One means of ascertaining reinforcers which mothers might enjoy is having them complete, with a worker, a pleasant activities schedule similar to the one developed by MacPhillamy and Lewinsohn[24] and modified for this study. Although *N* group mothers initially responded blandly to the questions regarding satisfying life events and interactions, as the interviewer's sincere interest in their opinions became evident, they became more involved in responding. This suggests that positive adult feedback may be of potentially high reinforcing value to mothers who have withdrawn socially. Too, it underscores the importance of structuring initial interviews to focus on mothers' own needs, daily frustrations, and feelings of uncontrollability rather than on accentuating, by lengthy review, the inadequacies of their nurturing behaviors.

Once reinforcers have been identified, conditions may be structured to provide positive reinforcement for small improvements in nurturing efforts and/or for mothers' engaging in activities with their children. Design and implementation of individualized intervention programs require considerable time and effort. However, pilot programs such as the Home and Community Treatment Team[25] currently being tested by the Milwaukee County Department of Social Services are endeavoring to establish that short-term, intensive, and individualized intervention efforts will produce long-term positive growth.

[24] D. J. MacPhillamy and P. M. Lewinsohn, *Manual for the Pleasant Events Schedule* (1974; available from P. M. Lewinsohn at Psychology Department, University of Oregon, Eugene, Oreg.; mimeographed).

[25] The Home and Community Treatment Team is an innovative behavior management training program currently being offered by the Milwaukee Department of Social Services to families whose children are "at risk" of being removed from the home. The team consists of three social workers, a supervisor, and a consulting psychologist who, together with the family, develop and implement the treatment plan. The social workers make daily visits to the home, providing immediate reinforcement for positive behavioral changes shown by the mother in the care of her children and for any increased efforts she makes to gain control of her own behaviors.

Alternatives to individualized intervention programs are assertiveness training groups or self-management, skills-training, or social skills development groups, structured to increase the interpersonal skills of mothers whose lives have become characterized by avoidance of any social interaction. The availability of these groups is increasing as their efficacy is being substantiated.[26]

This discussion of similarities in behaviors associated with maternal deprivation and those associated with learned helplessness suggests a new perspective from which to assess the dynamics of cases of child neglect. Researchers and practitioners have agreed for some time that the passivity and/or nonaction of mothers of physically neglected children is not a function of malicious intent.[27] However, it is only recently that professionals have begun to emphasize the necessity of developing distinctive treatment programs and predictive instruments to reach this problem population—a population which exceeds by a ratio of more than 10 to 1 that of abusing parents.[28]

Perhaps the most persuasive argument for considering behaviors of maternal neglect to be functions of learned helplessness is that considerable research has been done in developing and implementing, with success, techniques of intervention with individuals experiencing the latter condition. Finally, the theory of learned helplessness is itself predicated upon two optimistic principles of social learning theory: (1) if maladaptive behaviors have been learned, they can be unlearned; and (2) if certain adaptive behaviors never have been learned, given consistent and positively reinforcing environmental conditions, they can be learned.

[26] Sander J. Kornblight et al., "An Evaluation of the Contribution of Self-Reinforcement and Behavioral Assignments to the Efficacy of a Self-Control Therapy Program" (paper presented at the Behavior Therapy Conference, New Highlands University, Las Vegas, New Mex., 1979).

[27] Leontine Young, *Wednesday's Children* (New York, McGraw-Hill, 1964).

[28] Polansky, De Saix, and Sharlin, *op. cit.*, p. 4.

The Role of Parent-Child Visiting in Permanency Planning for Children

THE FULL potential of using parent-child visiting in foster care to meet the developmental needs of the child and the service needs of the family has not yet been realized.

The literature suggests that maintaining parent-child contact is critically important for the well-being of the child.[1] In interpreting the results of his five-year investigation of foster care in New York City, David Fanshel concludes: "Like the frequent monitoring of body temperature information for assessing the health of patients in hospitals, the visitation of children should be carefully scrutinized as the best indicator we have concerning the long-term fate of children in care."[2]

While the critical importance of visiting has been recognized, more needs to be known about the realities and underlying dynamics that actually shape the experience. Further work remains to be done in illuminating what Fanshel has called the unknown variables that affect the frequency

MARY S. WHITE is Child Welfare Coordinator, School of Social Work, University of Minnesota, Minneapolis.

This work was supported by Child Welfare Services Grant TEMN 9038 T21.

[1] David Fanshel and Eugene Shinn, *Children in Foster Care: a Longitudinal Investigation* (New York: Columbia University Press, 1978); E. A. Weinstein, *The Self-Image of the Foster Child* (New York: Russell Sage Foundation, 1960).
[2] Fanshel and Shinn, *op. cit.*

and quality of visiting.[3] To identify some of these variables, an exploratory study focusing on visiting was conducted at Hennepin County Community Services, Minneapolis. This article will report on the results of the study.

Information was gathered from interviews with social workers, natural parents, adolescents in placement, and foster parents. Their experiences and perspectives helped to identify factors that deter and those that facilitate visiting. Findings from the interviews suggest that visiting could be used more effectively as a natural vehicle for working with families and children. In cases where maintaining contact is appropriate, social workers should be encouraged to focus on the dynamics of the visiting experience as a major concern in the intervention process. This is in keeping with the growing national interest in permanency planning for children, increasing concern for client rights, and a new awareness of the importance of working with the natural family system.

DEFINITION OF VISITING

What is a "visit"? How would it feel to find yourself in the role of a visitor in your child's home?[4] Is it even possiible for a parent to "visit" his or her own child? Webster defines visit as a "short stay; a coming to stay with another temporarily and usually briefly; a brief residence as a guest; an official or professional call." Given these definitions, is "visiting" an appropriate term to designate the interaction between parents and children? Certainly, the notions of temporariness, brevity, and guest or official status do not fit with a parent-child relationship or with the current emphasis on the importance of permanency and continuity within changing but continuing family relationships.

Because current terminology is inadequate, it has been easy to disregard parent/child rights and needs by overlook-

---

[3] David, Fanshel, "Parental Visiting of Children in Foster Care: Key to Discharge?" *Social Service Review*, XLIX (1975), 513.

[4] Phyllis McAdams, "The Parent in the Shadows," *Journal of Public Social Services*, I, No. 4 (1970), reprinted in *Child Welfare*, LI, No. 1 (1972), 51–55.

ing the significance of visiting. If the full potential of using visiting to foster continuing parent-child interaction is to be realized, a new designation that more adequately expresses the essence of visiting is needed. However, in keeping with traditional usage and for lack of another term, this paper will continue to use "visiting" to mean parent-child visiting in the foster home and the child or adolescent visiting in his or her own home. Nevertheless, a broader interpretation which better connotes the essence of the permanency concept is intended.

SIGNIFICANCE OF VISITING WITHIN A PERMANENCY
FRAMEWORK

The importance of visiting cannot be understood as an isolated phenomenon but should be examined within the framework of permanency for children. The goal of permanency is to reduce foster care drift by developing a plan to reunite children with their families or free them for adoption or long-term foster care within a spcified period. The concept of permanency is significant because it integrates child development knowledge with legal, social, and cultural norms. The essence of the concept goes beyond the placement decision regarding the long-term fate of the child. Within permanency, the thrust is to meet the developmental needs of the child and to act in the best interests of the child.

Permanency has been defined by the Oregon Project, "Freeing Children for Permanent Placement," supported by the U.S. Children's Bureau as follows:

Permanency describes intent. A permanent home is not one that is guaranteed to last forever, but one that is intended to exist indefinitely. When the expectation of permanence is lacking, a child experiences doubt, uncertainty and hesitancy. Permanency planning means clarifying the intent of the placement, and during temporary care, keeping alive a plan for permanency. . . . Permanent homes give commitment and continuity to the child's relationships. . . . Permanent homes are rooted in and sanctioned by cultural norms and the law. . . . Children in permanent homes are recognized . . . as having a respected social status.[5]

A number of states are moving toward permanency through legislation to reduce the drift in foster care by mandating case planning and periodic court review. With the recent passage of the Adoption Assistance and Child Welfare amendments (H.R. 3434—now P.L. 96-272), the objectives of permanency will be imposed from the federal level. States will be encouraged to require practices that favor prevention and permanency and discouraged from the use of custodial foster care.

However, in implementing the law there is a new danger that we become concerned primarily with legal and agency procedures and overlook the substance of permanency as defined by the Oregon Project. Working within this context, the fundamental importance of parent-child visiting should not be underestimated. Visiting could become a cornerstone in the development of a permanent plan and in fostering a sense of permanency for the child whether or not the child returns home.

Despite the evidence that visiting is important for the well-being of both parent and child[6] and the best indicator of the outcome for the child,[7] studies have persistently documented the overwhelming failure of parents to visit their children in placement.[8] Natural parents report that they do not see their children as often as they would like.[9] While definitive proof is not available, a number of reasons have been put forth to explain the failure to visit. These include

---

[5] V. Pike *et al.*, *Permanent Planning for Children in Foster Care: a Handbook for Social Workers* (Portland, Oreg.: Regional Research Institute for Human Services, Portland State University, 1977), pp. 1–2.

[6] Fanshel and Shinn, *op. cit.*; Weinstein, *op cit.*

[7] Fanshel and Shinn, *op. cit.*

[8] Henry S. Maas and Richard E. Engler, *Children in Need of Parents* (New York: Columbia University Press, 1959); Alan Gruber, *Foster Home Care in Massachusetts* (Boston: Governor's Commission on Adoption and Foster Care, 1973); Edmund V. Mech, *Public Welfare Services for Children and Youth in Arizona* (Tucson, Ariz.: Joint Interim Committee on Health and Welfare, 1970).

[9] Gruber, *op. cit.*

discouragement by social workers, traumatic effects on the child, difficulties with the natural parents, inconvenience for the foster parents, transportation and scheduling problems.

In the short run, the arrangements for and the actual visit can be problematic for all those involved. Because visiting has not always been perceived as a basic right of parents and children, workers may have overlooked using it as an opportunity to meet needs related to the separation and to the ultimate fate of the child. However, if children in care are to benefit in the long run from new information about the importance of visiting, changes will have to be made in agency policies, attitudes, and practices. A commitment to change will strengthen permanency planning, insure the rights of the natural family, and provide the family with improved services.

EXPLORATORY STUDY ON PARENT-CHILD VISITING

Through the cooperation of Hennepin County Community Services, Minneapolis, group interviews were conducted with social workers, foster parents, and adolescents in placement. Adolescents were interviewed because it was felt that younger children would not be as able to verbalize their thoughts or feelings. Individual interviews were arranged with biological parents. Participants in the study were asked to identify factors that deter and those that facilitate visiting from their own experiences. It should be noted that difficulties were encountered in arranging interviews with natural parents and further work remains to be undertaken with this group.

A questionnaire was used to solicit information on the following topics:

1. Understanding the purpose and importance of visiting
2. Agency policies and procedures
3. Agency and worker encouragement and facilitation of visiting
4. Type of visiting plan and scheduling procedures

5. Visiting arrangements including place, time, frequency, transportation, geographic distance

6. Persons who have had contact, including parents, siblings, other family members, and friends

7. Expenses related to travel, child care for siblings, support for a child who visits at home, and activities associated with the visit

8. Types of activity pursued during the visit, including play, recreation, television, sharing meals, entertainment, shopping, household tasks, and participation in church, school, or other organizational activities

9. Communication, including discussion of everyday events, problems, and feelings

10. Feelings about visiting and separation

11. Quality of relationships among the parents, child, foster parents, and social worker.

DISCUSSION OF FINDINGS

Analysis of information gathered from the four groups show substantial areas of agreement about the problems and the benefits involved in visiting.

Results indicate that there is agreement in theory about the importance of parental visiting. However, in practice the significance of visiting is often overlooked. Social agencies and workers do not concentrate on visiting. The actual visit creates problems particularly for the foster parents and the child or adolescent. It causes a temporary worsening of the child's behavior and ability to function. Relationships between the natural parent and the child or the foster parent create conflict and bring to the surface negative feelings about separation and placement. Visiting is disruptive to family schedules and functioning. Results from the interviews are reported here in summary form.

Specific problems most frequently cited by foster parents. Visits are disruptive to the child and may result in changed behavior. The child may experience continuing fears of rejection and separation which result in anger, aggression, with-drawal, psychosomatic symptoms, acting out in the family or in school.

Behavior of the natural parents can be problematic. Parents may be uncooperative and unpredictable. Some use alcohol and drugs irresponsibly. They may make unrealistic promises to the child. Frequently, they are disorganized and have standards and schedules for the child that are different from those of the foster family. They often miss appointments without calling, arrive late, and return the child late. They do not seem to know what to do during the visit, particularly when visiting an infant or very young child. For example, instead of interacting with their child, they spend the time talking to the foster parents.

Agencies and social workers do not do enough to encourage visiting and to help the foster parents cope with the problems, particularly those resulting from the child's worsened behavior and the parents' behavior.

Foster parents feel ambivalent about visiting. They recognize its importance but were frustrated, confused, and often angered by the problems created by the visit.

Specific problems most frequently cited by adolescents in placement. Visits bring to the surface painful feelings about the realities of the situation. Rather than trying to cope with the realities of their family and the relationships with parents, adolescents may refuse or balk at visiting. Maintaining contact precipitates overwhelming feelings about separation and loss. They feel they are not helped enough in coping with these feelings. Those who are physically afraid of their parents fear the dangers involved in a visit home. For example, an adolescent reported that she always took a friend along on home visits, as a protective measure.

Visiting schedules and activities are arranged to meet the needs of the foster parents or natural parents and do not take into consideration the adolescent's needs.

The frequency and scheduling of visits are used by foster

or natural parents to reward or punish behavior. For example, foster parents restrict home visits if the adolescent is acting out or disobeying in-house rules.

Specific problems most frequently cited by natural parents. Parents report they are not helped to understand the importance of frequent visiting or the purpose for visiting.

Their child may refuse to visit home or may react negatively to a visit from the parent. As a result, parent-child contacts are often not permitted early in the placement and frequent visiting is not encouraged. Telephoning and other means of communication are not promoted.

Visiting brings out feelings of guilt, inadequacy, and anxiety. Parents suffer from ambivalent feelings about their ability to be parents and to give the child "as good a home as the foster family's." For example, a father stated that he worried about his child's adjustment upon returning home because he could not compete in material ways with the foster family.

Specific problems most frequently cited by social workers. There is a gap between the visiting plan and the reality of the visit. The purpose of maintaining contact needs to be better clarified for all those involved.

Worsening of the child's behavior as a result of visiting is disruptive in the treatment process. If visiting becomes too disruptive, it is difficult to retain foster homes.

Because of the problems involved, foster parents may not cooperate and may sabotage the visiting plan.

The low functioning level and behavior of some natural parents may make the visit problematic.

Problems created by geographic distances often occur when the child is placed in an institution. Lack of funding for travel and for support of the child who visits at home can also be a problem.

BENEFITS OF VISITING

Results show strong agreement among the four groups that maintaining contact is critically important because it allows the child, parent, and other siblings an opportunity to see each other realistically and to work out feelings related to separation and loss. For example, an adolescent reported that she initially rebelled at being required to visit home. However, with the support and help of her social worker, she was able to work through her feelings of grief and anger, and eventually accept the reality of her family situation. Dealing with the realities will lessen the tendency to repress separation feelings and to develop irrational explanations. The need to fantasize (both idealizing the good and exaggerating the bad) will be decreased.

Frequent visiting was also seen as beneficial because it provides opportunities for the parent and child to maintain or develop a relationship that meets developmental needs. An understanding of these needs can be helpful in determining the purpose of visiting, frequency, persons who visit, the place, and the activity. In discussing the benefits, the importance of providing appropriate social services was stressed by the four groups.

RECOMMENDATIONS

An analysis of the information from these interviews suggests that empirical studies have not yet had a substantial impact on practice. Visiting is not perceived by those involved in the foster care system as an essential part of permanency planning nor is it viewed as a natural vehicle for providing social services. Over all, what stands out as most significant is the lack of a common understanding of the importance of parents and children maintaining contact.

The following guidelines are recommended to help in the development of better visiting policies and practices.

1. *Agency policies.* Policies should be developed to encourage and facilitate visiting at all levels of the agency: administrative, staff development, supervisory, and line worker. Limiting or restricting visits should be prohibited unless specific reasons are communicated to all those involved. This is in keeping with current trends favoring client rights.

Visiting should be allowed during the early phase of placement. In general, the younger the child, the more frequent the visits should be. Visiting should never be allowed to be used as an award nor should visiting be refused as punishment for behavior.

A visiting plan that is incorporated into the over-all case plan should be required in all out-of-home placements. Foster parents, natural parents, and the child should participate in developing the plan and be educated about its importance. The plan should specify visiting arrangements, activities, and clarify how the visit will be used in the therapeutic intervention. A visiting log should be maintained, including an evaluation which can be used in case and court review.

Agencies should offer training to supervisors, workers, foster parents, natural parents, and children on the benefits, problems, and significance of visiting. A training model that focuses on visiting has been developed at Hennepin County Community Services for foster parents and workers.[10]

2. *Planning and arrangements.* Prior to the time the child is actually placed, the social worker should begin to prepare the natural parent, child, and foster parent for visiting. The negative and positive consequences should be discussed. In developing a plan, two visiting models can be considered. To meet changing needs, the models are offered as a continuum which recognizes the rights and needs of all those involved.

In the Open Model, foster parents, natural parents, and the child work out visiting arrangements informally and on demand. The social worker is kept informed and is involved in structuring activities for the visit, helping with problems, and assessing the quality of the visit.

In the Mediated Model, the social worker takes pressure

[10] Training for foster parents and social workers has been developed by Becky Richardson, Foster Parent Training Coordinator, Hennepin County Community Services, Minneapolis.

off the clients by facilitating or mediating the visiting arrangements. In addition, the worker carries out the other responsibilities listed above.

3. *Therapeutic use of visiting.* It is recommended that social workers time their appointments to precede immediately and/or follow the visit in order to help the natural parent, child, and foster parent cope with developmental and parenting issues.

Visiting provides natural opportunities to help the parent understand the child's needs within the framework of developmental stages and tasks. The purpose, type of activity, and interaction for each visit should be planned in keeping with developmental and individual needs. In some cases, role playing the visit might help reduce feelings of anxiety and inadequacy. The actual visit can be used to help the parent gain better parenting and child care skills. If the visits are in the foster home, some time for privacy with the child is recommended. Worker observation of the visit, with feedback, might be helpful in certain cases.

Natural parents need to be involved in problem-solving and decision-making about practical matters, whenever feasible. For example, foster parents should include them in making decisions with the child about purchase of clothing, school/social activities, peer relationships, and other concerns. Natural parents, siblings, and other family members might be included on special occasions, such as holidays, birthday celebrations, school conferences, and in church and other organizational activities. These efforts will help children and parents preserve their family identity and continuity and help them increase their sense of control over their situation.

New information about the effect of loss and change on the individual has important implications for children in foster care. Painful feelings of rejection, loss of identity, anger, and guilt, which are associated with the separation, place the parent and child in a highly vulnerable situation. There is evidence that the child exposed to sustained sepa-

ture and other opportunities on the one hand and to escape cruel and oppressive parents or masters on the other.

SOME CHARACTERISTICS OF RUNAWAYS

Recent research on runaways[2] has developed a definition of runaways as youth aged 10 to 17 who were absent from home at least overnight without parental permission. Using this definition, the National Statistical Survey of Runaways,[3] after corrections for underreporting, estimated that 733,-000 youths ran away in 1975. They note that if shorter runs of two hours or more are included, the figure approximates one million—a figure which appears frequently in the press.

Runaways are almost equally divided between males (53 percent) and females (47 percent). The largest proportion are 16 years of age (31 percent). Twenty-five percent are 15; 24.0 percent are 17; 9.0 percent are 14; 6.0 percent are 13; 3.0 percent are 12; 2.0 percent are 11; and 0.2 percent are 10. Some confusion has arisen concerning the sex and age of runaways because of reports from runaway shelters. The average age of the runaways who go to government-supported shelters is younger. The largest number are 15 rather than 16 and are composed more largely of females: 57.0 percent females and 43.0 percent males. It should be remembered that only about 5.0 percent of runaways use the shelters.[4]

Runaways are more likely to come from low-income families (the rate is about 40.0 percent higher), but the lowest rate comes not from the highest income families, but from those in the very middle of the income distribution.

The lowest rate occurs in four-person households; only 1.9 percent of these households experienced a runaway in 1975 compared to the average of 3.0 percent in all households with youth aged 10–17. In most instances these would

[2] Opinion Research Corporation, *National Statistical Survey of Runaway Youth* (Princeton, N.J.: the Corporation, 1976).

[3] *Ibid.*

[4] National Youth Work Alliance, *National Directory of Runaway Programs* (Washington, D.C.: the Alliance, 1979).

be two-parent, two-children households. Households with two people, ordinarily one parent and one child, have a much higher rate—5.1 percent. The highest rate of running away for any type of household is that of eight or more persons; 7.1 percent of such households had a runaway child in 1975. The rate for these households is four times that in the four-person households. Probably size alone does not account for all these differences, since a disproportionate number of single-parent and very large families are found in the low-income group.

Racial differences in running away are slight. The white rates is 2.9 percent; black, 3.2 percent; Hispanic, 4.6 percent. The higher rate for Hispanics may reflect, in part, a cultural difference that children are relatively free to leave their own household to live a while with a relative. White-collar and blue-collar families have identical runaway rates. Both central cities and towns have higher rates than suburbs and rural areas. However, the differences are of modest magnitude: city, 3.4 percent; suburbs, 2.8 percent; small towns, 3.4 percent; rural areas, 2.4 percent.[5]

The above data were for those who ran away during 1975. Cumulative data show that 8.4 percent of families in the 1975 national survey had at some time in the past experienced a runaway event, and among single-parent families and those households with eight or more persons, approximately 15 percent had had a child or adolescent runaway at some time in the past. Based on this national survey, it is estimated that about one child in eight will run away sometime before his or her eighteenth birthday.

CHARACTERISTICS OF THE RUN

Most runaways do not run far or stay long. Twenty percent travel less than a mile, 52 percent less than ten miles. Only 18 percent traveled farther than fifty miles. Forty percent ran only one day, and 60 percent were back by the third

[5] Opinion Research Corporation, *op. cit.*

day. Seventy percent had returned within a week, and 84 percent were back within a month. Nine percent were gone one to six months, and 5 percent had not returned at the time the national survey was made.

Although these researchers defined a runaway as any child under 18 who is gone overnight without parental permission, not all parents define the behavior in those terms. In 47 percent of the cases the parent did not consider the event as running away. They explained that they knew where the youths had gone and expected them to return. In less than a third of the cases did they report the event to police. Apparently parents reserve the term runaway for youths who plan to leave home permanently. Likewise, many youths who are gone overnight without parental permission have no intention of staying away indefinitely and do not consider themselves to be runaways.[6]

CLASSES AND TYPES OF RUNAWAYS

Brennan, Huizinga, and Elliott[7] from their extensive research describe two general classes and seven specific types of runaways.

CLASS I

The three types in Class I are defined as *not* highly delinquent and, in general, not alienated from family and school. They are not pushed out, rejected, or abused. Therefore, more positive motivations may be inferred, with attractions elsewhere being more powerful for this than for other groups of runaways.

In the case of Type 1, "young, temporary escapists," tight controls are maintained by parents accompanied by physical

[6] *Ibid.*
[7] Tim Brennan, David Huizinga, and Delbert Elliott, *The Social Psychology of Runaways* (Lexington, Mass.: Lexington Books, 1978).

and other types of punishment. Family life is not especially attractive, but these young adolescents have not rejected parents. Parents display indications of powerlessness and societal estrangment. Sixty percent of the runaways are boys.

The researchers call Type 2 "middle-class loners." These average just over 16 years of age. They are not alienated from parents. They have high self-esteem and do well in school. However, typically, they have few friends.

Type 3, "unrestrained, peer-oriented runaways," also average just over 16 years of age. They are independent and largely do not relate to parents. Family nurturance is low and freedom high. They have high interaction with a few friends. They are not highly delinquent. However, they dislike school and have no educational aspirations. Their lack of ties to family and school provides few ties to hold them. Dislike of school seems to be their primary negative reason for running. They run repeatedly, usually with one or more friends.

Class I composed 45 percent of the runaway sample.

CLASS II

Those in Class II are characterized as "delinquent, alienated runaways." This general class is characterized by high conflict with parents, rejecting and rejected parents, high commitment to delinquent peers, personal delinquent conduct, school problems, alienation from school, and low self-esteem. This class includes four types which vary by age and social class.

Type 4 is composed mainly of younger youths from low-income and low-education families (average age 14.4). They reject and are rejected by their parents, are highly involved with delinquent peers, and exhibit much personal delinquent behavior. Parents attempt high levels of control and punish frequently. Although these youths aspire to educational success, they rank low in achievment. The type includes many repeater runaways. Most parents of these runaways respond by trying to locate runaways and return them home.

"Rebellious, constrained middle-class drop-out girls," Type 5, resemble Type 4, except that they are older (average 15.2 years), exhibit outright rebellion, and are predominantly from middle-class families. This group rejects school as well as parents and reports a variety of parental rejection, abuse, and favoritism to siblings. They have high commitment to delinquent peers. Almost all planned their runaway episode.

Type 6 runaways, "homeless, rejected, unrestrained youth," also exhibit alienation from parents and school and high commitment to delinquent peers. These average 15.6 years of age, 62 percent boys, and largely middle class. Parents are not overprotective. These youth have relatively high educational and occupational aspirations but are uninvolved educationally and have no aspirations for involvement. Most did not plan a runaway episode, and many were not sure they were running away. Parents infrequently notified police. The picture is one of little parental commitment or control and little commitment of youth to anything except a few delinquent friends.

Type 7, "pushouts, socially rejected youth," is composed primarily of boys in lower-class families. Very high levels of rejection are characteristic both of parents toward youth and youth toward parents. The youths reject school and have almost ceased to participate. The only strong ties are to peers, who are involved in continuing delinquent behavior and who frequently pressure them to participate in deviant behavior. Most planned their runaway episode and run repeatedly. Few parents report episodes to police or try to have the youths return. Some can be truly characterized as "pushouts"; others have little if anything to prevent them from running.

Over all, the two general classes of runaways are quite different. Class I differs little from nonrunaways in relationship to parents and school and in achievement in school. This implies positive goals and interests as reasons for running away. Class II is characterized by high to very high alienation from parents and school and by high identification with delinquent peers and by personal delinquent behavior. These youths exhibit personal feelings of powerlessness, alienation, and low self-esteem. Both classes are differentiated into subtypes by different parental behaviors based on age and sex of the youths and the social class of parents.

In general, it appears that runaways are motivated by three groups of reasons for running away:

1. *Positive reasons.* There is a desire to explore, to meet new people, and to have new experiences. It appears that about 20 percent of runaways are of this type.[8]

2. *Negative experiences.* Youth may dislike school, feel parental control is too restrictive, and have had quarrels with parents or teachers. These range from minor matters of discipline or other disagreements to continued severe conflict and alienation from parents and school. This is by far the largest category, numbering perhaps 75 percent of the total.

It is useful to divide this very large group into two subgroups. One is composed of first-time runners, who run impulsively after a dispute with parents or because they anticipate being punished. Most of these do not run away again. Most of these do not exhibit other serious deviant behaviors such as delinquency, truancy, and drug abuse. The second subgroup has chronic conflict with parents and usually exhibits continuing deviant behaviors. Many of these are repeat runaways.

3. *"Pushouts."* These are youths who have been told to leave home or have been abandoned by parents or severely and repeatedly beaten. These feel they have no alternative but to leave. There are no exact estimates of the size of this

[8] William W. Wattenburg, "Boys Who Run Away from Home," *Journal of Educational Psychology*, XLVII (1956), 335–43; Brennan, Huizinga, and Elliott, *op. cit.*; Libertoff, *op. cit.*

group, but it may be about 5 percent of the total.[9] The Opinion Research Corporation in its national survey (1976) found that all but 5 percent of runaways had returned home.

EXPERIENCES ON THE ROAD

One of several motivations for running away is to have a good time—not to have to go to school, to be free to do as one pleases, see new places, meet new people, have new experiences. About one fourth of runaways report that in fact they did have a good time.[10] Much of this was because of more freedom and new experiences, but it also included a feeling of growth, of thinking through one's interests, goals, and plans. In contrast, about one in five reported unhappy experiences—hunger, cold, fear, boredom, and a lack of any positive experiences. That leaves over half who reported neither. When one recalls that over half were gone less than three days and that most of these traveled less than ten miles and stayed with a relative or friend, it is understandable why their experience lacked drama—either positive or negative.

A very small proportion, perhaps 3 percent, reported traumatic experiences—being beaten, robbed, raped, or being jailed with undesirable adults.[11]

But there is another less dramatic side of running away which may have serious consequences. If youth are gone for an extended period, they exhaust whatever money they may have. Most are not prepared to obtain and hold a job to support themselves. Thus, many of those who stay away for months become involved in delinquent behavior. Brennan, Huizinga, and Elliott[12] found that one third engaged in petty theft, one in six had stolen large sums of valuable property, one in ten had broken into buildings, one in five had sold marijuana, and one in ten had sold hard drugs

[9] Dobie Butler, *Runaway House: a Youth-run Project* (Washington, D.C.: U.S. Government Printing Office, 1974).
[10] Brennan, Huizinga, and Elliott, *op. cit.*   [11] *Ibid.*   [12] *Ibid.*

while on the run. Some became involved in prostitution.[13] Of course, some youth were involved in delinquent behavior before they ran away, but running away provides both more opportunity and a greater need for money.

PARENTS' RESPONSES TO RUNNING AWAY

Many parents (47 percent) did not consider that the child had run away, even though the youth was gone overnight without permission. Thirty percent thought they knew where the child was and expected a return the next day. Others guessed the youth was at a friend's or relative's home. About one in four did nothing but wait.

Of those who took action, 31 percent called the police. One in four called friends, one in six called relatives, and one in four talked with other people, including teachers or social workers. Three out of eight youths returned by themselves. Parents located 22 percent; police, 18 percent; and friends and relatives, 14 percent. Runaway shelters returned one percent and social agencies, 2 percent.

Just as reasons for running away reveal tremendous variations, so do the responses of parents to the event.

[13] Michael Baizerman, Jacquelin Thompson, and Kimaka Stafford-White, "Adolescent Prostitution," *Children Today,* September–October 1979, 20–24; Dorothy H. Bracey, *Baby Pros: Preliminary Profiles of Juvenile Prostitutes* (New York: John Jay Press, 1979).

The research on adolescent prostitution provides little support for the newspaper stereotype of the innocent child who arrives in New York to be seduced, beaten, and inducted by a pimp into prostitution. The research conducted by Dorothy Bracey in downtown Manhattan finds that most adolescent prostitutes began practicing in their own cities or in the satellite communities around New York. They came to Manhattan attracted by the excitement and glamour of the "Big Time." Pimps do not prefer minors, rather the contrary. They have found that if a minor is picked up by the police, it is much more difficult to obtain a speedy release. Also they report girls of 14–17 years of age commit more acts of violence against clients, such as "putting a knife into him to see him squirm." This usually brings the police and creates much expense and other problems for the pimp.

However, pimps do recruit minors, especially if they have few adult women working for them. Others "turn out" on their own. Police regard the downtown area as extremely dangerous for runaway minors. Many are robbed and beaten, some become addicted, and murders are not uncommon. Police try to intercept runaways at the bus terminal or, if not there, to pick them up as soon as possible and return them to their original communities.

SOME ISSUES FOR SOCIETY

RELATIONSHIPS WITH PARENTS

Four of the seven types of runaways reject their parents and their parents reject them. A fifth type is viewed negatively by parents, although the youths have not rejected their parents. Thus, a poor to an outright hostile relationship between youth and parents is characteristic of perhaps two thirds of runaways. This raises two issues for immediate attention and a third to be discussed later.

Olson et al.[14] report that some parent-child conflicts which become overt in adolescence have a history that goes back to the infant years of the runaways. Runaways were more likely to exhibit troublesome, unresponsive, and antisocial behavior accompanied by parental irritation, punishment, and favoritism toward the more attractive siblings of the runaway. This suggests that parent education is needed which alerts parents both to correct early lazy, negative, antisocial behavior of children and to guard against chronic favoritism and more severe punishment directed toward some children than to others. In more general terms, it means that parents need help in understanding how children can be effectively socialized.

Can behavioral scientists and practitioners provide guiding principles which would be helpful to parents and, if so, is there some way to transmit them to parents? (I am assuming that the quality of information supplied by journalists and film makers is presently of such low quality that it does not meet this need.) Current educational and counseling strategies seem to flow mainly from a humanistic or behaviorist paradigm, but since much of it is written by journalists or scriptwriters, it may not adequately reflect these strategies. Generally, these paradigms have seemed to contradict

---

[14] Lucy Olson et al., "Runaway Children Twelve Years Later: a Follow-up," in Nye and Edelbrock, eds., *op. cit.*, pp. 165–89.

each other. However, Greenspan[15] has shown that the prescriptions which are offered to parents if not identical are at least compatible. If Greenspan's analysis is correct, then a critical issue is how these helpful concepts and ·propositions may be made directly available to parents of children, preferably before these children reach adolescence.

Another issue involves support for parents from the community. Parents now receive less support from kin than formerly, since frequently they live at a distance from relatives. The school is perhaps as critical as supportive of parents. The decriminalization of runaways and rebellious youth largely removes the support for parents traditionally supplied by law-enforcement agencies. Corporal punishment by parents may now be defined as abuse and could become grounds for removing the child from the home. Thus, it appears that there is less and less support for parental authority, and schools and agencies actually are increasingly challenging parental authority. Is this one reason that many parents give up trying to control or even influence youths' behavior?

ISSUES FOR SCHOOLS

Five of the seven runaway types did poorly in school. While some retained high aspirations, their achievment or commitment to study was not consistent with high aspirations. Most runaways do poorly, dislike school, and become heavily involved in truancy.

Rejection of school and extensive truancy seem to be mainly characteristic of middle adolescence, as are runaway behavior and a variety of deviant behaviors. Do we retain all youths too long as full-time students (or, at least, attempt to retain them)? Would better results be obtained if, at about age fourteen three major alternatives were devel-

---

[15] Stephen Greenspan, *A Common Framework for Parent Education: Bridging the Gap between Humanism and Behaviorism* (Boys Town, Nebr.: Boys Town Center for the Study of Youth Development, 1980). See also, F. Ivan Nye, "Runaways: a Report for Parents" (Pullman, Wash.: Washington State University, Cooperative Extension Service, Bulletin Department, 1980). This educational bulletin explores some issues for parents and proposals for parent education.

oped, with one aimed at college preparatory work, leading eventually into white-collar occupations? A second, moving into vocational training and apprenticeship, would be aimed at early entry into skilled blue-collar occupations, and the third would involve immediate part-time entry into paid employment. (The quick-food industry and other businesses that require little advanced training offer such an opportunity.) Youths in the third alternative would be encouraged to continue part time either in college preparatory or vocational courses. Of course, those choices should be made *by* youths rather than for them and should be reversible at any time a youth decides that another alternative is preferable. All the Communist countries utilize this third alternative of part-time youth employment, and their experiences in working and living with youth have been notably more successful than our own.

Besides the issue of multi-alternatives in the educational system, size itself should be considered an issue. The literature on runaways provides much evidence of the difficulty of youth finding a place in our mammoth high schools. Only a small percentage can excel scholastically; likewise, there is a limit to the number who can play on athletic teams, be school officers, editors, and the like. In small high schools there is a place for every, or almost every, student who is willing to make an effort in scholarship or a school activity. Should not youth have at least an alternative of attending small junior and senior high schools—perhaps those with enrollments of 50 to 100? Small schools would also provide more oportunities for youth to know all the other students and to become better acquainted with teachers and administrators.

DELINQUENT PEER GROUP

Many studies of runaways comment on the influence of a delinquent peer group.[16] Especially is this characteristic of

[16] Deborah Klein Walker, *Runaway Youth: Annotated Bibliography and Literature Overview* (Washington, D.C.: U.S. Government Printing Office, 1975).

repeater runaways. These youth are also likely to be involved in drug and alcohol abuse and truancy.[17] The delinquent peer group supplies models for runaways, companions for the runaway episode, information about running away, and approval and support for running away. It appears that, in the late 1970s and 1980s, at least, a delinquent subculture exists in and out of school among middle adolescents (age 14–17). This culture is composed of antiparent, antischool, antipolice, and perhaps antiwork beliefs and values. It includes information and strategies to circumvent the authority and control of parents, schools, and law-enforcement agencies, and illegitimate strategies for meeting adolescent needs and goals. It provides a set of alternatives to conventional behaviors.

The delinquent peer group appears to be quite influential in encouraging and facilitating deviant behavior, including running away. In general, its effects seem to be detrimental for society, for parents, and, in long-term perspective, for adolescents. How can this counterculture be dismantled and this influence toward antisocial behavior be reduced? This is not the same question as how to eliminate deviant behavior, although to break up the culture and disband the delinquent peer groups would surely help reduce deviant behavior.

One strategy, of course, is to render legitimate alternatives more attractive (as previously mentioned), and to devise ways to increase the attractiveness and competence of adolescents so that they are more accepted by nondelinquent peers. Another is to try to develop more interesting recreation and better social relationships within the family, so that youths are less dependent on peers. These seem to promise the most lasting results. But beyond these, could society achieve some results by a more vigorous attack on the delinquent subculture and organized delinquent

[17] Craig Edelbrock, "Running Away from Home: Incidence and Correlates among Children and Youth Referred for Mental Health Services," in Nye and Edelbrock, eds., *op. cit.*, pp. 210–28.

groups? Recently, there has been a tendency to view the criminal as the victim and society as the culprit.[18] Does not this support delinquent groups and the delinquent culture by offering legitimization?

DECRIMINALIZATION

One might conclude that decriminalization of runaways and of incorrigible youth is not an issue in the 1980s, since the matter seems to have been decided in favor of decriminalization. However, the transfer of hundreds of status offenders from the justice to the social welfare department poses some new questions. For example, are sufficient funds also transferred to welfare or human services divisions to service these runaways?

Since the runaway per se is no longer an offender, how can he be detained if he or she seems in need of services? Two patterns are emerging, and doubtless there are others. One involves reclassification of the status offender; that is, if the runaway is a chronic delinquent, then he or she will be classified as a delinquent. Another pattern involves an order from a judge requiring the youth to remain in the nonsecure quarters, on penalty of contempt of court action if he or she leaves. The legality of this action is being tested in the courts.

There may be one latent consequence of decriminalization which is worth attention, even though it is not currently an issue. Formerly, parents could threaten rebellious adolescents with being taken to court if they did not change their behavior. Since this is no longer possible, more parents may completely lose control of adolescent children, which may result in an increase in the number of runaways and pushouts and, therefore, in the number who will require alternative living arrangements.

[18] John Taylor, "Prisons Are Monuments of Hatred," *Sunday World Herald Magazine of the Midlands* (Omaha), April 13, 1980.

ALTERNATIVE LIVING ARRANGEMENTS

Just as over a million couples each year find they cannot continue to live together, tens of thousands of adolescents and parents decide that it is best that they cease to live together. If families are sufficiently affluent, adolescents may be placed in boarding schools. Others run away, living independently or in a group care facility; some are in prisons and reformatories; some are in foster care. Some of these alternatives are chosen by adolescents, some by parents, and still others are prescribed by the courts.

American society must face the issue (with the assistance of professionals) of how many shall be given care away from their families; how those decisions shall be reached, and what alternative living arrangements shall be provided for homeless, alienated youth.

Obviously it is expensive. One boarding school advertised a staff of fifty to care for eighty youths. This would include teachers and perhaps guards as well as caregivers. Is a ratio of one caregiver to two or three youths reasonable? In addition, boarding schools require additional housing, utilities, meal preparation, clothing care, shopping, counseling, and other activities which intact families usually provide. On the positive side, it provides a "safety valve" for parents and youth who are alienated and for those who engage in physical conflict. Many nonindustrial societies provide a similar option by permitting children to live with a variety of relatives, not solely with parents.

THERAPY, EDUCATION, AND TRAINING FOR MID-
ADOLESCENCE

As America enters the 1980s it has a large population of youth with major, chronic, unmet needs. Brennan, Huizinga, and Elliott[19] find that about half of the runaway pop-

19 Brennan, Huizinga, and Elliott, *op. cit.*

ulation is involved in delinquent behavior on a continuing basis. About the same proportion has negative, conflictual relationships with parents, dislikes school, and is failing to achieve in school, and/or is involved in truancy. Edelbrock[20] has shown that these youths are also likely to be involved in drug and alcohol abuse, to have poor self-concepts, and to report powerlessness and normlessness. Many have poor living arrangements. Some are receiving therapeutic services, economic assistance, and are taking part in alternative educational programs.

The intriguing question for researchers and theoreticians is: what maladaptive behaviors on the part of parents and children underlie this complex of deviant behaviors and personal and social pathology? One can hardly think of a more challenging set of issues for theoretically oriented researchers, or for educators and practitioners who counsel with parents.

PERSONAL CONTROLS

The decade of the 1970s brought more and more autonomy to children and youth. Both scholarly and popular literature took the position that each individual should determine his or her own goals, with the assumption that all values and goals are of equal validity.[21] Schools at all levels have been influenced toward more and more autonomy for children. The same messages have been communicated to parents and other adults as well.

I am not convinced that society or its individuals can function effectively with this amount of responsibility transferred to each individual. But, if American society *is* to provide the autonomy of the 1970s, and even increase it in the 1980s, as seems very likely, when and how do we undertake the task of socializing children (and perhaps adults, too) to be sufficiently concerned with the needs, rights, and welfare

---

[20] Edelbrock, *op. cit.*

[21] Thomas Harris, *I'm O.K., You're O.K.* (New York: Avon Books, 1973); Robert J. Ringer, *Looking Out for #1* (New York: Funk and Wagnalls, 1973).

of other children, of spouses, and the public in general? So much of the literature, training, and teaching of the 1970s has focused on the needs and rights of one's self—how to advance and achieve one's own goals—and so little on how to understand, be concerned with, and protect the rights of others, individually and collectively. If we do not cope with these tasks effectively, American society seems in danger of becoming a social jungle.

CONCLUDING NOTE

Running away from home during mid-adolescence creates some problems for youths, parents, and society, in that youths escape parental supervision and are deprived of parental supports before they are mature enough to function effectively as adults. However, for those who travel only to a friend's or a relative's home and return in a day or two, the consequences are usually not great. In some instances it actually results in resolution of parent–child problems, or the youth comes to appreciate more the security provided by one's home and family. In other instances of protracted and repeated runs, the consequences are serious.

Beyond the immediate issue precipitated by running away, the magnitude of the phenomenon calls attention to the prevalence of parent–youth conflict, the prevalence of school failure, alienation and truancy, of juvenile delinquency, and drug and alcohol abuse. It should say to professionals, policy-makers, and citizens that youths and younger children require a larger share of the attention of researchers and theoreticians than they have received.

The research on runaways highlights the need for an effective parent-education program in the United States. It will be most effective if it can be timed when young people become parents—when they feel a need for information and can immediately apply its principles. It needs to be based on valid theory and research. Much advice to parents in the 1970s (in my opinion) has been misadvice, which is worse than folk knowledge. The preparation of valid parent-education materials will require time to search the professional literature exhaustively and care in organization and writing. Finally, when valid, effective materials are available, the means must be developed to disseminate it effectively to the millions of parents rearing children.

It seems also that a thorough reexamination of the permissive, humanistic theories and practices of the 1970s should be conducted by professionals and policy-makers. Should not the prime responsibility for deviant behavior remain with the person who commits the act rather than with society or some other group? Have the theories created more problems for youth and families than they have solved?

However, youth and others need maximum opportunities to meet their needs legitimately. The decade of the 1970s has been one of declining economic opportunities for youth which has restricted not only job opportunities but opportunities to create their own businesses, to buy decent houses, and rear families. It is hard to defend government policies which predictably create unemployment and depression.

Finally, and most difficult, American society urgently needs new leaders at the top (President, Cabinet, Congress, and the like) who are willing to put personal advantage second to the welfare of all citizens. Only thus can respect for our governing institutions be restored.

Hospice Care and the Care Giver

BERNICE CATHERINE HARPER

T HE PLACE OF dying in the United States has been changed by medical, social, and health practices. Most individuals no longer die in the privacy of their homes with families and friends. Generally, individuals die in hospitals, nursing homes, and convalescent and long-term-care facilities. Data reveal that 70 percent of the deaths now take place in these facilities, including some 300,000 deaths annually in nursing homes, as compared to 49 percent some thirty years ago. According to Feifel, "care of the dying has been relegated to third-party professionals. Unwittingly, institutional dying further serves as a means whereby society dissociates itself from the problems of dying and death."[1] Americans have attempted to cope with death by disguising it and acting as if death is not a part of the continuum of life. In addition, dying in present-day society has been shaped mainly by present-day social developments, changes in the meaning of death, and outstanding advances in medical science and technology. The idea of death is not a very comfortable one for twentieth-century American men and women.

To aggravate further the situations that some dying persons must face, stated Butler, "currently, less than one per-

BERNICE CATHERINE HARPER is Medical Care Advisor, Office of Professional and Scientific Affairs, Health Care Financing Administration, Department of Health and Human Services, Washington, D.C.

[1] H. Feifel, "The Meaning of Dying in American Society," in *Dealing with Death* (Los Angeles: University of Southern California, Ethel Percy Andrus Gerontology Center, 1973), pp. 1–3.

cent of the hospitals in the United States have any type of organized programs related to the care of the dying."[2] Staffs in health care facilities must, therefore, develop ways of helping their patients to live fully and die gracefully.

Health workers and professionals who are willing to invest themselves can become comfortable in working with dying patients and improving the quality of life in this area of our health care delivery system. This is further supported by the fact that in the past the psychosocial aspects of death and dying have been overlooked. They now require special attention in an environment that is conducive for mourning and grieving by all who are involved—the dying and the surviving.

The growing recognition of, and interest in, the whole area of death and dying, the beginning acceptance of death as a part of the individual's life continuum, and the identification of the five stages of death by Kubler-Ross;[3] use of the Harper schematic comfort-ability growth and development scale in coping with professional anxieties in terminal illness;[4] the removal of the myth of the Dark Ages concept of death and dying; workshops, symposia, consumer needs, the articles about death without dignity, newspaper reports, death with dignity bills and other Congressional concerns, and the hospice movement all have contributed to the current surge of interest in death.

Therefore, the quality of life of the twenty-first century is going to be judged by the way health workers administer to dying patients and their families. There is a continual growing concern and an impetus for comprehensive care and treatment of the individual from birth to death. There is also strong evidence to lead one to believe that humanization of the health care delivery system must include atten-

[2] Robert N. Butler, *A Humanistic Approach to Our Last Days* (Bethesda, Md.: National Institutes of Health, 1977), pp. 1–2.

[3] Elisabeth Kubler-Ross, *On Death and Dying* (New York: Macmillan Co., 1969), pp. 32, 51, 83, 87, 113.

[4] Bernice Catherine Harper, *Death: the Coping Mechanism of the Health Professional* (Greenville, S.C.: Southeastern University Press, 1977).

tion to the development of health workers who are academically, emotionally, and psychologically prepared to deal with dying patients and their families.

A humanization revolution in medicine is long overdue. But it is coming, and it promises to be as profound as the science-oriented revolution that began fifty years ago. Medicine is the discipline at the interface of science and human needs, and medical and allied health professionals must adapt to these needs.

There is beginning to be a science of hospice care in North America, and dying patients and their families will be able to receive appropriate and comprehensive care. Maturational principles in relation to death and dying care are emerging based on empirical data and rational premises, thus bringing together fragmentary hypotheses. Concepts and principles have been promulgated and are being utilized for program planning and continuing education. Others are still in conceptualization and will be emerging for future utilization. It is these aspects of the process and the literature that will be discussed here.

PAST AND CURRENT VIEWS ON COPING WITH DEATH

A review of the literature reveals that death and dying are too important to be left totally to any one discipline, and that health professionals generally are not trained to do death work from a psychosocial or psychological viewpoint. Patients, especially children and their families (rather than professionals who serve dying patients), have undergone study in relation to death but only recent literature reports investigations regarding health professionals and their reactions to death and dying.

Early recorded history indicates that human beings from the beginning of time have been preoccupied with death. Fear has been the predominant emotion. The conscious explicit efforts to reduce this fear have subordinated intellect to emotions; that is, the explicit ideas about death have served primarily to demonstrate the emotion-motivated concept of immortality. Expressions of the immortality theme are abundant, ranging from the crude animism of early human beings (and modern aborigines) to the sophisticated and closely reasoned theologies which are important parts of the modern cultural fabric. The nonexplicit efforts of human beings to cope with death may be of greater evolutionary importance. The subtlety of such presumed efforts renders them difficult to study, as reported by Natterson and Knudson.[5]

Freud[6] speculated that the rudiments of society were established by rivals who ceremoniously agreed to coexist, each motivated by a fear of death at the hands of others. In later writing, Freud attributed much of the cohesiveness and structure of modern society to repression of the death instinct, that is, death avoidance. In the main, studies of the explicit and nonexplicit efforts to cope with death have been fragmentary. The problems of how death affects human motivation and integration at the individual level have been discussed by Freud,[7] who cited aggression, guilt, incorporation, and identification with the death-love object.

Lindemann[8] considered the effects on survivors of the death of loved ones. The author emphasized the pathologic consequences of death for the survivors and also stressed primarily interpersonal problems.

Quint and Strauss,[9] in their sociological approach concerning the problems of nursing faculties and students with the dying patient and death, observed that in talking to staff nurses in hospitals about their experiences with dying pa-

[5] Joseph M. Natterson and Alfred G. Knudson, "Observations Concerning Fear of Death in Fatally Ill Children and Their Mothers," *Psychosomatic Medicine,* XXII (1960), 456–65.
[6] Sigmund Freud, "Totem and Taboo," in *The Complete Psychological Works of Sigmund Freud* (London: Hogarth Press, 1955), XIII, 1912–13.
[7] Sigmund Freud, "Mourning and Melancholia," in *Collected Papers* (London: Hogarth Press, 1950), p. 1917.
[8] E. Lindemann, "Symptomatology and Management of Acute Grief," *American Journal of Psychiatry,* CI (1944), 141.
[9] J. Quint and A. Strauss, "Nursing Students' Assignments and Dying Patients," *Nursing Outlook,* XII (1964), 24–27.

tients, one becomes aware that this aspect of nursing care is not viewed as particularly pleasant or as something that is sought out. Many nurses say they prefer a surgical service where, generally speaking, patients get well and go home. This imagery still holds despite the fact that changes in surgical techniques have increased the number of hazardous operations performed. The authors further noted that recent advances in diagnostic and treatment techniques hospitalize many persons who have fatal illnesses though they may not yet be near death.

Terminal illness and death represent trauma which can bring forward deep emotional anxieties for the professional person. In the helping process, the professional persons need to: (1) understand the dynamics of behavior of the patients who will not recover; (2) relate to the actions of patients and relatives; (3) give counseling, support, and strength to the patients and relatives; and (4) understand and deal with their own feelings and anxieties. However, if the professional person reaches the point where he or she has become "nonfeeling," or if the patient is "just another terminally ill case," then that person may become damaging to the patient and the patient's family. Members of the helping professions must recognize and accept their obligations to the patient whose condition is terminal and who is dying.

THE MEANING OF DEATH

Definitions of death. Webster defines death as a permanent ending of all life in a person. But death is more than that. Death is always with us and it is a certainty. Death is a part of us; death is here to stay—men, women, and children are not. Dying and death involve the demise of one's self, one's being, and one's presence here on earth; the leaving of one's family and friends and going to the great beyond, the great unknown, back to dust, back to ashes and the earth. All this has many connotations for each individual. This episode of one's life is as important as birth, perhaps more so because of life's experiences and involvements. Therefore, the psychosocial needs of the dying patient and the family unit must receive attention. The term "terminal illness" has been coined by professionals in order to avoid the word "dying." The word "terminal" is less anxiety producing than the word "dying." Men and women have no control of death and are helpless when death comes despite their vast storehouse of knowledge and abundant skills. Professionals may predict that death is imminent, but they cannot pinpoint the exact time of death. Therefore, they feel uncomfortable and compensate in various ways, such as their choice of terminology. Professionals appear to know instinctively what is meant by "terminal illness," and seldom is an explanation required. Terminal illness denotes the feeling that there is nothing in the way of treatment that can be attempted. The diagnosis of an illness, with all that it conveys for the patient and the family, poses a multiplicity of problems for professionals as they encounter patients with serious life-threatening diseases and illnesses in their practices.

DEATH AND THE HEALTH CARE TEAM

A major anxiety point for the patient and family when facing a catastrophic disease is the diagnosis. Further, there is still the debate regarding who should tell the patient, when, and how much. This, then, becomes an important area of the illness to which the health professionals must relate, thus creating anxiety for them because they do not know how the patient and family will react or relate. The important factor is that all members of the health team know what information has been given. Knowing what the patient and family have been told, the team is in a position to support and reinterpret the physician's plan of treatment and care. In this way the staff is cognizant of the emotional support which will be needed when the impact of the diagnosis is realized. All members of the health team must share information which may aid in the care plan for the patient.

How a patient feels about his illness affects the entire course of his medical treatment. If the patient denies that he has a terminal illness, he or she may refuse to carry out the physician's recommendations. If the illness is considered a punishment, the patient may exaggerate the symptoms. Patients, then, have a variety of reactions—depression after being told the diagnosis; denial of illness; denial of anxiety or concern; guilt for having delayed in seeking medical care; fear of becoming dependent on others; fear of pain; fear of mutilation; difficulty in giving up employment; feelings of loneliness; feelings of inadequacy as a spouse, mother, or father; fear of rejection; and threats to commit suicide. Thus, for one individual, terminal illness may mean suffering, relief from anxiety, and escape from an intolerable situation, while to another it means giving up one's life work. Each one's reaction to illness is an individual matter based upon one's life's experiences and one's method of handling crises in the past.

Kubler-Ross identified five stages that patients pass through when faced with a terminal illness. These are denial, anger, bargaining, depression, and acceptance. In *Death and Dying* she explains that while patients greatly appreciate sharing their concern with others and talk freely about death and dying, they will signal when the topic of conversation should be changed, when more cheerful subjects should be discussed.[10]

THE HOSPICE CONCEPT

Definitions of hospice. According to Webster, a hospice is "a place of refuge . . . a home for the sick and poor." A hospice may be defined as not a place, but as a way of dealing with a dying patient where he or she wants to be, probably at home. The place of care should be left to both the patient and the physician.

[10] Kubler-Ross, *op. cit.,* p. 113.

The hospice concept was started in the middle of the nineteenth century by Mother Mary Aikenhead, founder of the Irish Sisters of Charity, to care for the dying poor in Dublin.

In 1905, St. Joseph's Hospice was established on the east side of London. Two other hospices were founded, one by Anglican nuns and the other by the Methodist West London Mission. Currently there are 30 such hospices in England with a total of almost 1,000 beds. In 1967, Cicely Saunders, M.D., founded St. Christopher's Hospice, London, a 54-bed inpatient facility and home care program for people who are in the advanced stages of neurological and malignant diseases.

The United States has a unique opportunity to create unique hospice services designed to meet the unique community needs of terminally ill and dying patients and their families in all diagnostic categories, settings, and age groups. The uniqueness is based on knowledge, and on resources related to the successes and failures, strengths and weaknesses of the past and present health care delivery systems. America must, at all cost, avoid the development of fragmentary hospice services coupled with the lack of human dignity and human caring.

According to the National Hospice Organization (Vienna, Va.), as of January, 1980, there are 116 active provisional hospices throughout the fifty states and the District of Columbia. These are organized in several different ways, including:

1. Free-standing hospice facilities that provide inpatient services

2. Home care programs, which may be affiliated with a hospice, hospital, or nursing home

3. Hospice teams within a hospital that provides services to dying patients throughout the facility

4. Hospice units within a hospital or nursing home.

Hackley states that the full-service hospice offers home,

day, and in-patient care.[11] The common basic characteristics that any hospice program should include are:

1. The patient/family is the unit of care.
2. Emphasis is placed on symptom control.
3. There is over-all medical direction of the program.
4. Home care and inpatient programs are coordinated by the autonomous hospice administrator.
5. Services are provided by an interdisciplinary team approach.
6. There is twenty-four-hour, seven-day-per-week coverage, with emphasis on the availability of medical and nursing skills.
7. Volunteers are used as an integral part of the health care team.
8. Care of the family extends through the bereavement period.

DEVELOPING A COPING MECHANISM

Health professionals who would be successful in working with the dying patient and that person's family must come to grips with personal feelings about their own immortality, life's end, and the in-between life processes. This writer dealt with these areas in *Death: the Coping Mechanism of the Health Professional.*[12] The premise of this thesis is rather simply stated: Professional anxieties in catastrophic diseases and terminal illnesses are observable phenomena for which a coping mechanism can be developed. The health professional who is helped to come to grips with his or her own feelings is enabled to give strength and support to patients and relatives. The patient can be helped to die with dignity and self-respect. Families can be helped to come through a

[11] John A. Hackley, "Full-Service Hospice Offers Home, Day, and Inpatient Care," in *Hospitals* (*Journals of American Hospital Association,* LI, No. 21 [1977], 84–87).
[12] *Op. cit.*

traumatic experience with some semblance of mental health.

Central to this thesis is a development scale for professionals who deal with death and dying. It identifies the stages a care giver will and should go through, describes the activities and emotions associated with each stage, and suggests coping mechanisms to ease the transitions through a demanding experience of learning, growth, and human responsibility. These stages are identified in a schematic comfort-ability growth and development scale as follows:

Stage 1: Intellectualization (1–3 months). Care givers come to know terminal illness and its consequences. Frequently, during this stage, they will examine the facts rationally without regard for emotional considerations.

Stage 2: Emotional Survival (3–6 months). During this stage, health professionals have their emotional feelings aroused by the knowledge gained in stage 1. They may exhibit fear, anger, and various mental and physical manifestations in reaction to this knowledge of the patient's approaching death.

Stage 3: Depression (6–9 months). A decrease in functional activity together with pain and mourning are exhibited by the health professionals in stage 3. The emotional excitement of stage 2 becomes sorrow and distress.

Stage 4: Emotional arrival (9–12 months). At this stage, health professionals have learned to accommodate within themselves their feelings of sorrow and grief and to achieve an understanding of these strong feelings about the dying. The extreme and excessive behaviors exhibited in stages 2 and 3 are moderated. As the health professionals progress through stage 4, they become more helpful to the patient/family and more willing to provide services.

Stage 5: Deep compassion (12–24 months). The health professionals accept the sufferings of others, accompanied by an urge to help and deep empathy. At this last stage, the care givers are most able to help the patient/family.

The learning process for the professional, whether audiologist, social worker, nurse, physician, occupational therapist, clergyman, or aide, is continuous as each situation provides new insight, new problems, new challenges, and the opportunity to contribute, to grow, and to develop in the caring process. There is in every stage a new progressive unfolding of self which constitutes a new hope and new responsibility for the care giver.

The integration takes place in the form of ego mastery with the accrued experience of the ego's ability to integrate all identification with the vicissitudes of the dying process, with the aptitude developing out of the emotional investment, and with the opportunities offered to the professional in becoming a helping person. The sense of ego mastery, then, is the accrued confidence that the inner strength and growth of the professional evidenced in working successfully with dying patients and their families. The strength acquired at any stage is tested by the necessity to transcend it in such a way that the professional takes chances in the next stage with what were most vulnerably precious in the previous stage.

The professional develops the capacity to commit himself/herself to concrete affiliations and partnerships and develops the ethical strength to abide by such commitment even though it calls for significant sacrifices and comprises trauma, pain, mourning, and grieving. Similarly, the professional finds gratification and satisfaction in helping and accepting the challenge to assist patients to die with dignity and self-respect.

Learning to cope in the area of hospice care, death, and dying involves knowledge development and building on the part of the health professional. The understanding of the fundamentals of the technology in the day-to-day tasks, external and internal hindrances in the use of new capacities, and the technological ethos of the hospital environment must be part and parcel of the growth process. Knowledge building takes place through: (1) sharing feelings in supervisory relationships; (2) attending teaching conferences; (3)

participating in patient and family conferences; (4) reading charts, medical records, and professional literature; (5) conferring with other health professionals; (6) attending workshops; (7) participating in seminars and symposia; (8) conducting research; (9) making maximum use of staff development programs; (10) recording inputs and evaluating outcomes.

The health professional must also develop: (1) knowledge about the philosophy and ideology of the facility; (2) knowledge about the patient and his family; (3) knowledge about community resources; (4) knowledge about lacks and gaps in programs and services.[13] Thus, these activities constitute the basic substance of knowledge building and aids the professional to gain security in relation to practice and to perform with dignity and competency.

The heightened interest in hospice care, death, and dying is a good sign—a sign of man's and woman's growing toward maturity, a sign of the humanizing of the health care delivery system, a sign of man's and woman's humanity to each other. The future holds a great deal for those individuals who have a commitment and dedication to help another human being cross over to his/her final resting place with dignity, with someone who is willing to hold a hand; to die in love, unafraid to take the final step that completes the continuum of the life cycle.

[13] Bernice Catherine Harper, "Social Aspects of Cancer Recovery," *Cancer*, XXXVI, No. 1 (1975), 274–76.

Underlying Agendas in the New Social Work Code of Ethics

JOSEPH R. STEINER and *GERALD M. GROSS*

THE CODE OF Ethics in social work summarizes idealized standards of professional conduct. It is a public testament which guides the behavior of social workers both in and out of practice and it serves as a tool for helping the profession gain public respectability.[1] The code represents a general contract that social workers accept when they identify themselves as professionals. And yet, it does not remove decision-making responsibility from individuals since many specific decisions that social workers must make do not lend themselves to precise applications of a code. The code reveals much about the profession of social work and the values upon which professional workers base their professional conduct.

The phrase "underlying agendas" in the National Association of Social Workers new Code of Ethics refers to non-articulated and perhaps unrecognized contrasting beliefs which make it difficult for social workers to attain ethical consensus, that is, to determine what is right and wrong. These underlying agendas may block progress and cause groups with the task of making ethical decisions to blame

JOSEPH R. STEINER and GERALD M. GROSS are professors, Syracuse University, Syracuse, N.Y.

[1] Charles Levy, "On the Development of a Code of Ethics," *Social Work*, XIX (1974), 207–16.

their collective difficulties upon personality conflicts, age, sex, or race differences, or some other variable which has little to do with the ethical controversy being discussed. Being more aware of contrasting beliefs within the profession will reduce difficulties in implementing the new Code of Ethics.

Two contrasting belief systems underlie the new Code of Ethics and many other ethical controversies within the profession. One system is based upon the premise that persons have a positive inclination, and that they possess virtue by nature of their being. The other belief system is based upon the premise that persons by nature have a negative inclination, and that their attainment of virtue is dependent upon the success of socialization and regulation. These contrasting systems and the way they are revealed are developed in the first part of this article. The second part utilizes these two conceptions of persons as the basis for a content analysis of the new Code of Ethics. Special attention is given to what is implied about the conceptions of persons in the roles of "social workers," "clients," and "colleagues."

Dedicated background work, the fact that the former code was clearly inadequate, and much skillful negotiation made it possible for the 1979 NASW Delegate Assembly to approve overwhelmingly a new Code of Ethics. This approval for the new code does not discount the dissension which existed as the old code was being discussed and as the new code was being developed and ratified. It is anticipated that further disagreements will take place as the new code is implemented. Raising ethical dilemmas into the consciousness of social workers does not guarantee that they can work together effectively to achieve ethical consensus. Rather, it does increase the likelihood that underlying conflicts will be clarified and that constructive negotiation becomes possible.

CONTRASTING CONCEPTIONS OF PERSONS WITHIN SOCIAL
WORK

The contrasting conceptions of persons found within social
work are also found within society and the cultural and
philosophical foundations upon which it is based. Numerous philosophers and theologians have presented contrasting arguments which contend that persons by nature have
positive inclinations, have negative inclinations, or are inclined toward neither positive nor negative attitudes and behavior. For example, David Hume believed that persons
were innately motivated by a moral sentiment which caused
them to feel good when they saw useful things being done
to others.[2] Hobbes, who believed that a person's moral nature was neutral, also believed that one's basic motivation
was one of self-interest. In situations of scarce resources,
this causes persons to have short, nasty, brutish lives unless
social contracts (laws, customs, standards) can be established
and enforced. He further believed that a contract which
could not be enforced by a soverign party ceased to be a
contract.[3] John Calvin summarized his conceptions of persons when he concluded: "Man is so enslaved by sin, as to
be of his own nature incapable of an effort, or even an inspiration, toward that which is good."[4]

Carl Rogers and Sigmund Freud have had a direct effect
upon the social work profession regarding the two contrasting conceptions of persons discussed here. Carl Rogers believed that persons are basically "positive, forward-moving,
constructive, realistic, and trustworthy."[5] In addition, he believed that their

[2] David Hume, "Treatise on Human Nature," in W.T. Jones *et al.*, eds., *Ap-proaches to Ethics* (New York: McGraw-Hill Book Co., 1977), pp. 198–213.
[3] Thomas Hobbes, "Leviathan," in Jones et al., *op. cit.*, pp. 174–88.
[4] John Calvin, *A Compend of the Institutes of the Christian Religion*, Hugh Thomson Kerr, ed. (Philadelphia: Presbyterian Board of Christian Education, 1939), p. 51.
[5] Carl Rogers, "A Note on the Nature of Man," *Journal of Counseling Psychology*, IV (1957), 200.

deepest characteristics tend toward development, differentiation, cooperative relationships; whose life tends fundamentally to move from dependence to independence, whose impulses tend naturally to harmonize into a complex and changing pattern of self-regulation; whose total character is such as to tend to preserve and enhance himself and his species, and perhaps to move it toward its further evaluation.[6]

The ideal social environment which corresponds to this positive view of human nature is revealed in what Rogers prescribes for persons needing help: "safety, absence of threat, and complete freedom to be and to choose."[7] Little emphasis is placed upon social control and conformity, much emphasis is placed upon individual freedom and creativity.

Sigmund Freud clearly communicated a contrasting conception of persons and ideal social conditions when he wrote:

Civilized society is perpetually menaced with disintegration through this primary hostility of men toward each other. . . . Culture has to call up every possible reinforcement in order to erect barriers against the aggressive instinct of men. Hence . . . its ideal command to love one's neighbor as oneself, which is really justified by the fact that nothing is so completely at variance with original human nature as this.[8]

Persons are not only hostile toward other persons, according to Freud, they are also hostile toward society and its institutions.

It seems more probable that every culture must be built up on coercion and instinctual renunciations; it does not even appear certain that without coercion the majority of human individuals would be ready to submit to the labor necessary for acquiring new means of supporting life. One has, I think, to reckon with the fact that there are present in all more destructive, and therefore anti-social and anti-cultural, tendencies, and that with a great number

    [6]*Ibid.*, p. 201.   [7]*Ibid.*
    [8]Sigmund Freud, *Civilization and Its Discontents* (New York: Jonathan Cape and Harrison Smith, 1930), pp. 86–87.

of people these are strong enough to determine their behavior in human society.[9]

There are many competing conceptions of persons which are communicated in social work literature. They are communicated directly as persons are being described or, indirectly, as ideal family, agency, community, or other social conditions are being advocated. And yet, some concepts of persons have wide support, either because they are demonstrably true or because they must be believed if one is to do social work. Levy clarified one such conception when he said that "man can change—individually and collectively, attitudinally and behaviorally. The social worker must regard man as changeable in these terms or what are his ministrations for?"[10]

There is also broad support for the belief that the well-being of persons is heavily dependent upon social conditions, that social work practice should be purposeful (directed toward objectives, goals, or purposes), that clients should have the right of confidentiality and self-determination, and that factors which degrade from the virtue and dignity of persons should be minimized. These general beliefs, however, have contrasting specific interpretations based upon one's view of human nature. Alan Keith-Lucas recognized this in his critique of client self-determination when he said that "the so-called principle is by no means unitary, that it is a sort of verbal umbrella covering quite different and even contradictory concepts and ideas that exist in different categories of thought."[11]

The dependence upon social conditions for persons' well-being is interpreted in contrasting ways based upon one's conception of persons. For those who believe that persons

[9] Sigmund Freud, *The Future of an Illusion* (London: Hogarth Press, 1949), pp. 10–11.

[10] Charles Levy, "The Value Base of Social Work," *Journal of Education for Social Work,* IX (1973), 39.

[11] Alan Keith-Lucas, "A Critique of the Principles of Self-Determination," *Social Work,* VIII (1963), 66.

by nature have positive inclinations, the perceived requirements for families, schools, social agencies, professions, and
other societal institutions are to provide social conditions
which do not corrupt their basic nature. The leading cause
of such corruption is the extension of factors which produce order and conformity (customs, standards, laws) at the
expense of factors which permit creativity (knowledge,
choice, encouragement). Most attempts to create order and
conformity are seen as:

artificial impositions of alien conditions which keep man from becoming what it is his nature to be. No wonder man in society is
corrupt, enslaved, guilt ridden, neurotic, miserable, unhealthy,
and discontent. The whole notion of what order is necessary for
man to live communally has been misconstrued so that his natural
instincts will be repressed, not liberated; his freedom can be
usurped, not explored; his strength used for the benefit of others,
not himself; his inventiveness suppressed, not encouraged.[12]

Society, its rules, laws, and procedures (perhaps even a code
of ethics) are seen as influences which may corrupt the positive inclinations of persons which exist in a more natural
state.

The primary view of persons and the ideal social environment is
expressed by William Gordon when he describes the social
work profession's highest possible sense of mission:

Maximum realization of each individual's potential for development throughout his lifetime is a basic value. . . . The faith that
man when freed can be trusted to grow and develop in desirable
directions is probably the highest expression of a belief in human
dignity, and thus an encompassing value for social work to proclaim and use as an ultimate criterion to judge that which is good
and desirable for people.[13]

The primary purpose of social work, to those with this
view, is to emphasize the quality of human participation

[12] Charles J. Brauner and Hobert W. Burns, *Problems in Education and Philosophy*,
Prentice-Hall Foundations of Education Series, Hobert W. Burns, ed. (Englewood
Cliffs, N.J.: Prentice-Hall, Inc., 1965), p. 137.
[13] William Gordon, "Knowledge and Value: Their Distinction and Relationship
in Clarifying Social Work Practice," *Social Work*, X (1965), 38.

more than static predetermined methods or outcomes. Emphasis would be given to increasing the responsibility and capacity for human choice and self-actualization, the development of human knowledge and potentialities, assisting others in more challenging and enriching experiences, and permitting individuals to adapt creatively to an ever-changing world.[14] The principles of confidentiality/self-determination would exist more as absolutes to persons with this conception rather than being relative—for example, deciding that "compelling professional reasons"[15] are acceptable causes for disclosing confidences or that self-determination is respected "until it is well demonstrated that the exercises of this right would be highly detrimental to himself" or to others.[16] David Soyer supports the right of self-determination being more absolute even if it means that clients will fail. In fact, he felt the right to fail must accompany meaningful self-determination.[17]

Those who believe that persons by nature are negatively inclined see human dependence upon social conditions, the purpose(s) of social work, client rights of confidentiality/self-determination, and factors which degrade human virtue and dignity in a contrasting way. An emphasis upon social order and conformity is seen as a prerequisite for human creativity, freedom, virtue, and dignity. Persons must have rules, laws, and standardized procedures which are enforced or their natural human faults, ineptness, hostility, or generally antisocial behavior will prevail.

Rules of conduct, cultures, and institutions, like the Ten Commandments,

[14] Carl Rogers and B. F. Skinner, "Some Issues Concerning the Control of Human Behavior," *Science,* CXXIV (1956), 1057–65.

[15] "Compelling professional reasons" are listed as acceptable reasons for a worker to disclose confidential material about a client in the new NASW Code of Ethics. No such overt qualification is given to limiting client self-determination in certain situations.

[16] Florence Hollis, *Social Case Work in Practice: Six Case Studies* (New York: Family Welfare Association of America, 1939), p. 5.

[17] David Soyer, "The Right to Fail," *Social Work,* VIII (1963), 72–78.

they seek to extend order into moral activity. "Thou shalt not kill" . . . "Thou shalt not steal" . . . for example, can be viewed as unambiguous directives which prescribe certain things never to be done in any circumstances, or they can be seen as wholly ambiguous, vague, and general statements which prescribe an attitude toward certain activities but apply only under certain conditions. . . . The literal application of them as absolute principles leaves no room for interpretation. . . . Viewed literally . . . they leave only one choice—acceptance or rejection; and acceptance almost always means violating them at some time or another.[18]

On the other hand, rules of conduct can be interpreted as general guides which might allow conditions under which specific rules could be discarded, such as killing in time of war or in self-defense. To those who view persons as having negative inclinations, individuals cannot be left to their own freedom and personal judgment to decide when and how a rule applies.

There must be a seer, a priest, or other arbiter—someone free of animal frailties of human nature—to tell ordinary humans what to do. Wherever the issue is important, unguided choice is so likely to lead to error that order in the form of absolute commandments, or in the form of absolute authority which interprets commandments, must be extended to cover the situation.[19]

The purpose of social work to those with this view focuses more upon end states, such as working with individuals so that they become "happy, informed, skillful, well-behaved, and productive."[20] Equally important is the development of "good" social institutions which provide the right mix of control and conformity so that persons gain virtue and dignity. The principles of confidentiality and self-determination are more relative than absolute, and are conditional upon such things as the worker's interpretation of "the client's own good" or the welfare of society. The absence of "good" social institutions makes human virtue and dignity impossible.

In summation, social contexts with less structure, fewer expectations for conformity, and more opportunity for self-

[18] Brauner and Burns, *op. cit.*, pp. 133–34.   [19] *Ibid.*, p. 135.
[20] Rogers and Skinner, *op. cit.*, p. 1061.

direction are generally valued by those who believe that persons by nature have positive inclinations. If persons really have positive inclinations, the ideal social context will help free the constructive urge. Social contexts with more structure, more expectations for conformity, and less freedom for self-direction are generally valued by those who believe persons by nature have negative inclinations. Controlling and channeling this destructive urge into acceptable channels becomes the norm against which social structures are judged.

This conflict extends into the arena of how much freedom individual social workers should have for self-directed practice versus the limits of practice freedom imposed by the profession, agencies, licensing groups, peer regulation, and so forth. These contrasting conceptions of persons are represented both within the social work profession and within its new Code of Ethics. On the one hand, the preamble of the code says:

The ethical behavior of social workers results not from edict, but from a personal commitment of the individual. This code is offered to affirm the will and zeal of all social workers to be ethical and to act ethically.[21]

On the other hand, the preamble says:

It offers general principles to guide conduct, and the judicious appraisal of conduct. . . . It provides the basis for making judgments about ethical actions before and after they occur. . . . Ethical behavior in a given situation must satisfy not only the judgment of the individual social worker, but also the judgment of an unbiased jury of professional peers.[22]

CONTRASTING CONCEPTIONS OF PERSONS AND A CODE OF
ETHICS CONTENT ANALYSIS

The two contrasting conceptions of persons developed earlier were the basis for a content analysis of the new NASW Code of Ethics.[23] The principal question was: Do the specific statements of ethical principle which make direct ref-

[21]"The NASW Code of Ethics," *NASW News*, XXV (1980), 24.
[22]*Ibid.*   [23]*Ibid.*, pp. 24–25.

erence to the roles of the social worker, client, and colleague vary with regard to what is implied about the nature of persons who occupy these roles?" To the extent that such variance exists, clarification of its nature may facilitate communication about ethical issues and dilemmas.

The inquiry employed content analysis methods. Each of the sixty-nine specific statements of ethical principle comprising the Code of Ethics served as a unit of analysis. The conceptual framework which developed contrasting conceptions of persons was used to derive a coding plan. That plan utilized three nominal categories designed to tap the latent content regarding the conceptions of persons in regard to each of the sixty-nine statements of ethical principle. An ethical principle was assumed to imply that persons were *positively inclined* when their morality, dignity, and worth were affirmed by such means as directing that they be given information, access, cooperation, devotion, loyalty, respect, and unqualified confidentiality and self-determination. An ethical principle was assumed to imply that persons were *negatively inclined* when it prescribed what a person should/should not do in language which implied they would do the wrong thing if the rule did not exist. An ethical principle was assumed to be *neutral or unclear* when it applied nothing about the positive or negative inclination of a person or when contrasting inferences about a person's nature could be made from two or more phrases in the principle.

The authors independently rated each ethical principle using these procedures: the roles (social worker, client, colleague) to which each principle makes direct reference were noted; the implied conception of the person who occupies that role was identified by using the coding plan described above; and independent ratings were compared to identify items of agreement and disagreement. Items on which there was disagreement regarding the implied conception of the role occupant were debated until consensus as to rating was reached.

At the conclusion of the independent rating phase, the

authors were in full agreement that 69 ethical principles made direct reference to the social worker role, 20 made direct reference to the client role, and 14 made direct reference to the colleague role. They were in 88 percent (91 of 103 ratings) agreement as to the implied conception of the role occupant evidenced in the 69 statements of ethical principles. Forced consensus debate yielded agreement on the remaining 12 ratings (12 percent).

The findings of this analysis are based on the consensus of the authors on completion of the procedures. In brief, the findings demonstrate substantial variance in the conception of persons based upon whether they are social workers, clients, or colleagues. Eighty-eight percent of the references to social workers implied that they were "negatively inclined," while only 10 percent of the references to clients and 7 percent of those to colleagues implied they were so inclined. Conversely, 4 percent of the references to social workers implied they were "positively inclined," while 70 percent which referred to clients and 71 percent which referred to colleagues implied they were so inclined.

IMPLICATIONS

These findings and their implications are worthy of further debate, and they also raise additional questions: Do social workers have different beliefs concerning the basic nature of persons based upon the roles they occupy? Do social workers generally view others as having a more positive nature than they themselves have? What is the association between preferred conceptions of persons that specific social workers have and the fields of practice or specific methodologies they prefer? What are the underlying beliefs within social work which associate the right of a profession to intervene in, control, and bring about more conformity of individual practitioners and the rights and responsibility of practitioners to intervene in, control, and bring about more conformity in clients? Answers to these questions may uncover additional underlying agendas which block social work groups charged with making ethical decisions.

The new Code of Ethics will fulfill its mission to the extent that it improves the conduct of social workers and helps the profession gain public respectability. These functions can be accomplished without consensus regarding specific conceptions of persons. And yet, contrasting conceptions of persons and contrasting beliefs about ideal social conditions within and beyond the profession are significant agendas as the new Code of Ethics is being implemented. Recognizing these contrasting beliefs facilitates both collective and rational decision-making.

Developing, ratifying, and implementing a new code represents an opportune time for social workers to reawaken, analyze, and critique their beliefs and to revitalize discussions of social work knowledge, values, and practices. The new code represents a major improvement over the previous one both in terms of guiding professional conduct and in helping the profession gain public respectability. The efforts which went into its development and ratification are to be applauded, and it is hoped that this discussion will help clarify problematic issues in its implementation.

Appendix A: Program

PLENARY SESSIONS

OPENING PLENARY SESSION
Speaker: The Honorable Patricia Roberts Harris, Department of Health and Human Services, Washington
Presentation of Distinguished Service Awards

THE FUTURE OF OUR CHILDREN
Speaker: Richard H. De Lone, Corporation for Public/Private Ventures, Philadelphia
Discussant: Alvin Schorr, Case Western Reserve University, Cleveland

THE INDEPENDENT SECTOR AND VOLUNTARY ACTION
Speaker: Brian O'Connell, Independent Sector, Washington

THE PROFESSIONAL AS PARENT: VALUES AND ETHICAL DILEMMAS IN BENEVOLENCE
Speaker: David J. Rothman, Columbia University, New York
Discussant: Nancy Amidei, Food Research and Action Center, Washington
Presentation of NCSW Membership Awards

SOCIOCULTURAL CHANGES IN THE 1980s AND THEIR IMPACT ON WOMEN AND CHILDREN
Speaker: Marian Wright Edelman, Children's Defense Fund, Washington
Discussant: Shirley Jenkins, Columbia University, New York

TOWARD A HUMANIZED ECONOMY
Speaker: Gar Alperovitz, National Center for Economic Alternatives, Washington
Discussant: Melvin A. Glasser, United Automobile Workers, UAW, Detroit

WHITNEY M. YOUNG, JR., MEMORIAL LECTURE
Speaker: Robert C. Weaver, Hunter College, New York
Presentation of NASW Social Worker of the Year and Public Citizen of the Year Awards

SECTION I: ECONOMIC INDEPENDENCE

DOES RETIREMENT HAVE A FUTURE?
Speakers: Barbara Torrey, President's Commission on Pension Policy, Washington,
Bert Seidman, AFL-CIO, Washington
James R. Storey, Urban Institute, Washington

THE ENERGY CRISIS AND SOCIAL WELFARE
Speaker: David Sweet, Cleveland State University

FINDING JOBS FOR YOUTH: A CHALLENGE FOR THE 1980s
Speakers: David H. Swinton, Urban Institute, Washington
Joseph E. Garcia, Rural Opportunities, Inc., Seattle

FISCAL PROBLEMS AND SOCIAL WELFARE: OUTLOOK FOR THE 1980s
Speakers: John T. Dempsey, Michigan Department of Social Services, Lansing
Alair A. Townsend, Department of Health and Human Services, Washington

IS IT TIME FOR GUARANTEED JOBS—OR DEBATE?
Speakers: Garth Mangum, University of Utah, Salt Lake City
Isabel Sawhill, Urban Institute, Washington

SOCIAL EXPERIMENTATION: A WAY TO PLAN THE FUTURE
Panelists: Robert G. Spiegelman, SRI International, Palo Alto, Calif.
James P. Zais, Urban Institute, Washington
David O'Neill, General Accounting Office, Washington

WOMEN, WORK, AND SOCIAL WELFARE: ISSUES FOR THE 1980s
Speakers: Robert Crosslin, Department of Labor, Washington
Nancy M. Gordon, Congressional Budget Office, Washington
Carol Lee Jusenius, National Commission on Employment Policy, Washington

SECTION II: PROBLEMS OF EFFECTIVE FUNCTIONING

EFFECTIVE FUNCTIONING OF THE ELDERLY
Speakers: Barbara Morrison, Hunter College, New York
Julianne Oktay, University of Maryland, Baltimore
Howard A. Palley, University of Maryland, Baltimore

EFFECTIVE FUNCTIONING OF WOMEN
Speakers: Prudence Brown, Columbia University, New York
Elinor Polansky, State University of New York at Stony Brook

EFFECTIVE SOCIAL FUNCTIONING
Panelists: Werner Boehm, Rutgers University, New Brunswick, N.J.
Siri Jayaratne, University of Michigan, Ann Arbor
Rona L. Levy, University of Washington, Seattle

ETHNICITY AND SERVICE DELIVERY
Speakers; Shirley Jenkins, Columbia University, New York
Emelicia Mizio, State University of New York at Stony Brook
Leon Chestang, University of Alabama, University

FAMILIES AND PUBLIC POLICIES
Speakers: Nancy A. Humphreys, National Association of Social Workers, New Brunswick, N.J.
Robert M. Rice, Family Service Association of America, New York

FUNCTIONING UNDER STRESS
Speakers: Jona Rosenfeld, Columbia University, New York
Sister Mary Paul, Center for Family Life, Brooklyn, N.Y.

TRAINING AND EDUCATION OF CHILD WELFARE WORKERS
FOR EFFECTIVE WORK WITH FAMILIES AND CHILDREN
Panelists: Ann Hartman, University of Michigan, Ann Arbor
Anthony N. Maluccio, University of Connecticut, Hartford
Nolan Rindfleisch, Ohio University, Columbus

SECTION III: SOCIAL ASPECTS OF HEALTH

ADVANCES IN WOMEN'S HEALTH
Speakers: Miriam B. Rosenthal, M.D., University Hospitals of Cleveland
Sidney H. Sachs, M.D., American Cancer Society, Cleveland

HOSPICE CARE AND THE HEALTH PROFESSIONAL: A
METHODOLOGY FOR LEARNING HOW TO CARE
Speaker: Bernice Catherine Harper, Department of Health and Human Services, Washington

NATIONAL HEALTH INSURANCE AND HEALTH SERVICE
PROGRAMS: PROSPECTS FOR THE 1980s
Speakers: Allen N. Kopelin, M.D., New Jersey Department of Health, Trenton
Thompson Fulton, University of Missouri, Patterson

NEW APPROACHES TO ADOLESCENT PREGNANCY
Speaker: Marion Howard, Grady Memorial Hospital, Atlanta

PROMOTING CHILD HEALTH IN AN ERA OF SHRINKING
PUBLIC SUPPORT
Speakers: Lisbeth Bamberger Schorr, Select Panel for the Promotion of Child Health, Washington
Faustina Solis, University of California, La Jolla

USING THE MEDIA IN MENTAL HEALTH
Speaker: Roy H. Schlachter, Cuyahoga County Hospital System, Cleveland
Reactor: Jane Temple, WEWS TV Channel 5, Cleveland

SECTION IV: LEISURE-TIME NEEDS AND THE QUALITY OF LIFE

THE CONTINUED PRACTICE OF CLOSET GROUP WORKERS
Speakers: Bernard M. Shiffman, Community Council of Greater New York, New York
Ruth Middleman, University of Louisville, Louisville, Ky.

ISSUES IN GROUP WORK: HIGHLIGHTS FROM THE FIRST
GROUP WORK SYMPOSIUM
    Speakers: Paul Abels, Case Western Reserve University, Cleveland
    Sonia Leib Abels, Cleveland State University, Cleveland

THE PUBLIC AGENCY AS A COMMUNITY-CARING RATHER
THAN CONTROLLING AGENCY: WHAT CHANGES NEED TO
BE MADE
    Speaker: Thomas H. Walz, University of Iowa, Iowa City

THE REEMERGENCE OF GROUP WORK AS A VIABLE
COMMUNITY SERVICES INSTRUMENT
    Panelists: Bernard M. Shiffman, Community Council of Greater New
    York, New York
    Mary Lynch, Ramsey County Community Corrections Department,
    St. Paul
    Paul Abels, Case Western Reserve University, Cleveland
    Thomas H. Walz, University of Iowa, Iowa City

SERVICES TO FAMILIES IN THE COMMUNITY: A BRIDGE
BETWEEN THE THERAPEUTIC AND DEVELOPMENTAL
STRATEGIES
    Speaker: T. George Silcott, Urban Research Planning and Conference
    Center, New York

WOMEN'S ISSUES IN THE WORLD OF WORK AND LEISURE
    Speaker: Mary Lynch, Ramsey County Community Corrections De-
    partment, St. Paul

    *SECTION V: PROVISION AND MANAGEMENT OF SOCIAL
    SERVICES*

FUTURE OF SOCIAL SERVICES FINANCING: STRATEGIES
FOR COPING
    Speakers: William C. Copeland, Seneca Corporation, Minneapolis
    Thomas Rhodenbaugh, Institute for Economic Development, Wash-
    ington

FUTURE OF SOCIAL SERVICES FINANCING: WHAT'S GOING
TO HAPPEN IN THE EIGHTIES
    Speakers: Ernest L. Osborne, Department of Health and Human Ser-
    vices, Washington
    Allen Jensen, U.S. House of Representatives, Washington

HOUSING THE "COMMUNITY MISFITS": THE PROMISE OF
COMMUNITY-BASED CARE
    Speakers: Ralph Brody, Federation for Community Planning, Cleve-
    land
    Kathleen A. Raffo, Federation for Community Planning, Cleveland

HUMAN SERVICES MANPOWER IN THE 1980s
    Speakers: Bertram M. Beck, Community Service Society, New York
    Burton Gummer, State University of New York at Albany

THE LAW AND HUMAN SERVICES: A GROWING
RELATIONSHIP
> *Speakers:* Adele Blong, Center on Social Welfare Policy and Law,
> Washington
> Patricia S. James, Case Western Reserve University, Cleveland

SERVICES INTEGRATION REVISITED
> *Speakers:* David Pingree, Florida Department of Health and Reha-
> bilitative Services, Tallahassee
> Robert Morris, Brandeis University, Waltham, Mass.

SECTION VI: SOCIETAL PROBLEMS

EXPERIENCES WITH UNDOCUMENTED ALIENS: WEST
COAST ASIANS, MEXICAN NATIONALS, CENTRAL AND
SOUTH AMERICANS
> *Speaker:* Royal F. Morales, Asian-American Community Mental
> Health Training Center, Los Angeles
> *Panelists:* Ramon Salcido, University of Southern California, Los An-
> geles
> Adriana Di Nardo, Family Reception Center, Brooklyn, N.Y.
> Raul Ramirez, Arizona State University, Tempe

INJUSTICE AND SOCIAL INTERVENTION FOR ETHNIC
MINORITIES, WOMEN, AND CHILDREN
> *Speaker:* Phyllis Freeman, Columbia University, New York
> *Discussant:* Cosme Barcelo, National Council of La Raza, Washington

ORGANIZATION AND DELIVERY OF SERVICES IN PUBLIC
WELFARE AGENCIES
> *Panelists:* Fred J. Buscaglia, Erie County Welfare Department, Buf-
> falo, N.Y.
> John P. McGinty, Cuyahoga County Welfare Department, Cleveland
> Keith L. Colbo, Montana Department of Social and Rehabilitation
> Services, Helena

ORGANIZING SERVICES TO MEET SOCIAL NEEDS: PUBLIC
AND PRIVATE AGENCY PERSPECTIVES
> *Speaker:* Leon H. Ginsberg, West Virginia Department of Welfare,
> Charleston
> *Discussants:* Jack Wedemeyer, California Department of Social Wel-
> fare, Sacramento
> John Wedemeyer, Community Congress, San Diego

PLANNING FOR UNDERSERVED POPULATIONS: RUNAWAYS,
BATTERED SPOUSES, AND CHILDREN
> *Panelists:* Linda Silverman King, Center for Women Policy Studies,
> Washington
> F. Ivan Nye, Runaway Project, Boys Town, Nebr.

POLICY AND SERVICE ISSUES IN THE ORGANIZATION OF
SOCIAL SERVICES
> *Panelists:* Elmer J. Tropman, United Way, Pittsburgh

John Tropman, University of Michigan, Ann Arbor
Peter Tropman, Wisconsin Department of Health and Social Services, Madison

STRATEGIES FOR ASSESSMENT OF SERVICES
Speaker: Robert Teare, University of Alabama, University
Discussants: James A. Goodman, International Institute of Public Management, Washington
Jill Kagle, University of Illinois, Urbana-Champaign

AUTHORS' FORUM

CHANGING PUBLIC AND PRIVATE SECTOR RELATIONSHIPS
Speakers: George Hoshino and Susan Nassar, University of Minnesota, Minneapolis (coauthors)
Douglas A. Spicka, American Red Cross, Dayton, Ohio, and James Scott Fraser, Wright State University, Dayton, Ohio (coauthors)

CONSUMER HEALTH AND SERVICES EVALUATION
Speakers: John P. Myers, New Mexico State University, Las Cruces
Julia M. Norlin and Wayne A. Chess, University of Oklahoma, Norman; Siri Jayaratne, University of Michigan, Ann Arbor (coauthors)
Angela E. McGuire and Lee Troy, Ohio Department of Mental Health and Mental Retardation, Columbus (coauthors)

CULTURAL AND LINGUISTIC ISSUES IN HUMAN SERVICES
Speakers: Peter C. Y. Lee, San Jose State University, San Jose, Calif.
James T. Decker and Richard A. Starrett, University of Texas at El Paso (coauthors)
Raju Varghese, University of Maryland, Baltimore, and James N. Thistel, Youth Services, College Park, Md. (coauthors)

CULTURAL DIVERSITY AND INNOVATION
Speakers: Louis A. Colca, Shirley A. Lord, and Susan Boline, State University College at Buffalo, N.Y.;
Carole D. Colca and Debra Lowen, State University of New York at Buffalo (coauthors)
Martha Rodgers Graf, John R. Howmiller, and Christine Martinez, San Jose State University, San Jose, Calif. (coauthors)
Daniel S. Sanders, University of Hawaii at Manoa

EMERGING DATA ON THE HANDICAPPED AND DISABLED
Speakers: Harris Chaiklin, University of Maryland, Baltimore, and David M. O'Hara, John F. Kennedy Institute, Baltimore (coauthors)
Jane Pfouts and Donna G. Nixon, University of North Carolina, Chapel Hill (coauthors)
Rebecca Van Voorhis, Ohio State University, Columbus, and Carolyn J. Shoemaker, Franklin County Mental Health and Retardation Board, Columbus, Ohio (coauthors)

EMPLOYMENT AND RELATED POLICY OPTIONS
Speakers: John H. Ramey, University of Akron, Akron, Ohio
Gwendolyn C. Gilbert, Columbus Urban League, Columbus, Ohio

FORMAL AND INFORMAL HELPING NETWORKS
Speakers: Virginia M. Schuster, Aileen E. Widman, and Charles R. Wilt, St. Paul-Ramsey Medical Center, St. Paul (coauthors)
Murali D. Nair, Marywood College, Scranton, Pa.
Lambert Maguire, University of Pittsburgh

FOSTER CARE EVALUATION AND EDUCATION STUDIES
Speakers: Mary S. White, University of Minnesota, Minneapolis
Edward A. Brawley, Pennsylvania State University, University Park; Ronald M. Feinstein, Community College of Philadelphia; and Anne M. Wagner, Claymont Community Center, Claymont, Del. (coauthors)

HUMAN SERVICE LEADERSHIP AND MANAGEMENT
Speakers: William E. Berg, University of Wisconsin-Milwaukee
Marion Wijnberg, Western Michigan University, Kalamazoo, and Bertha Laury, State University of New York at Buffalo (coauthors)
George Hoshino, University of Minnesota, Minneapolis
Gary Haselhun, Minnesota Department of Public Welfare, St. Paul

HUMAN SERVICES MANPOWER CONSIDERATIONS
Speakers: Salvatore Imbrogno, Ohio State University, Columbus
Miriam Clubok, Ohio University, Athens
Wilburn Hayden, Jr., Department of Human Services, Chapel Hill, N.C.

NEGLECT, DEPRIVATION, AND LOSS
Speakers: Joan M. Jones and R. L. McNeely, University of Wisconsin-Milwaukee (coauthors)
James N. Thistel, Youth Services, College Park, Md., and Raju Varghese, University of Maryland, Baltimore (coauthors)
Roy T. Denton, University of Southern Mississippi, Hattiesburg
Donald W. Green, Gulf Coast Junior College, Biloxi, Miss.

PHILOSOPHICAL AND ETHICAL ISSUES
Speakers: John D. Collins, Summit County Welfare Department, Akron, Ohio
Joseph R. Steiner and Gerald Gross, Syracuse University, Syracuse, N.Y. (coauthors)

PLANNING FOR THE ELDERLY
Speakers: Nick L. Linsk and Elsie M. Pinkston, University of Chicago (coauthors)
Alejandro Garcia, Syracuse University, Syracuse, N.Y.
Michael E. Tindall, Crozer-Chester Medical Center, Chester, Pa.

RURAL SERVICE DELIVERY: BOOM TOWNS AND CULTURAL VARIATIONS
Speakers: Judith A. Davenport and Joseph Davenport, III, University of Wyoming, Laramie (coauthors)
Murali D. Nair, Marywood College, Scranton, Pa.
Emilia E. Martinez-Brawley, Pennsylvania State University, Univer-

sity Park, and Carlton E. Munson, University of Houston, Houston, Texas (coauthors)

SEX-ROLE PERCEPTIONS AMONG HUMAN SERVICE WORKERS
Speakers: Wallace J. Gingerich, University of Wisconsin-Milwaukee, and Stuart A. Kirk, State University of New York at Albany (coauthors)
John H. Behling, Caroletta Curtis, and Sara Ann Foster, Ohio State University, Columbus (coauthors)
Carlton E. Munson, University of Houston, Houston, Texas

SOCIAL WORK PRACTICE EVALUATION
Speakers: Lester B. Brown, University of Wisconsin-Milwaukee
Elizabeth Mutschler, University of Michigan, Ann Arbor
William D. Eldridge, Ohio State University, Columbus

VULNERABLE POPULATIONS AND ALCOHOLISM
Speakers: Susan Berger, Prevention Center of the North Shore Council on Alcoholism, Danvers, Mass.
Babu Suseelan, Marywood College, Scranton, Pa.
Lenore A. Kola and Jordon I. Kosberg, Case Western Reserve University, Cleveland, (coauthors)

WOMEN AND MEDICAL CARE
Speakers: Joyce A. Brengarth and Linda Hoshino, University of Pittsburgh, Pittsburgh
Theresa A. Masciantonio, Craigh House-Technoma, Pittsburgh

NATIONAL CONFERENCE ON SOCIAL WELFARE

COMMUNITY EMPOWERMENT
Speakers: Arthur J. Naparstek, University of Southern California, Washington
Juan Patlan, Mexican-American Unity Council, San Antonio
Presentation of VISTA Award to NCSW by Mary King

EMPLOYMENT OF THE HANDICAPPED
Speaker: Alice H. Randolph, Kent State University, Kent, Ohio
Reactors: Douglas Randolph, Cleveland Society for the Blind
Ferguson Meadows, Kent State University, Kent, Ohio
Dora Teimouri, Kent State University, Kent, Ohio

HEALTH SERVICES FOR REFUGEES
Panelists: Richard A. Goodman, M.D., Center for Disease Control, Atlanta
Gordon Soares, Department of Health and Human Services, Region IX, San Francisco
Sandra DuVander, Department of Public Welfare, St. Paul

THE HISPANIC FAMILY IN THE 1980s
Speakers: Guadalupe Gibson, Our Lady of the Lake University, San Antonio
Luis Miranda, Community Service Society, New York

INDOCHINESE HOUSING PROBLEMS OF THE PAST AND PROPOSED SOLUTIONS FOR THE FUTURE
Speakers: Wade R. Ragas, University of New Orleans
Anne Heald, Indochinese Refugee Action Center, Washington

INTERNATIONAL AND DOMESTIC POLICIES REGARDING REFUGEES
Speakers: Victor H. Palmieri, Washington
Richard F. Celeste, Peace Corps, Washington

MENTAL HEALTH SERVICES FOR REFUGEES
Panelists: Barry Miller, Eastern Pennsylvania Psychiatric Institute, Philadelphia
Cynthia Coleman, Eastern Pennsylvania Psychiatric Institute, Philadelphia
Le Xuan Khoa, Eastern Pennsylvania Psychiatric Institute, Philadelphia

MULTIETHNIC ISSUES IN THE 1980s
Speakers: Kenneth J. Kovach, Ohio Historical Society, Cleveland
Joseph Giordano, American Jewish Committee, New York

MUTUAL ASSISTANCE ASSOCIATIONS' ROLE IN REFUGEE RESETTLEMENT
Speakers: Nguyen Dinh Thu, Vietnamese American Association, Oklahoma City
Tou-Fu Vang, Illinois Governor's Center for Asian Assistance, Chicago
Kan-Oum, Cambodia's Association of Ohio, Cincinnati

TRAIN THEM OR SUPPORT THEM: A DISCUSSION OF ESL/EMPLOYMENT SERVICES FOR REFUGEES
Speakers: Joyce Schuman, Indochinese Education Program, Arlington, Va.
Synthia Woodcock, Prince George's Community College, Adelphi, Md.
Ruth Petkoff, Northern Virginia CETA Skills Center, Arlington

ALUMNI ASSOCIATION OF THE SCHOOL OF APPLIED SOCIAL SCIENCES, CASE WESTERN RESERVE UNIVERSITY

DEINSTITUTIONALIZATION: THE PLIGHT OF THE MENTALLY ILL AND HUMAN SERVICE SYSTEMS
Speaker: Leona L. Bachrach, University of Maryland, Baltimore
Reactor: Stuart A. Kirk, State University of New York at Albany

ASSOCIATE GROUPS

AMERICAN RED CROSS

INTEGRATING THE HOSPICE INTO THE HEALTH CARE SYSTEM
   Speakers: Linda Miller, Washington
   Thomas Kickham, Department of Health and Human Services, Baltimore
   David Ehrenfried, Blue Cross and Blue Shield Association, Chicago

CLEVELAND SPONSORING COMMITTEE

THE PRIVATE SECTOR: FORMULA FOR EFFECTIVE HUMAN SERVICES
   Panelists: Morton L. Mandel, Premier Industrial Corporation, Cleveland
   Cheryle Wills, House of Wills, Cleveland
   Lyman H. Treadway, Union Commerce Bank, Cleveland

COUNCIL ON SOCIAL WORK EDUCATION

QUALITY ASSURANCE IN PROFESSIONAL SOCIAL WORK EDUCATION
   Speaker: Sidney Berengarten, Council on Social Work Education, New York

TEACHING VALUES AND ETHICS IN SOCIAL WORK EDUCATION PROGRAMS: A NEGLECTED RESPONSIBILITY?
   Speaker: Gary Lloyd, Council on Social Work Education, New York

NATIONAL ASSOCIATION OF SOCIAL WORKERS

CHILD-PROTECTIVE SERVICES: STANDARDS AND GUIDELINES FOR SERVICE DELIVERY
   Panelists: Isadora Hare, National Association of Social Workers, Washington
   Joanne Selinske, American Public Welfare Association, Washington

CLINICAL SOCIAL WORK AND FEDERAL LEGISLATION IN THE 1980s
   Panelists: A. Stephen Du Bois, Gowanda Psychiatric Center, Helmuth, N.Y.
   Ruth I. Knee, National Association of Social Workers, Washington

THE DRYING UP OF TITLE XX TRAINING FUNDS, OR A NEW DAY?
   Panelists: Richard Verville, Esq., White, Fine & Verville, Washington
   John A. Yankey, Case Western Reserve University, Cleveland
   Michio Suzuki, Department of Health and Human Services, Washington

SOCIAL WORK IN THE YEAR 2000
Panelists: Chauncey A. Alexander, National Association of Social Workers, Washington
Bertram M. Beck, Community Service Society, New York

SOCIAL WORK PERSPECTIVES ON THE JOINT COMMISSION ON ACCREDITATION OF HOSPITALS
Panelists: Jacqueline Fassett, Sinai Hospital, Baltimore
Lawrence Shulman, Long Island Jewish Hillside Medical Center, New Hyde Park, N.Y.
Arthur Katz, University of Kansas, Lawrence

TRANSRACIAL ADOPTION: DREAM OR NIGHTMARE?
Panelists: Sandi Christofferson, Human Services Center, Rugby, N. Dak.
Charlotte Goodluck, Jewish Family and Children's Service, Phoenix

OHIO COMMISSION ON AGING

CONTINUUM OF CARE FOR OLDER PEOPLE IN OHIO
Speakers: Jack Fox, Ohio Commission on Aging, Columbus
Michael Rust, Western Reserve Area on Aging, Cleveland

REGIONAL COUNCIL ON ALCOHOLISM

THE CHALLENGE OF ALCOHOLISM TREATMENT FOR SOCIAL WORKERS
Speakers: Bonnie Long, Hitchcock House, Cleveland
Seth Nieding, Loraine Community Hospital, Loraine, Ohio
Renee Spiegel, Veterans Administration Hospital, Cleveland

SALVATION ARMY

REDEFINING A MORAL AND ETHICAL BASE FOR SOCIAL SERVICES
Speaker: Allen Keith-Lucas, University of North Carolina, Chapel Hill

U.S. COMMITTEE, ICSW

DETERMINANTS OF PUBLIC WELFARE POLICY IN SWEDEN AND THE UNITED STATES
Speakers: Hans Berglind, Case Western Reserve University, Cleveland
M.C. "Terry" Hokenstad, Jr., Case Western Reserve University, Cleveland

VETERANS ADMINISTRATION

BURNOUT IN HEALTH CARE PROFESSIONALS
Speaker: Emily Adams, Training Interventions Association, Inc., Baltimore

INTERNATIONAL EXCHANGE PROGRAMS FOR SOCIAL
WORKERS AND SOCIAL WORK EDUCATORS
  Speakers: Thomas Hatcher, Council of International Programs for
  Youth Leaders and Social Workers, Inc., Cleveland
  Joan Smith, St. Louis University, St. Louis
  Reactor: Mary Catherine Jennings, Department of Health and Human
  man Services, Washington

INTERRELATIONSHIPS OF AGING CONFERENCES
  Panelists: Clark Tibbitts, Department of Health Services, Washington
  William E. Oriol, International Center for Social Gerontology, Washington
  ington
  John Anderson, Ministry of Community and Social Services, Toronto
  ronto

NORTH AMERICAN POLICIES AND PROGRAMS INVOLVING
INDOCHINESE REFUGEES
  Speakers: Mary C. Spillane, Department of Health and Human Services, Washington
  vices, Washington
  Michael J. Molloy, Canadian Employment and Immigration Commission, Quebec
  mission, Quebec

Appendix B:
Organization of the
Conference for 1980

COMMITTEE ON NOMINATIONS

Chairman: Walter L. Smart, New York
Vice-chairman: Sam Grais, St. Paul
Term expires 1980: Glenn Allison, Washington; Diane Bernard, Tallahassee, Fla.; Corazon Esteva Doyle, Phoenix; Mary K. Lazarus, Columbus, Ohio; Marian H. Miller, Chicago; Harriet H. Ruggles, Dallas, Pa.; Morton I. Teicher, Chapel Hill, N.C.
Term expires 1981: Robert S. Burgess, North Dartmouth, Mass.; Ismael Dieppa, Tempe, Ariz.; Hans S. Falck, Topeka; Sam Grais, St. Paul; Marjorie W. Main, Cleveland; Mary Ripley, Los Angeles; Walter L. Smart, New York
Term expires 1982: Anna V. Brown, Cleveland; Nancy Coleman, New York; Mary Hoffer, Columbus, Ohio; Jule Johnson, Springfield, Ill.; Frank Ladwig, Sante Fe, N. Mex.; David L. Neal, Ann Arbor, Mich.; Aaron Sacks, Pittsburgh

COMMITTEE ON PUBLIC RELATIONS

Chairwoman: Elly Robbins, New York
Vice-chairwoman: Elma Phillipson Cole, New York
Ex officio: Don Bates, New York
Term expires 1980: Inez Almond, New York; Elma Phillipson Cole, New York; Herbert S. Fowler, Washington; Rae M. Hamilton, Washington; Ronald E. McMillen, Washington; Mary Jane O'Neill, New York; Guichard Parris, New York; Fred Schnaue, New York; Frank Strauss, New York; Owen T. Wilkerson, New York
Term expires 1981: Adele Braude, New York; Ann Gropp, Washington; Betty Leslie Lund, Southbury, Conn.; Elly Robbins, New York; Anne R. Warner, New York

EDITORIAL COMMITTEE

Chairman: H. Frederick Brown, Chicago
Chairwoman-elect: Bernice Catherine Harper, Washington
Members: Jane Collins, Denver; Ronald A. Feldman, St. Louis; Charlotte Nusberg, Washington; William Ray, Washington; Carl Schoenberg, New York

U.S. COMMITTEE OF ICSW

Chairwoman: Ellen B. Winston, Raleigh, N.C.
Vice-chairman: Michio Suzuki, Washington
Secretary: Maureen Didier, Albany, N.Y.
Treasurer: John Twiname, New York
Representatives of National Organizations: American Public Welfare Association, Edward T. Weaver, Washington; Council of International Programs, Paul Unger, Cleveland; Council on Social Work Education, Arthur Katz, Lawrence, Kans.; Department of Health and Human Services, Ernest L. Osborne, Washington; National Assembly of National Voluntary Health and Social Welfare Organizations, Rosalind Harris, New

York; National Association of Social Workers, Jacqueline Fassett, Baltimore

Members at Large: Mark G. Battle, Washington; Evelyn Blanchard, Portland, Oreg.; Werner Boehm, New Brunswick, N.J.; John Charnow, New York; Catherine S. Chilman, Milwaukee; Guadalupe Gibson, San Antonio; Shelton B. Granger, Philadelphia; Bernice Catherine Harper, Washington; Helen Howerton, Washington; Carolyn Hubbard, New York; Kate Katzki, New York; Kenji Murase, San Francisco; Bernard E. Nash, Washington; Charlotte Nusberg, Washington; C. C. Patrick Okura, Rockville, Md.; William E. Oriol, Washington; Samuel J. Silberman, New York; Morton I. Teicher, Chapel Hill, N.C.; Daniel Thursz, Washington; Eloise Waite, Washington

Subcommittee Chairs: Margery P. Carpenter, Washington; Frank Gordon, Baltimore; Iris Gordon, Baltimore; Margaret Hickey, Tucson; Helen Howerton, Washington; Ruby Pernell, Cleveland

Liaison: Inter-American Conference, Mary Catherine Jennings, Washington; NCSW Program Committee, Catherine S. Chilman, Milwaukee; New England Committee, Pearl Steinmetz, Cambridge, Mass.

Members of Committee of Representatives, ICSW: Ernest L. Osborne, Washington; John B. Turner, Chapel Hill, N.C.

Officers of ICSW (residing in U.S.): Alden E. Bevier, New York; Dorothy Lally, Washington; Charles I. Schottland, Tucson; Edward T. Weaver, Washington

Secretary General ICSW: Ingrid Gelinek, Vienna, Austria

NCSW STAFF

FULL-TIME

Executive Director: John E. Hansan
Associate Executive Director: Benjamin O. Hendrick
Administrative Assistant to the Executive Director: Marie Waite Fiske
Director of Publications: Maureen Hassett Herman
Staff Associates: Sunny Harris, Carole J. M. Perkins

PART-TIME

Consultant, International Activities: Margery P. Carpenter
Secretary: Helen G. Whetzel
Typist: Elizabeth H. Dolan
Financial Clerk: Jennie M. Porrazzo

COMMITTEE ON PROGRAM FOR THE 107TH ANNUAL FORUM

President and Chairman: Mitchell I. Ginsberg, New York
Members at Large: Mark G. Battle, Washington; Bertram M. Beck, New York; Leon W. Chestang, University, Ala.; Jane Collins, Denver; Peter Forsythe, New York; Merl C. Hokenstad, Jr., Cleveland; Marta Sotomayor, Rockville, Md.; Paul Unger, Cleveland; Duira B. Ward, Cos Cob, Conn.; Edward T. Weaver, Washington

Representatives of National Social Welfare Organizations: American Public Welfare Association, Edward T. Weaver, Washington; Council on Social Work Education, Samuel O. Miller, New York; National Assembly of National Voluntary Health and Social Welfare Organizations, Raymond DeVera, New York; National Association for Statewide Health and Welfare, Sara Ellison, Hartford, Conn.; National Association of Social Workers, George D. Metrey, Union, N.J.

Liaison Members: NCSW Executive Director, John E. Hansan, Washington; NCSW Editorial Committee, H. Frederick Brown, Chicago; NCSW Public Relations Committee, Elma Phillipson Cole, New York; U.S. Committee, ICSW, Catherine S. Chilman, Milwaukee; U.S. Department of Health and Human Services, Jerry Turem, Washington

SECTION LEADERS

I. *Economic Independence:* Ronald B. Dear, Seattle; Robert Harris, Washington

II. *Problems of Effective Functioning:* Shirley Jenkins, New York; Emelicia Mizio, Stony Brook, N.Y.

III. *Social Aspects of Health:* Eleanor Klein, Los Angeles; Elizabeth L. Watkins, Chapel Hill, N.C.

IV. *Leisure-Time Needs and the Quality of Life:* Livingston S. Francis, New York; Thomas H. Walz, Iowa City

V. *Provision and Management of Social Services:* Abe Lavine, Tallahassee; Stephen P. Simonds, Portland, Maine

VI. *Societal Problems:* James A. Goodman, Washington; Charles Guzzetta, New York

Index